Life Line

LIFE LINE

The Merchant Navy at War 1939–1945

Peter Elphick

CHATHAM PUBLISHING

LONDON

Dedication

This book is dedicated to all merchant seamen who
served during the Second World War.

It is especially dedicated to two of them:

Captain Selwyn Capon CBE for so ably commanding the
gallant crew of *Empire Star* during the evacuation of Singapore;

and, in the hope that it will in a small way compensate for the fact
that his bravery has never been officially recognised,
Fourth Engineer Samuel Elsby Harper of *Automedon* in recognition of
his escape whilst a prisoner of war.

Copyright © Peter Elphick 1999

First published in Great Britain in 1999 by Chatham Publishing,
61 Frith Street, London W1V 5TA

Chatham Publishing is an imprint of Gerald Duckworth & Co Ltd

British Library Cataloguing in Publication Data
A catalogue record for this book is available from the
British Library

ISBN 1 86176 100 7

Typeset by Dorwyn Ltd, Rowlands Castle, Hants

Printed and bound in Great Britain by The Cromwell Press, Trowbridge, Wilts

Contents

List of Plates

Acknowledgements

A wide range of people and organisations have helped, directly or indirectly, during the research for this book, and my thanks go out to all those listed below and to any others I may have inadvertently left out.

Captain Peter Adams, Captain Ralph Armstrong, H W F Baynham (Canford School), Harry Beaton (Nestorian Association), William Bowden, Tom Brown, Frank Carter, James E Cowden, Captain Mike Curtis, John Dagleish, Brigadier Ian Dobbie, Redmond Faulkner (New Zealand), Edward Green, Peter Guy, Reg Hanson (MN Association), Geraldine Harper, Sam Harper, George Heads, W R Henke, the late Bill Heslam, Anthony J Higgins, Alf Johnson, Pat Jones (Archivist, Exmouth Association), Captain T A Kent, J K Kerr, the late Captain William McVicar, Ken Maguire, G V Monk, J R Munday, George Musk, Winifrid Mutimer, Dennis Naylor, Lettice Nichols née Capon, Captain S F Nicolson, Ray Parker, Alex Parsons, Edward Pearlman (Israel), Pat Phillips née Tenow, Tom Pritchard, Dr Doreen Rippon, Captain Philip Rivers (Malaysia), the late Chief Petty Officer Charles Rogers, Tom Simpkins, Donald Stewart, Captain D A Stokes, Mairi Stronach, Gabe Thomas, Commodore John Wacher, Jim Waggott (*Milag* Association), Frank Walker, and Ross Woods (Australia).

Admiralty Library (Jennie Wraight); Apostleship of the Sea (Tim Maguire, National Director); Blue Star Line; Canadian Pacific (UK) Ltd; City of Hull Museums (Arthur G Credland); Commonwealth War Graves Commission (Helen M Chapin); Guildhall Library; Honourable Company of Master Mariners (J A V Maddock, Clerk to the Company); Imperial War Museum (Roderick Suddaby); John Swire & Company Ltd (Charlotte Havilland); Merseyside Maritime Museum (J Gordon Reed); The Missions to Seamen (Anne Haines, Registrar); P & O Group (Stephen Rabson, Information Department); Public Record Office (William Spencer); Registry of Shipping & Seamen (Neil Staples); South Street Seaport Museum, New York (Norman Brouwer); Western Mail & Echo Library (Julie Gordon).

Quotations from documents in the archives of the Imperial War Museum appear by permission, as do quotations from documents under Crown Copyright in the Public Record Office.

Special thanks go to Roderick Suddaby, Keeper of Archives at the Imperial War Museum for his ever-friendly guidance into the Museum's files.

The photograph of the Merchant Navy Memorial at Tower Hill would not have appeared without the co-operation of the present owners of the Port of London Authority Building at Ten Trinity Square, which overlooks the memorial. Not only did the Willis Corroon Group PLC allow me onto the roof of their offices, they also supplied an escort in the shape of Sergeant Barry Codling of the Corps of Commissionaires to make sure I did not fall off.

Abbreviations Used

AMC	Armed Merchant Cruiser
BEM	British Empire Medal
CAM	Merchant ship fitted with catapult and aircraft
CBE	Commander of the Order of the British Empire, a decoration a rank above OBE
DBS	Distressed British Seaman
DEMS	Defensively Equipped Merchant Ships. Gunners aboard merchant ships were therefore known as DEMS gunners
DSC	Distinguished Service Cross
DSM	Distinguished Service Medal
DSO	Distinguished Service Order
EWOMN	Essential Work Order, Merchant Navy (dating from 1942)
HE	High Explosive(s)
HMIS	His Majesty's Indian Ship
MAC	Merchant Aircraft Carrier
MBE	Member of the Order of the British Empire, a decoration a rank lower than the OBE
MSA	Marine Safety Agency
OBE	Order of the British Empire
OSS	Office of Strategic Services (US)
RA	Royal Artillery
RAAF	Royal Australian Air Force
RIN	Royal Indian Navy
RINVR	Royal Indian Navy Volunteer Reserve
RNR	Royal Navy Reserve
RNVR	Royal Navy Volunteer Reserve
SCI	Seamen's Church Institute, New York
SOE	Special Operations Executive
SO, E	Senior Officer, Escort
WAAF	Women's Auxiliary Air Force

Author's Note

The name Blue Funnel Line has been used throughout this book instead of the more proper Alfred Holt & Company or Ocean Steam Ship Company.

The anglicised spellings of Asian place names are those that were in use at the time of the Second World War.

Introduction

After the First World War Admiral of the Fleet Lord Fisher wrote about the preponderance of young, rather than old, officers of the fighting services who had been killed. He went on:

> There is, however, a very splendid exception – when all hands, old and young went to the bottom; and that is in the magnificent Merchant Navy of the British Nation. Seven million tons sank under these men, and the record of so many I've seen who were saved was, 'Three times torpedoed'. And remember! for them no Peerage or Westminster Abbey. They didn't even get paid for the clothes they lost, and their pay stopped the day the ship sank.

Later on he wrote 'of the great Merchant Navy that saved our country'.

Admiral Fisher's words were echoed in the Second World War by General Sir William Dobbie, Governor of Malta at the time that island earned the George Cross. In a foreword to his daughter's book, *Grace Under Malta*, published in 1943, he wrote:

> . . . there is one Service to which I must make special reference. It has not been and is not classified as a fighting Service, and yet it has to face the same perils as some of the others but with less chance of hitting back. I refer, of course, to the Merchant Navy. The work which this magnificent Service did, in conjunction with the Royal Navy, in bringing supplies to Malta cannot be over-estimated. Without that help Malta could not have held out. It was, however, terribly difficult at times to bring the supplies. Many brave men and many fine ships were lost in these operations. But the supplies did get through, in just sufficient quantities to help Malta to turn the corner. The debt the Empire owes to the Merchant Navy is immense.

The Malta convoys mentioned by General Dobbie, important as they were for the Maltese people and for British strategy in the Mediterranean, formed but a fraction of the Merchant Navy's overall contribution to the war effort. On every ocean and every sea, British merchant ships formed the principal life-line of the Empire and its Allies. Throughout the war, even after the United States entered it, Britain's merchant fleet provided the main conduit for Allied food, oil, arms, tanks, and troops, in every theatre of war save the North Pacific where their colleagues in the American Merchant Marine played the predominant role. Two thousand Allied merchant ships were used to support the D-Day landings in June 1944, and most of them were British. Most troop movements in the war were made by British ships, and Churchill is on record as saying that the trooping movements of the *Queen Mary* and *Queen Elizabeth* shortened the war by two years.

Another Second World War soldier, arguably the most famous of them all, Field Marshal Viscount Montgomery of Alamein, in a speech at a Chamber of Shipping meeting in London in 1950, said,

> . . . victory was won in Hitler's war not only by the courage and skill of the Fighting Services, but also by the quality of the ships and men of the Merchant Navy who transported us to our overseas bases and battlefronts, and maintained us there till the job was done. All this is quite apart from the fact that our country could never have survived either of the two world wars if our imports from overseas had not been maintained. And they were maintained in spite of the most determined attacks by the enemy to disrupt our sea communications.

In a message to seamen in July 1941 Winston Churchill said:

> We are a seafaring race and we understand the call of the sea. We account you in these hard days worthy successors in a tradition of steadfast courage and high adventure, and we feel confident that the proud tradition of our Island will be upheld wherever the ensign of a British merchantman is flown.

Later he wrote, 'We never call on the officers and men of the Merchant Navy in vain', and elaborated further in his Victory in Europe broadcast in May 1945 when he said:

> My friends, when our minds turn to the North-western approaches we will not forget the devotion of our merchant seamen . . . so rarely mentioned in the headlines.

He was right about the comparatively small amount of publicity given to the work of the Merchant Navy during the war years, and it has been so ever since. Books about the campaigns of the war in which the three armed services took part are legion, but comparatively few have been written about the role of the unfashionable and unarmed fourth service.

A few years ago, during various 50th anniversary celebrations of Second World War events, any observer too young to have been around between 1939-45 could have been forgiven for thinking that the Merchant Navy had played a non-essential role in those events; even that the Royal Navy and the U-boats were out there fighting each other with nothing in between. The truth is, of course, that merchant seamen were there, playing the parts of piggies-in-the-middle.

And here is more food for thought. At the annual Remembrance Day march past at the Cenotaph in Whitehall, no men of the Merchant Navy and Fishing Fleet are to be seen. None have ever been invited. The distinctive white berets of the contingent representing the Arctic convoys are worn by men of the Royal Navy escort ships and not by anyone from the ships they were escorting. At that great and moving ceremony the only recognition of the part the Merchant Navy played in the war is the wreath laid by its single representative who stands alongside the leaders of the armed services. (Every year the British Department of Transport, through its presently styled Marine Safety Agency (MSA) which controls the Registry of Shipping and Seamen located in Cardiff, requests the Honourable Company of Master Mariners and other Merchant Navy organisations to select the person to lay that wreath at the Cenotaph. Those bodies are also asked to select representatives to take up three or four seats in Westminster Abbey at the Service of Remembrance which follows the Cenotaph ceremony.) It is said that the ceremony commemorates the fighting services only, yet nurses, firemen, Bletchley Park code-breakers, London bus drivers and other non-belligerents take part, and quite rightly too.

Instead, therefore, at that same 11th hour when the military war dead are being commemorated by the great and the good in Whitehall, merchant seamen congregate about their own memorial hard by the Tower of London. Not much pomp and circumstance there as the forgotten navy remembers its own. But its representatives stand in pride in the Portland stone-walled sunken garden among the bronze-emblazoned names of 23,837 of their comrades who have no grave but the sea and who are listed under the names of the ships they died with. (The graves of another 8000 of their comrades lie in cemeteries scattered around the globe.)

British merchant seamen were well and truly in the front line of the Second World War from its very beginning. The last few months of 1939 have been described as the 'phoney war', and except for the unfortunate Poles it might have been 'phoney' on land, but it was a very different matter at sea. Less than nine hours after hostilities began on 3 September 1939 the liner *Athenia* (Donaldson Atlantic Line) commanded by Captain James Cook, en route from Belfast to Montreal, was torpedoed by the German submarine *U-30*, commanded by Lieutenant Fritz Lemp. Of the 1418 passengers and crew on board, well over 100 were lost, including 19 members of the crew. Between that date and the end of the year 215 merchant ships, totalling 748,000 tons, were lost.

Merchant seamen were up to their eyes in the war right to the end. On 7 May 1945, the day of Germany's unconditional surrender and the day before VE-Day, the steamship *Avondale Park* was torpedoed by a U-boat in the Firth of Forth.

During almost six years of hostilities against the Axis powers, the war at sea never ceased. Those years saw the loss of nearly 2500 British merchant ships and 116 fishing vessels, amounting to some 12,000,000 tons. (Great Britain began the war with nearly 9000 merchant ships of all classes, amounting to 21,000,000 tons.) 'British' in this context, and in the manner of the times, includes all ships under the British flag and those on

UK, Dominion, Indian, or Colonial Registers, together with foreign vessels either on charter or which had been requisitioned. The figures shown here are those given in the Admiralty publication *British Merchant Vessels Lost or Damaged by Enemy Action During the Second World War*, published in London in 1947. British merchant ships that were commissioned for naval service, including fishing craft used as minesweepers, and other ships used as Royal Fleet Auxiliaries, are not included. That publication is not a wholly reliable source – all depends on how the phrase 'lost or damaged from enemy action' is defined – and so statistics based on it are likely to be on the low side. (According to the Commonwealth War Graves Commission a total of 4786 merchant ships were lost during the war, although that appears to be an over-estimation.) Some of those lost were victims of the ordinary perils of the sea, a few more were lost to war causes other than to enemy action, and some were seized by the enemy, but 69 per cent of them were sent to the bottom by submarines, and others to attacks by enemy surface units or aircraft or to the hazards posed by the magnetic, contact, and acoustic mine. A further 900 vessels were damaged by enemy action. Nearly 32,000 of the 185,000 merchant seamen who served in the war either went down with their ships, died subsequently as a result of those sinkings, or were otherwise killed in action or died while interned as prisoners of war. The British Merchant Navy lost proportionately more men than did any of the three armed services; moreover, more than a few of those who died were barely sixteen years old and some were even younger than that. Some of the merchant 'seamen' lost were women. There were three stewardesses, for instance, aboard *Ceramic* (Shaw Savill & Albion) when she was torpedoed and sunk with the loss of all 295 members of her crew on 6 December 1942. (*Ceramic*, Captain H C Elford, holds the record for most crew members lost on any one British merchant ship in the Second World War. The tragedy does not end there, for she was also carrying 378 passengers and only one of those, Sapper A E Munday of the Royal Engineers, was saved.) During the conflict, merchant seamen gained 6500 awards for gallantry.

Full details of ship sinkings were not officially published during the war as such information might have helped the enemy. However, with survivors, many of them injured, coming ashore or being brought ashore in ports all over the world including neutral countries, news got around the international press; the epic story of the sailors Tapscott and Widdicombe from *Anglo-Saxon* (see Chapter 3) is a case in point, for it made the newspapers in the United States. During the worst period for sinkings, losses of ships and cargoes were appalling enough, but what happened to the crews and sometimes passengers on the ships involved were often the subject of horrendous headlines. Survivors told of the terror of those often too brief minutes between an explosion deep down in the bowels of the ship and its final plunge to the bottom. They spoke of losing their mates, of having to fight their way clear through twisted steel, scalding steam, and fire, in an effort to reach a lifeboat, sometimes only to find that the boat had been destroyed. When tankers blew up, survivors found themselves struggling in a blazing sea of oil. Even when in a lifeboat, the horrors were not yet over. In those boats, unless they were lucky enough to be picked up quickly, seamen watched helplessly as their comrades died of injuries, or from exposure or thirst; on top of that survivors in boats sometimes suffered the additional horror of being machine-gunned by the enemy.

The worst month of all for ship losses was December 1941, when a total of 120 vessels were lost, 98 of them seized or sunk in the South China Seas when Japan entered the war. The worst twelve months were those between June 1940 and May 1941, during which 806 vessels were lost at the rate of over two a day, the majority to U-boat action in the North Atlantic. The havoc created by U-boats is best illustrated by the record of that ace among U-boat commanders, Otto Kretschmer. Firstly in *U-23* and then in *U-99*, in sixteen patrols covering the first year and a half of the war, Kretschmer sank forty-four ships totalling 266,029 tons. For every day he spent at sea in that period he sank 1000 tons of shipping, a record never equalled. Not for Kretschmer the usual firing of salvoes of four or six torpedoes from 3000 yards; he preferred to act like a sniper, picking off individual ships at close range. Fortunately for British merchant seamen, *U-99* was sunk by HMS *Walker* in March 1941. (Kretschmer and all but three of his crew were picked up and became prisoners of war in Canada. In 1965, the by then Flotillenadmiral Otto Kretschmer was appointed Chief of Staff, NATO Naval Forces, Baltic Approaches.)

The war experience of J & C Harrison Ltd, a London-based firm of trampship owners formed in 1888, is perhaps typical of the experiences of the genre of shipping companies that made up the bulk of the British merchant fleet of the time. On the outbreak of war, 'Hungry Harrisons' as they were known (a not unique allusion to the standard of food served on board and, in this case, to the black 'H' funnel markings the ships carried), possessed a fleet of twenty-three tramps. During the war years they took on the management of four wartime-built ships, two 'Forts' and two 'Libertys', and a requisitioned Yugoslav freighter, *Frederico Glavic*, renamed *Radport*. In peacetime, ships of the Harrison fleet might be found on any ocean or sea, though there was a tendency to specialise in the 'coal out, grain home' trade to and from the River Plate; the fleet lost none of this ubiquity during the war years, in which no less than nineteen of them were lost.

Two of the nineteen were mined within a few of days of each other in the Thames Estuary. Two others were torpedoed on the same day while serving in an Arctic convoy and went down with eighteen members of their crews. A further two were lost in other Arctic convoys, one of them taking with her all but seven of her crew. With the loss of over two hundred lives, ten of the company's ships were sunk in other parts of the North Atlantic, one of them, the *Harlesden*, to an attack by the German raider *Gneisenau*, and the rest to submarines. Amongst the latter was *Harpagus* which had earlier on the day of her sinking and at great risk to herself, plucked forty-eight survivors from *Norman Monarch* out of the water; twenty-six of those together with thirty-two of her own crew later went down with *Harpagus*. One ship was torpedoed in the South Atlantic. The other two losses took place on opposite sides of the Indian Ocean. *Harpasa* succumbed to an attack in the Bay of Bengal by aircraft from a Japanese carrier fleet working in tandem with their Burma-based 11th Air Fleet. The other, *Hartismere*, fell to torpedoes and gunfire from the Japanese submarine *I-10* under its crack captain, Commander Nakajima Seiji who, operating in the Mozambique Channel, sank a total of eight Allied ships amounting to 40,000 tons during a five-week period in June/ July 1942. One more Harrison ship, *Harpenden*, was severely damaged by a torpedo attack in the Atlantic, though she managed to limp to safety.

As with the British armed services, the Merchant Navy entered the Second World War largely unprepared. It had suffered grievously from years of depression since the last conflict, those years witnessing many rivers and lochs choked with laid-up ships. Many seamen had perforce left the sea, in some years the loss in manpower exceeding 15,000, and many deck officers had taken seamens' jobs in the fo'c'sle, finding that better than the alternative of trying to obtain one of the rare jobs ashore.

In 1938, when the writing on the wall was fortunately being read by a handful of unblinkered men in Whitehall, a register of volunteers ready to return to sea should the need arise was compiled. It was as well the precaution was taken, for when war came in September 1939, about 12,000 serving merchant officers and men who were either in the Royal Naval Reserve (RNR), or who were serving on ships such as *Jervis Bay* which became armed merchant cruisers or, in the case of the Fishing Fleet, when many trawlers were requisitioned, to become minesweepers, went at once into the Navy. The Admiralty's demand for officers in particular was such that it caused the Board of Trade, the government department with central responsibility for the Merchant Navy at the time, to urge a go-slow in the transfer of merchant seamen into the Royal Navy until the already depleted numbers could be made up.

In view of the immense and important task the Merchant Navy undertook in the war years it is worth recalling that its total strength in 1942, perhaps the worst period of the war, was only about 120,000 officers and men. This number was small in comparison with the total number of men in the Royal Navy, for a merchant ship needs only a fraction of the complement necessary to man a fighting ship, and furthermore merchant seamen were not required to man shore bases. Nevertheless, the total number of merchant ships vastly exceeded the total number of warships.

At various stages of the war merchant ship losses and, of course, losses of men required to man them, became a major, perhaps *the* major, source of concern for Winston Churchill and his Whitehall colleagues as they went about the business of managing the war. It is said that the first thing Churchill required to see as he began work each day during the bad times of 1940-1943 was a summary of merchant shipping losses.

Under international convention merchant ships, even those engaged in blockade-running as we shall see, were permitted to carry only sufficient armament for their own protection; that is, such guns that were provided were for defensive and not offensive purposes. In fact the guns provided little protection with no real scope for hitting back, though a few ships did manage to do so, especially when they were manned by the professionals of the Maritime Regiment of Royal Artillery, the Royal Marines, the Royal Navy and, aboard some troopships, men of the RAF, who were collectively known as DEMS (Defensively Equipped Merchant Shipping) gunners. Many of the 38,000 DEMS men were pensioners who had volunteered to return to the colours, and nearly 4000 of them lost their lives during the conflict. (For administrative and pay purposes most naval DEMS gunners were listed as being attached to HMS *President*, a naval drill ship, each personal record then being endorsed with the name of the merchant ship actually being served on. For legal purposes they 'signed on' the ship's Articles of Agreement at a nominal wage of one shilling a month.)

There was another dimension to the 'hitting back' problem. Long forgotten ashore but very much remembered by shipmasters was the case of Captain Charles Fryatt of the Great Eastern Railway's cross-channel steamer *Brussels* during the First World War. In late March 1915, whilst making for the Hook of Holland from Harwich, Fryatt sighted *U-33* on the surface and making for his ship at top speed. *Brussels* could not outrun the submarine, but it could attack, and Fryatt headed straight for the submarine. After scraping down the side of the ship, the now listing U-boat made off. As a result of this Fryatt became a marked man, and in June the following year *Brussels* was intercepted by German torpedo-boats and escorted into Zeebrugge. On 27 June 1916 he was tried by a Naval Court, sentenced to death as a *franc tireur* and was taken out and shot that same night. In the Second World War a shipmaster taking on a submarine could not be certain, therefore, that if captured he would not face a similar fate. (In 1919 Captain Fryatt's body was brought back with much pomp and ceremony to Dover, then taken to St Paul's in London, where a service was held, before being transported to Fryatt's home town, Dovercourt near Harwich, to be buried.)

Although largely without the means to protect themselves, seamen manned the ships and kept on manning them throughout the war, despite the fact that about one in four of the number serving at sea at any one time were to meet with watery graves. Their depth of commitment is well illustrated by the many who, after having their ships blown from under them and spending hours, days, even weeks afloat in open lifeboats before being rescued or before reaching land under their own efforts, went back for more of the same almost immediately. Even that is not the end of the story. During the first part of the war, until the Essential Work Order for the Merchant Navy (EWOMN) was promulgated in May 1941 making it illegal for anyone to leave the service but balancing that by guaranteeing wages between voyages, merchant seamen received no pay when 'off articles'. Seamen signed Articles of Agreement when they joined a ship and from that moment they were 'on pay'. When eventually they arrived back at a home port they 'paid off', the Articles officially coming to an end, and prior to May 1941 the seaman was then 'off pay' until he joined another ship or signed new Articles on his last one. There was one other circumstance which brought Articles and therefore wages to an end, and that was when a ship was lost for whatever reason, including enemy action. In other words, until the advent of EWOMN, a seaman could have his ship blown from under him and then spend weeks in a lifeboat in the knowledge that he was 'off pay' from the time of the sinking. There was an equally objectionable corollary to that. A seaman at the time of signing articles could allot part of his salary to his next-of-kin, and those monthly allotments, too, came to an end at the time of the sinking. It was a system scarcely designed to ease the mind of a seaman fighting for his life in an open boat, to say nothing of the effect the allotment cessation must have had on his next-of-kin who often would have no firm knowledge of what had happened to the husband or son involved.

Although the May 1941 changes were beneficial, they did nothing, of course, to diminish the dangers the seaman had to face; they merely eased some of the consequences. Those dangers had been recognised from the second week of the war when on 15 September 1939 a War Risk Payment was added to the basic pay of all merchant seamen. It was paid at the rate of £10 per month to everyone over the age of eighteen, and £5 per month to those under that age. (The latter seems a rather strange arrangement for, from an actuarial point of view, the youngsters had more to lose.) This extra payment helped to keep sailors from leaving the sea during the period before the EWOMN made it illegal for them to do so, and furthermore, by calling it 'War Risk Payment', that prevented other industrial workers ashore from making matching wage demands.

The Essential Work Order was one of several innovations which helped raise the status of merchant seamen generally, something that was very much needed. The low regard in which merchant seamen had been held in some circles until then is perhaps best illustrated by the case of the *King City*. This ship belonging to Reardon Smith Line and under the command of Captain H W Marshall, was requisitioned by the Admiralty early in the war for service as a collier to the fleet. On 24 August 1940 she was sunk in the Indian Ocean by the German raider *Atlantis*. The survivors, including Captain Marshall, were landed in Italian Somaliland and placed in a prisoner of war camp. They were rescued in 1941 when the British Army captured Somaliland but, instead of being greeted like returning heroes, they were treated like lepers. The *King City* incident was not an isolated case, but the advent of the EWOMN brought some change for the better.

What manner of men went down to the sea in merchant ships? The bulk of seamen came from Merseyside, Clydeside, Newcastle, Hull,

London, South Wales, and that historic source, the West Country. Yet, any place in the British Isles was capable of breeding a sailor, and many did so. Furthermore, not all seamen manning British merchant vessels came from the home islands. A fair proportion were Lascars from India, West Indians, Chinese from Hong Kong, Somalis from Africa, Irish from Eire, and Arabs from various parts of the British Empire. Others came from the Dominions. Also amongst them were seaman from occupied Allied nations who had found themselves cut off in Britain, or had escaped there. A number of American citizens also served in the Merchant Navy (just as some of their compatriots did in the RAF, Royal Navy, and British Army, a handful even serving as officers in the Indian Army). Richard Maury, a descendent of Matthew Fontaine Maury, the hydrographer and oceanographer, joined the Merchant Navy in 1940, and until Pearl Harbor when he transferred into the US Merchant Marine, helped to train crews in Canada. Special mention must be made of seaman of the Jewish faith, from Britain itself or from other countries, who were considered to be under special risk if captured by the Germans. They were given the option of sailing under names other than their own; if the option was taken up they were issued with identity papers in that false name.

No matter his place of origin, the merchant seaman of those days was independent of mind and character and inclined to be a bit 'bolshie'. Not for him the rules and regulations of the Royal Navy; he much preferred the more easy-going ways aboard a merchantman. Not for him, except for the comparative few who served aboard liners, the wearing of uniform; more often than not he was allowed to wear exactly what he pleased. The ordinary sailor in peacetime had no job security. Indeed, it sometimes suited him to be paid off at the end of Articles for he could then do just as his fancy directed him, take a spell ashore or sign on another ship which would carry him to a part of the world he had never been before – always providing of course, that he could find one with an empty berth. If he found a happy ship with good shipmates he might stick with it if he could, his loyalty being directed towards his mates and the ship itself rather than to the rather remote shipping company which owned it.

Even masters, engineer and deck officers, who, in general, did tend to stay with a particular shipping line and who therefore owed some sort of allegiance to that company, had no real security of tenure, especially with the many less-than-decent companies around. The Merchant Navy Journal of October 1941 carried the story of the British master who had been awarded the George Medal for saving his ship from a German raider. He was dismissed by the company with only a fortnight's notice because he had been compelled to incur heavy engine-room repair bills in a foreign port. (The shipping line involved was later forced to make amends by the officers' union.)

Together with the merchant sailor's independence of character went a sense of adventure, which was, however, more apparent in the young seaman than in the old hand. As the sense of adventure in the older men diminished its place was taken, rather paradoxically, by a propensity towards the extremes of habitual behaviour; despite his independence of mind he became used to and liked a life regimented by the sound of the ship's bell striking the half-hours, a life of monotonous regularity and routine, of taking meals and tea and coffee breaks (called 'muggoes'), at set times. He accepted the sameness of long periods at sea that were just occasionally interspersed by usually much shorter periods of hectic 'making whoopee' ashore. Some of the older men came not to bother with the 'whoopees' at all, and it was not unknown for a few to stay on board without stepping a foot ashore for the entire period the ship was away from Britain, which could be for up to two years.

The attitudes developed in peacetime tended to be carried over into wartime. Life at sea is dangerous at any time, and the new dangers the war brought with it did not faze the seamen all that much; it was a matter of taking more care than usual and often sailing in convoy rather than independently. They were practical men and realists. The chief engineer of a tanker carrying benzine, which aside from ammunition was arguably the most dangerous of wartime cargoes, said it was not so bad serving in a tanker because for half of her voyaging, the outward half, she was in ballast which made her the safest thing afloat. At the same time, war or no war, the seaman was still more than willing to stick up for what he considered his just rights. He might not make too much fuss when in mid-winter he learned his ship was joining one of those most dangerous of convoys, those to Northern Russia, but beware any person who expected him to sail on that voyage with a dirty mattress on his bunk.

Though these men were in the front line of war, some, from both ends of the age spectrum, would not have been allowed to join the armed services, or if they had been, would not have been sent into a battle zone. Many rather ancient ex-masters and chief engineers were called out of retirement to serve again under the Red Ensign, and some cadets, apprentices, deck and cabin boys were just sixteen, although this minimum age was raised by a year later in the war. There are records of some deck and cabin boys being only fifteen and at least one was a year younger than that.

There would have been many more merchant navy deaths had not the majority of ships on the most dangerous routes sailed in convoys, so something must be said here about the history and implementation of the system. The convoy system is of hoary tradition but it had fallen out of favour with the British Admiralty by the time of the First World War. As late as November 1916, in the face of mounting shipping losses caused by U-boat attacks, Admiral Jellicoe declared at a War Committee meeting that he did not approve of convoys, arguing that they offered too large a target and that it would be impossible to keep them in close enough formation to be effectively screened by a few destroyers. He went on to say that the larger the convoy, the greater chances of U-boats' success against it. Much better, was the Admiralty view, to attack U-boats in their home lairs. Most admirals fought against the convoy concept with the obstinacy of entrenched experts, and were not alone in that. Top shipowner Walter Runciman was also opposed to the concept, saying that as all vessels in a convoy would have to keep to the speed of the slowest, it made for a waste of tonnage. Runciman's views may have been coloured by the fact that the convoy system subjected the private maritime industry to more than an element of State control.

Shipmasters of the time were none to keen on the concept either. At an Admiralty-sponsored conference of masters it was agreed that the standard of station-keeping and discipline required in a convoy would be impossible to obtain, so they advised against it. One can speculate that this decision owed more to the independent nature of shipmasters and to pressure placed upon them by shipowners like Runciman, and perhaps to the age-old and not always friendly rivalry between the Royal and Merchant Navies, than to any implied self-criticism of their seamanship and ship-handling abilities.

Then, in February 1917, in the knowledge that if their U-boats could devastate British trade routes Britain must surely collapse, the Germans began a campaign of unrestricted submarine warfare, sinking ships without warning. In that month shipping losses, measured in both number of ships and in tonnage, more than doubled the average for the previous six months, and by April had trebled. Almost at the twelfth hour, let alone the eleventh, Jellicoe and the Admiralty changed their minds, and a system of convoying was implemented, which slowly brought the number of losses down.

Despite the lessons of 1917-1918, at the outbreak of the Second World War Britain's anti-submarine forces, such as they were, were deployed in long-planned anti-submarine patrols in areas considered particularly at risk. The inter-war planners considered that the defensive armament of merchant ships, coupled with routing ships away from danger areas, would be sufficient precaution unless Germany again began unrestricted submarine warfare. The sinking of the liner *Athenia* within hours of the start of the war (the U-boat commander involved had in fact exceeded his instructions), put paid to all that. The Admiralty immediately introduced a system of convoy in the Western Approaches and this was gradually extended to cover most major Atlantic shipping routes. By 1943, Atlantic convoy routes formed a huge interlocking pattern, and linked to it was the convoy route in the Indian Ocean, from the Cape of Good Hope to the Red Sea and Persian Gulf, though in general most ships traversing the Indian Ocean (and also the Pacific) were expected to sail alone. Prior to the fall of Singapore in February 1942 there was a major convoy route between Bombay and that island fortress.

From early in the war on all routes (except that between Britain and Gibraltar where ships with a minimum speed of 8 knots were included), only ships that could steam at between 9 and 14.9 knots were placed in

convoys, the slower and faster vessels being required to sail independently. The upper speed limit was based on the surface speed of a U-boat,
estimated to be 15 knots. The slower of the independently routed ships
were, of course, in grave peril. As time passed the system underwent
refinement and experiment. In late 1940 for instance, slow North Atlantic
convoys for ships of between 7.5 and 9 knots were instituted. (In practice
it was found that for all convoys the actual speed made good was on
average between 0.5 and 1 knot lower than the declared lowest speed.)
Ships too slow for even those convoys were given a life expectancy of less
than a year. In the autumn of 1940 the upper speed limit was reduced to
13 knots in an attempt to speed up imports by faster passages from ships
capable of that speed. The experiment lasted only nine months, for it was
found that heavy losses among the slower of the independently routed
'fast' ships had resulted in an overall reduction of imports. Taking the
Second World War as a whole, 60 per cent of the ships sunk by submarine
were sailing independently.

Apart from adjustments to routes – evasive routing as it was called –
based upon reports of enemy attacks, U-boat wireless activity and, later
on, information stemming from Bletchley Park, the secret British code-
breaking facility with the ability to read German Enigma naval codes,
route changes were made in keeping with the tides of war and with the
development of new convoy protection techniques. If it can be said of
Lieutenant Fritz Lemp that he began the war at sea, it can also be said
that he was responsible, albeit unintentionally, for ensuring Allied victory
over the U-boats. On 9 May 1941, Lemp, now a Lieutenant-Commander
and commanding *U-100*, after sinking two ships in convoy HX123, was
forced to the surface by depth-charges from the corvette HMS *Aubrietia*.
U-100's crew abandoned ship but Lemp, seeing that his craft was not
sinking after all, tried to reboard, no doubt set on destroying the Enigma
code machine she carried, but he was killed by a machine-gun bullet.
U-100 was boarded by a party led by Lieutenant Balme from HMS *Bulldog*
and taken in tow. Two days later, on the way to Iceland, the submarine
sank but not before the Enigma and additional rotors and daily keys for
it, along with documents relating to the machine's setting and operation,
had been taken aboard *Bulldog*. That piece of good fortune turned out to
be decisive in the process of breaking German naval codes by Britain's
code-breakers at Bletchley Park, and had a decisive influence on the
winning of the Battle of the Atlantic.

The North Atlantic, across which the great majority of convoys sailed,
provides the best illustration of the change in techniques. The fall of
France in June 1940 necessitated the routing of London-bound ships
around Scotland instead of through the English Channel. From April
1941, Iceland became available as an Allied aircraft base and for the
refuelling of escort ships, and so convoy routes tended to move northward, especially during the northern summer. In August of that same year
came the first of the Arctic convoys to Russia. In the following month the

United States, although not then officially in the war, began assisting in the escort of convoys to and from her shores, thus easing the Royal Navy's overall burden. One remarkable example of this was Convoy WE12X. It was remarkable in that all eighteen ships involved, troopships and escorts, were American although the troops being carried were British. The British 18th Division, originally meant for service in the Middle East but which ended up in Malaya, left Britain aboard British ships and reached Halifax, Nova Scotia, in the first week of November 1941. There they transferred into six American troopships, including the crack liner *America*, now renamed *West Point*. The convoy left Halifax on 10 November escorted by the aircraft carrier USS *Ranger*, two cruisers and ten destroyers. It was a month later, and after the convoy had reached South African waters, when the news came of Pearl Harbor and America was officially in the war.

The improvements in North Atlantic convoy techniques continued. In June 1942 escorts began refuelling at sea. New and longer-ranged aircraft became available in the spring of 1943, which, operating from Britain, Canada, and Iceland, were able to cover most of the convoy routes except for an area known as the mid-Atlantic gap. By the summer of that year the gap was being filled by a new class of ship, the escort carrier, and by Merchant Aircraft Carriers, or MAC ships, each of the latter having a short flight deck and a complement of four Swordfish aircraft in addition to her normal cargo-carrying capability. There were also CAM ships which carried a catapult and a plane, usually a Mark I Hurricane, which once catapulted off was, of course, irretrievable. (There is no record of direct successes against submarines by planes from either MAC or CAM ships; but their presence undoubtedly caused U-boat commanders to be more circumspect.) In October of that year more southerly convoy routes were developed when Portugal, Britain's oldest ally, permitted air bases to be set up in the Azores.

One aspect of the convoy system much appreciated by merchant seamen was the incorporation of rescue ships into the convoy formation. From the beginning of 1941, small, specially-selected vessels manned by RNR crews and carrying medical teams performed excellent service picking up survivors. Six out of a total of twenty-nine of these ships were themselves lost, but overall they managed to save over 2000 British seaman and a similar number from Allied ships. It made a world of difference to a seaman's state of mind if he knew that there was at least a chance of being picked up quickly if his ship was sunk.

It is easy to forget in any account of the Merchant Navy at war that, in addition to being the life-line of the armed services wherever they might be, British merchant ships were still engaged in transporting ordinary non-military cargoes around the globe, just as they had been doing in peacetime. Ordinary trade had to go on to help pay for the war. It had been the same in the First World War, although this time round ship-owners were not permitted to make the fortunes that that war had brought them. The Ministry of War Transport (and its predecessor the Ministry of Shipping) took control of virtually the whole of the British merchant fleet and fixed the freight rates paid, which were considerably lower than those paid to neutral ships on the same run. For example, the 'neutral' rate between the UK and the River Plate was 55 shillings a ton whilst the British rate was 40 per cent lower; the difference in the two rates for cargoes to and from North America was even more marked, at nearly 60 per cent.

Ordinary hazards of the sea did not, of course, cease during the war years; indeed they were aggravated by the fact that lighthouses were switched off and buoys removed. Marine casualties from storms and strandings accounted for the loss of an average 265 ships a year. Along with all types of British capital equipment, ships were being run down for lack of proper maintenance, and this also caused losses.

On top of everything else, hazards for merchant ships did not cease once they had reached port. We shall see that two of the most catastrophic incidents of the war took place in what were considered to be reasonably safe havens.

Whatever the causes of ship losses, they had to be made good by new construction, but the war was half-way through before the Allied building programme completely bridged the loss gap and before the total tonnage available began to grow. By far the greater part of this new tonnage came from the United States, which produced an average monthly build of half a million tons between September 1939 and April 1945, Britain and the Dominions being able to produce less than a quarter of that amount. So it came about that a large number of British seamen ended the war sailing in American-built ships and especially in the so-called 'Liberty' ships. Of the 2710 Liberty ships built, over 200 sailed under the Red Ensign. The names of those on loan to Britain were all prefixed with 'Sam' (*Samderry* and *Samtampa* are two examples), probably as a reminder of who the ships belonged to and from whom those which survived the war had to be purchased after the war (at an average cost of £140,000 each). These ships, admirably suited to their purpose and largely pre-fabricated to cut construction time to the barest minimum, were at one stage being launched from American yards at the rate of three a day. One of them, the *Robert E Peary*, took only 111 hours to assemble after its keel had been laid. The Liberty ship building programme was only made possible by American know-how, management skills and industrial might, but it is worth remembering that the design used was a British one, based on the 1939 plans for a ship called *Dorrington Court* by the Sunderland shipbuilder J L Thompson & Sons Ltd. To facilitate pre-fabrication techniques, the Americans altered the internal lay-out of the ship, which resulted in all the accommodation being in one block amidships rather than the original 'two-island' concept. (Standard ships of a different type were built in Canadian dockyards. Their names included either the prefix '*Fort*' or the suffix '*Park*'.)

Many were the adventures of British merchant seamen and their ships during the war and the stories that appear in the following pages touch on only a few of them. The choice of stories is necessarily subjective, although an attempt has been made to include examples which cover all classes of ship and every war zone. Some of the better-known stories are not repeated here, except in asides. Amongst those omitted is the saga of the *San Demetrio* which has been made into a film. Operation 'Pedestal', the most famous of the convoys to Malta has also been left out, as has PQ17, the infamous convoy to Murmansk in which twenty-four merchant ships were lost, two-thirds of the number which set out. Both those convoys have been well documented elsewhere.

In recent years the exploits of the so-called 'Forgotten Army', the 14th British, which fought the longest land campaign of the Second World War in Burma, have rightly become better known. It is hoped that this book will help to remind people of those civilian sailors who were involved in keeping the sea life-lines open during the longest battle of all, the Battle of the Oceans, and who did so without having much of the wherewithal to hit back at the enemy.

CHAPTER 1

Ropner's Navy

Founded in 1874 by a migrant from Germany and based at West Hartlepool, Ropner & Company, together with its associates, had grown to be Britain's largest tramp ship fleet by the mid-1930s. Apart from their funnel mark and house-flag, company ships could be distinguished by their names, for with only a few exceptions, all ended with the suffixes '*-pool*' or '*-by*'. When war came on 3 September 1939, and despite having suffered during the shipping depression of the immediate pre-war years, the company owned forty-five ships amounting to over 400,000 tons.

The first of these to be sunk, a bare eight days after war began, was the 4800-ton *Firby*. She was torpedoed and then finished off by gunfire from a U-boat. The crew had no chance of hitting back because at that early stage of the war she was amongst those British merchant ships not yet armed. Captain Thomas Prince and his crew took to the lifeboats and were soon rescued by the destroyer HMS *Fearless*.

The next ship to be sunk was *Heronspool*, but she did not go down without a fight. On a voyage from Swansea to the St Lawrence with a cargo of coal, on 12 October 1939 she had lost contact with other ships in the convoy due to bad weather. That afternoon a French tanker (the *Emile Miguet*) was sighted some six miles away being shelled by a U-boat. In accordance with the standing instructions for 'stragglers', as ships accidentally detached from convoys were called, Captain Sidney Batson turned his ship away. As night fell Batson doubled the lookouts and placed his gunners on standby around the single 4-inch gun on the poop. At about 2000 hours a signal light was seen flashing from astern, ordering the ship to stop. Instead, Batson rang for full revolutions at the same time sending out an SOS. The U-boat, for that is what it turned out to be, opened fire and the ship fired back. The U-boat dived, but two hours later surfaced on the port quarter to fire again. *Heronspool*'s gunners got in one shot before the submarine submerged for a second time.

An hour later the submarine went through the same routine again. With his engineers coaxing every last ounce of horsepower from the engines, Captain Batson tried to outguess the U-boat commander. He had to keep the submarine astern in order to present the smallest possible target for its torpedoes and also to give his own gunners a chance. The chase and the guessing game went on until about midnight when a torpedo exploded prematurely about 10 feet from the ship before striking it. The U-boat then surfaced once more and exchanged shells with the ship before re-submerging. The cat-and-mouse game ended when the submarine at last managed to get the ship beam on, and its second torpedo slammed into the ship in way of No.1 hold. The explosion broke *Heronspool*'s back and Captain Batson ordered abandon ship. As the sun came up, he and his crew watched from the lifeboats as the ship slipped beneath the waves. A few hours later they were picked up by the American cargo liner *President Harding* and were subsequently landed in New York. For gallantly fending off the submarine for over four hours, Captain Batson was awarded the OBE, and Gunner George Pearson the BEM.

During the first months of the war there was not much cause for laughter during the proceedings of the House of Commons, but when, during a debate on the Merchant Navy on 15th November 1939, a scion of the Ropner family rose to his feet to speak, part of what he had to say brought not only loud laughter but also cheers from that assembly. In his speech Colonel David Ropner MP first paid tribute to the protection afforded merchant ships by the Royal Navy. He then went on to say that two of his company's ships had already been lost to submarines. However, two other company ships, he reported, had given such good accounts of themselves when attacked by U-boats on the surface, that both submarines had been disabled and, after breaking off engagements with the Merchant Navy, had within hours been despatched to the bottom by His Majesty's destroyers. He ended his speech thus: 'At the Admiralty "Ropner's Navy" is almost as well known as that of His Majesty.' It was that which brought the house down. The term 'Ropner's Navy' became a catchphrase and one which was still in use long after hostilities at sea ended in 1945. The incidents which gave birth to it came in the same month, October 1939, in which *Heronspool* was lost.

On 13 October *Stonepool* had detached from her convoy – the same one as *Heronspool*'s – to make southward for the Cape Verde Islands on her own, when suddenly a submarine was sighted on the surface about three miles off. Captain Albert Angell White, at thirty-five one of the company's youngest masters, sent out an SOS as he altered course away and as the submarine opened fire with its gun. The ship fired back with its 4-inch but not in time to prevent two enemy shells from striking home. One of them hit the hull just above the waterline and the other damaged the port lifeboat. The submarine then dived.

Shortly afterwards the ship's lookout spotted a torpedo and Captain White had just time enough to alter course to parallel the torpedo's track so that the missile passed harmlessly by. The submarine then surfaced and there was another exchange of shellfire. Shrapnel from a near-miss made smithereens of *Stonepool*'s second lifeboat. The submarine captain (Lieutenant-Commander Dau, commanding *U-42*) then commenced a series of strange and rather dangerous tactics, dangerous for him that is, of manoeuvring from one quarter of the ship to the other and presenting itself broadside on to *Stonepool* at the end of each such turn as it fired its gun. Gunner Frederick Hayter aboard *Stonepool* must have thought it was his birthday when the full length of the submarine entered his sights. One of Hayter's shells seemed to strike the side of the submarine, after which it dived only to resurface on the same bearing a few minutes later. By then *Stonepool* had put some distance between herself and the enemy despite the water that was coming in fast through the damaged hull. Through his binoculars Captain White could see that the submarine's gun was lying at an irregular angle and he realised that Hayter's shell must have made a direct hit on it. For an hour the German tried to keep up with *Stonepool* but eventually seemed to give up the chase.

Captain White now set about making his ship seaworthy for by then she was noticeably down by the head. By clearing away some of the coal cargo, the hole made by the shell was reached and a patch was rigged over it. Meanwhile, just in case it was needed, the ship's carpenter set about repairing the port lifeboat. Having assessed the hull damage Captain White decided to make back for the Bristol Channel. It was not long after coming round on the homeward course when a British destroyer was sighted and the submarine's last position was relayed to it. In a cloud of spray the warship turned and raced off in that direction and a few hours later returned. She carried survivors from the U-boat, for the craft had scuttled as soon as the destroyer hoved in sight.

Later that day Captain White received a radio message from the C-in-C, Western Approaches, congratulating him and his crew on directly contributing to the destruction of the submarine. Captain White passed the message around the ship, and now under escort of their very own destroyer, *Stonepool*'s proud crew thought their immediate adventures were over, but they were wrong. The ship's lookout suddenly spotted a U-boat surfacing in a position where *Stonepool*'s hull hid her from view of the destroyer. Captain White immediately flashed the sighting to the warship which turned at speed to engage. The U-boat met its end from depth charges. *Stonepool* had therefore had a direct hand in the destruction of one submarine and an indirect one in the destruction of another and that went some way to balance the books over the loss of *Firby* and *Heronspool*. By that time, however, Captain White had more things to worry about than mere submarines, for the weather had worsened and the temporary patch over the hole in the hull had worked loose and water was coming in so fast that the ship's pumps could barely cope. After battling against the elements for two days they finally reached the safety of Barry Roads. Captain White was awarded the OBE and Gunner Fred Hayter the BEM. The honours for Ropner's Navy that October were mounting up.

The second engagement referred to by Colonel Ropner concerned the *Rockpool*. On the very same day that *Stonepool* was battling with the U-boat, *Rockpool*, on passage from Halifax, Nova Scotia, to England, had lost contact with her convoy during a storm. She never caught up with it, and on 19 October entered the dangerous waters known as the Western Approaches alone. It was Captain William Harland himself who spotted a U-boat on the surface to starboard. Ordering hard-a-port he called all hands to action stations and sent off a radio signal. The submarine opened fire with its gun without scoring a hit and *Rockpool*'s gunner, ex-Colour Sergeant Tom Watkins, Royal Marines, returned fire as the submarine submerged.

In his report Captain Harland wrote:

> After three or four minutes [the submarine] commenced to rise. As soon as his periscope came above the surface we opened fire. He fired several rounds of shrapnel, the shells bursting just clear of the bows. We got close to him. Through the binoculars you could see the spray from our shells going over his conning tower. He again submerged for a few minutes. The battle went on like this until 1345. He was working out a very good bracket and at any moment I expected to be hit. When we dropped our shells close to him he dived. At 1345 I ordered smoke floats to be thrown over the side. At 1350 the smoke screen was effective and we got away without damage to the ship or crew. I must in concluding say the morale of the crew was astonishing, there was no panic, every man carried out instantly the orders that were given. At 1600 I put the firemen on double watches and kept them doubled until we passed Lundy Island. This was the only way they could keep up a full head of steam.

After reaching port Captain Harland added the following postscript.

> Since writing the above letter I have been informed by the Admiralty that we so damaged the submarine that he could not submerge. A destroyer coming in answer to my radio captured the survivors and sank the submarine.

That brought Ropner's Navy's tally in both submarines and OBE's to three. A BEM went to Colour Sergeant Tom Watkins.

Of the forty-five ships Ropner's began the war with, no less than thirty-four had been lost by its end. The company also took over the management of about the same number of requisitioned and wartime-built ships for the Ministry of War Transport, and many of those were also lost. Over 600 Ropner seamen lost their lives during the conflict. In April 1940 the company lost two vessels. *Haxby* was sunk by the German raider *Orion* with the loss of sixteen crew members. Next to go was *Hawnby*, commanded by the redoubtable forty-seven year-old Captain Harland OBE. The ship struck a mine and sank in the Thames Estuary, but fortunately without loss of life.

The destruction went on. After surviving two earlier aircraft attacks in 1940, *Otterpool* succumbed to a torpedo in June of that year. Twenty-three crew members went down with the ship, including Captain Thomas Prince who had survived the sinking of *Firby*.

Not all the story is of destruction, however. In September 1940, *Pikepool*, commanded by Captain J B Atkinson, was involved in the rescue of survivors from two ships in the North Atlantic. *Pikepool* was sailing west on a designated route when around midnight on the 20th radio messages were received from two ships somewhere ahead which were part of an eastbound convoy; both reported that they had been torpedoed and were sinking. Two hours later *Pikepool* almost ran into the eastbound convoy, not an unusual occurrence in the early part of the war when experience of convoy management was still being gained. After extricating his ship from this dangerous situation, Captain Atkinson posted extra lookouts and closed up his gun crew as they neared the reported positions of the torpedoed vessels.

At daybreak the *Blairangus* was sighted; her stern had been blown off and she lay low in the water with her deck awash aft. Two lifeboats were spotted and Captain Atkinson stopped his ship and took twenty-eight survivors on board, even hoisting the boats on deck. Only after receiving confirmation from Captain Hugh Mackinnon that the missing members of the *Blairangus* crew had perished in the attack, did Atkinson leave the scene.

Captain Atkinson's report is typical of the war reports of most shipmasters. It was a plain, straightforward account, understating both the danger involved and the courage called for in such incidents. This is what he wrote about the other torpedoed ship, the *Elmbank*:

> Shortly after, a second steamer was sighted ahead, evidently in a sinking condition. As before, all due action was taken for *Pikepool*'s own safety on approach, and simultaneously with seeing three lifeboats under sail steering for us, a large ocean-going class U-boat was sighted some two miles distant in surface trim. Our gun's crew were still closed up, of course, at the ready, and the submarine was brought to bear astern in our gun sights whilst the occupants of the three boats were got on board as quickly as possible.

That was followed by this prime piece of understatement:

> Owing to the nearness of the submarine, *Elmbank*'s boats were abandoned and with all possible speed we proceeded executing scatter zig-zags. When last seen the enemy was gradually submerging some three miles distant.

This time he had picked up fifty-five survivors and also the dead body of the *Elmbank*'s captain who had lost both his legs. Captain Atkinson and his crew, in conformity with the best traditions of the sea and under the very eyes of the enemy, had risked their lives to save from possible death a total of eighty-three fellow seamen. All the survivors were later safely landed in Newfoundland. This story also illustrates two of the war hazards confronting merchant seamen apart from the obvious one of enemy attacks. Only fine seamanship prevented a collision when *Pikepool* ran in amongst the ships of a blacked-out convoy; and the commodore of that convoy, which had no rescue ship attached, acting in accordance with standing orders (often more honoured in their breach than in their observance), had decided not to detach a ship to pick up survivors from *Blairangus* and *Elmbank*, but instead had perforce left them to their own devices.

In March 1941 another Ropner vessel, *Ullapool*, was particularly unlucky. Lying alongside Princes Stage at Liverpool only a few hours after arriving at the port with a cargo of grain from Canada, there was an air raid. A parachute mine landed squarely on her deck and exploded. The ship broke in two and sank, taking the captain and fifteen members of the crew with her.

About a month after that, the *Thirlby*, under Captain Birch, underwent a week of remarkable adventures. She was in an eastbound convoy in the Atlantic when her sister-ship *Alderpool* was torpedoed, her crew taking to the boats. Standing orders or not, Captain Birch was not about to leave other Ropner men to the mercy of the sea and so manoeuvred his ship to take aboard survivors. In the middle of doing so, a surfaced submarine was spotted and Captain Birch altered course to present the ship's stern and its poop-mounted gun to the enemy, at the same time managing to position his ship so that the sinking *Alderpool* lay between him and the U-boat.

It was a little before noon when the last survivor climbed aboard and Captain Birch rang full ahead. He managed to dodge two torpedoes, one passing ahead and the other astern. In the subsequent chase it appeared there were two submarines taking part, and Birch strove to keep them astern whenever a periscope was sighted. At one stage *Thirlby* was struck by a torpedo which failed to explode, and some time after that the ship's gunners took a pot-shot at a submarine which surfaced astern. The gunners appeared to have tasted blood, for Captain Birch's log entry for 1630 hours read '. . . gun manned all through and now crew anxious for further action'.

As night fell, *Thirlby*, pounding along at well over her normal maximum speed, finally managed to elude the chasers, and another memorable episode had been written in the annals of Ropner's Navy. But there was still more to come for Captain Birch and the two crews he now had on board. Early on a morning near the end of that voyage, *Thirlby* came under attack from a German aircraft which had arrived unseen out of the clouds. Cannon fire damaged the bridge and a bomb fell on the fore deck bringing down the foremast. The plane roared in for a second time and a bomb wrecked the fo'c'sle, killing two men. Captain Birch ordered abandon ship, hoping that the bomber would think his ship was sinking and so fly off. After circling overhead the bomber did fly away, and the crew immediately reboarded. There were fires on deck and water was entering No.1 hold through a gaping hole in the side, but Birch concluded that the ship could be saved. As fire-fighting teams dealt with the fires, others worked on patching the ship's side. About an hour later the bomber returned and the game was played out again, the crew once more taking to the boats. It did not attack and flew off again, this time for good. Back aboard went Birch and his men, and by mid-afternoon *Thirlby* was underway. She crept safely into Loch Ewe the following afternoon.

No description of Ropner's war adventures would be complete without mention of *Empire Starlight* and her master, Captain William Henry Stein. Born in West Hartlepool and therefore a natural recruit for a shipowner based in that port, Stein passed the examination for his master's certificate at Newcastle in 1930. He took command of *Empire Starlight* on 18 December 1941 at the age of thirty-five.

The ship was a little under 7000 tons and had been built in Hong Kong and placed under Ropner's management by the Ministry of War Transport, and had a crew of seventy-seven, consisting of fourteen British officers, twelve DEMS gunners, and fifty-one Chinese ratings. She sailed from Reykjavik, Iceland, for Murmansk on 20 March 1942 as one of the twenty-one merchant ships forming Convoy PQ13. There were eight other ships flying the Red Ensign in the convoy (including *Lars Kruse* which was later to be lost in the Bari disaster in 1943, see Chapter 21), and four American freighters, the remainder coming from other Allied nations. A gale blew up the first night and the following morning a rough sea and frequent snow squalls made close station-keeping impossible; indeed, any attempt to keep the convoy in close contact would likely have resulted in collisions. The gale developed into a full Arctic storm and the laden ships were soon covered in thick ice, this extra top-hamper causing the ships to roll ever more sickeningly. The convoy began to break up, and *Empire Starlight* found herself in company with six other merchant ships but with no escort vessels in sight.

The weather eased somewhat on the third day but that brought a new form of tension. Improved weather meant a better chance of being discovered by the enemy, and sure enough late that morning the seven-ship flotilla came under attack by a German bomber. The ships opened fire but missed. Bombs struck one ship and it had to be abandoned, survivors from it being picked up by one of the others. The next day, 23 March, tension rose again when shells, coming from light German surface craft that could be seen in the distance, fell amongst them. The ships fired back, more in the hope that such defiance might keep the attackers at bay than in the expectation of hitting anything at that distance. Then suddenly the cruiser HMS *Edinburgh* arrived to swiftly dispose of the threat. After that the weather again grew worse. Aboard *Empire Starlight* Captain Stein's worries were not eased when a radio message came in reporting that two other ships of the original convoy had gone down.

On the 24th, and once more sailing unescorted, the ships were attacked by a dive-bomber but no hits were sustained. The day after that brought a different kind of grief. Usually there are two reliable signs of pack ice ahead. One is so-called ice blink, the characteristic light effects of which in the sky, even at night, is one of those natural phenomena once seen, is never to be mistaken. The second is the abrupt smoothing away of the sea, even a gradual lessening of the underlying swell. Sometimes, however, neither warning sign is apparent, and it was so on this occasion. Whilst being shadowed by enemy planes the ships suddenly found themselves running into heavy ice. After a signalled consultation the captain of the senior ship decided that the designated course must be maintained despite Stein's suggestion that it would be better to go round the ice-field even if that took them closer to enemy airbases. The ships pressed on, but by mid-day *Induna* in the lead was stuck fast in the ice with four others beset and stopped behind her. Only *Empire Starlight* was still navigable, and Captain Stein, ordering full ahead and gallantly putting his own ship at risk, ground his way around the other ships for over four hours so cutting a channel to free them. After that Captain Stein decided to proceed alone, and two days later his ship reached Murmansk Roads. On the way he learnt that *Induna* and another ship in the convoy had been lost. The voyage had been typical of the Arctic convoys or, to put it another way, it had been a nightmare.

On the first morning *Empire Starlight* was alongside at Murmansk, the harbour came under heavy air attack and though the ship suffered no direct hits, near misses caused some leaks in the hull. During another air raid a few days later the ship was hit by a 500lb bomb which exploded in No 1 hold and caused fires in No 2. Several Russian stevedores were killed, and some of the ship's precious cargo of Hurricane fighters and military trucks destroyed. *Empire Starlight* fought back with its guns and Russian sources confirmed later that the ship had brought down a plane. From then on Captain Stein and Chief Engineer B Morgan led the crew in an eight-week-long battle to save the ship and its cargo, a battle waged against rising water in the holds and more air attacks. Despite all these efforts and after another air raid during which the ship sustained no less than four direct hits, the ship finally settled on the bottom on 1 June.

Through all the ship's vicissitudes only one crew member lost his life, and he was not killed on board; one of the Chinese stewards had died in an air-raid shelter ashore which suffered a direct hit. Captain Stein and his men were soon repatriated home. On 20 January 1943, both he and Chief Engineer Morgan were awarded the OBE.

After *Hawnby* was sunk, Captain Bill Harland OBE joined the *Empire Bison*, a 5600-ton vessel managed by Ropners on behalf of the Ministry of War Transport. In the North Atlantic on 1 November 1940 the ship was torpedoed and sunk by a German submarine. Harland, together with thirty-seven members of his crew, was killed, the only survivors being Second Mate Carlton and three seamen who spent eight days on an open raft before being rescued.

In late November 1940, *Pikepool*, with Captain Atkinson still in command, struck a mine about 22 miles off the Smalls Light in the Bristol Channel. She went down with 17 men, but Captain Atkinson and the remainder of his crew were picked up from waterlogged rafts two days later.

Thirlby, the ship involved in the saving of survivors from *Alderpool*, was not among the eleven Ropner ships to survive the war. She was torpedoed in 1942 with the loss of three of the crew. *Stonepool*, the ship involved in the double sinking of U-boats, did not make it either. She was torpedoed in September 1941 and blew up with flames shooting 150 feet into the air. Only six of her crew survived.

Captain Stein's next command after *Empire Starlight* was the *Fort Rampart*. She was torpedoed in April 1943 and Stein was awarded the Lloyd's Medal for bravery at sea for his actions during the incident. After that he safely saw out the war aboard *Fort Coulonge*.

CHAPTER 2

Harry Tate's Navy

'Harry Tate's' is Royal Navy jargon for anything amateur, and it dates from the First World War, deriving from a popular music hall entertainer of the times whose act was built around the theme of bungling everything he touched. It was applied during that war, and the next one, to the drifters, trawlers, and other small craft requisitioned into the Royal Navy Patrol Service. Very soon after the start of both world conflicts there was nothing at all amateur about their war effort, but as with other such names that start life as jocular and somewhat disparaging ('Old Contemptibles' is one such), the term 'Harry Tate's Navy' came to be looked upon with justifiable pride by those who were part of it.

The title Merchant Navy was officially introduced in 1922 in place of the hitherto used terms Mercantile Marine or Merchant Service. (Notwithstanding that, the Government offices in large ports at which seamen signed on or off articles carried on being called Mercantile Marine Offices.) In February 1928, King George V conferred upon the Prince of Wales the title of Master of the Merchant Navy and Fishing Fleets in recognition of the important roles these closely associated organisations played in the prosperity of the nation.

This close association is often forgotten, to the detriment of fishermen. If the Merchant Navy can be described as the forgotten service, then the Fishing Fleet is its unremembered arm. Yet the association has always been a very close one. Many young sailors began their nautical careers in fishing boats and afterwards joined ships in either the home-trade or foreign-going branches of the Merchant Navy. Shipowners and shipmasters were very pleased to have such men, for life aboard a trawler or drifter not only breeds toughness and resilience in the face of adversity, but also expert seamen.

Lessons had been learnt from some of the improvisations made in the First World War for guarding Britain's coastline, so that when war came again in 1939 plans were already in hand to requisition trawlers and drifters into the Royal Navy as minesweepers or patrol craft, along with their skippers and crews. (The rank of Skipper RNR had been introduced into the Navy List during the First World War for just that purpose.) They joined that part of the Navy called the Royal Navy Patrol Service. Some skippers and some of their men had continued to receive occasional naval training in the inter-war years, and a few had taken part in the Non-Intervention Patrol in Spanish waters during the Civil War there. Britain therefore began the Second World War much better prepared for anti-mine warfare than she had been at the start of the earlier conflict and much of this preparedness was thanks to the men and boats of the fishing fleet.

Minesweeping may have been the main task of requisitioned fishing craft but it was far from being the only one. Some were used as auxiliary patrol vessels or as armed escorts for both inshore and offshore convoys, including those to Russia; some became boom-defence vessels; and perhaps most dangerously of all, some were used as decoy vessels to keep submarines and E-boats busy whilst their mates were about other tasks. Two anti-submarine trawlers, the *Northern Gem* and her sister-ship *Arab*, took part in the Norway campaign, and later became stalwarts of the convoys to Murmansk.

If merchant seamen are a very independent lot, then fisherman have got independence of spirit down to a fine art, and they took that with them into the Navy. They did not take kindly to naval routine, discipline, and form-filling, and the more enlightened Naval Commanders in charge of the minesweepers based at a port soon learnt to put up with the foibles of the rather strange men under their command; in return they eventually received back a measure of co-operation over the routine 'nonsense'. There is a story that on the day war broke out, one Commander pointed out that it was the Skipper's duty to read out the Articles of War to his crew. The Skipper fished the articles from the drawer into which he had thrown them unread on first receiving them, took one look at the many-claused document and then called his crew on deck. Without once glancing at the document in his hand, and beginning his talk with the words 'Now lads', he told them that the war had started and the ship was now their home, that minesweeping was hard and dangerous work and that no-one-knew-that-better-than-him-for-he-had-been-blown-up-twice-in-the-last-lot, and that he and the Commander expected every man to do his duty in return for their pay and certain privileges they could enjoy ashore. 'Do yer duty', he ended, 'And me and the Commander 'ere will see you gets those privileges. That's all.' The Commander was wise enough to let things be. From those, shall we say, rather informal beginnings, the patrol service was to grow into a closely-knit band of men which gained in naval discipline as time went on and as new RNVR officers and men were trained and brought in to man specially-built ships as well as requisitioned ones, although the service lost very little of its colourful nature in the process.

Not all the vessels requisitioned as minesweepers were fishing boats. A number of paddle-steamers which had enjoyed a pre-war existence as ferry-boats or excursion vessels also joined the ranks. These were known as 'Smoky Joes' and included the famous *Medway Queen* and *Waveney*. They, also, took their peacetime crews to war with them.

It is as well the Navy were prepared to an extent at least for anti-mine warfare right from the start of the war, for almost immediately ships began to be sunk by mines. The very first to go was Brocklebank's

Magdapur, which struck a mine on the seventh day of the war and sank off Aldeburgh on the Suffolk coast with the loss of six lives. Between 8 and 22 November 1939, no less than fifteen merchantships were lost to mines. Two of those were neutrals, one being the Japanese *Terukuni Maru*. Her sinking off the Sunk Light Vessel on the 21st caused a flurry of diplomatic activity between London and Tokyo, although all 206 persons on board were saved.

Minesweeping has been called a war without glory. There is little doubt that the sweepers' battle could be lonely and monotonous for long stretches of time, but it was also highly dangerous. Each day every channel had to be swept because of the minelaying activities of German aircraft, submarines, and surface craft, including E-boats. For days on end flotillas of sweepers plodded up and down the same old routes waiting for their gear to snag a mine. If a mine evaded the sweep it often meant the destruction of another sweeper or of a merchantman coming up behind. It was not really a war without glory, as we shall see, and even the monotonous periods were broken whenever it was found that the Germans had altered the design or operating characteristics of the several different types of mines they used, for every such change necessitated the development of new sweeping or mine-destruction techniques. A sweeper can be likened to a bomb-disposal unit, a floating one. Indeed, from time to time a sweeper would carry an officer specially trained to examine mines before their destruction in case the Germans had come up with another innovation, a task much like that of bomb-disposal experts ashore.

A special duty fell the way of some of the minesweeping fleet in May 1940 during Operation 'Dynamo', the evacuation of Dunkirk. Several of the 'Smoky Joes' were among the many craft gathered together for the task, and so were some requisitioned drifters. The paddle-sweepers were amongst the ships which crossed and recrossed the Channel during the rescue, whilst the drifters were amongst the smaller craft acting as ferries between the beaches and moles and the larger ships offshore. One paddle-sweeper, the *Waveney*, was sunk during the operation. One of the drifter/minesweepers involved was *Feasible*, which in 1998 was undergoing restoration work as an historic vessel at Weymouth. The record for the number of cross-Channel voyages among the paddle-sweepers went to *Medway Queen*, which made no less than seven round-trips.

But Dunkirk was only a diversion for some of the requisitioned vessels. The standard duties of minesweepers and patrol craft were equally as dangerous, if not so spectacular, and they went on all around the British coast. This point is illustrated by the losses the service sustained during the three-month period beginning the end of July 1940. On the 28th of that month, HM trawler *Staunton* struck a mine off Brightlingsea on the Essex coast and was lost with all hands. A week later, on a single day (4 August), the service lost three trawlers, the *Drummer* also off Brightlingsea, the *Oswaldian* in the Bristol Channel, and the *Marsona* off Cromarty on the coast of Scotland. On 20 September, the anti-submarine decoy trawler *Comet* was lost off the Lizard with all but two of its crew.

The *Stella Rigel* was one of several Grimsby trawlers taken into the minesweeping service in September 1939, along with Skipper T H Spall RNR and his crew. She was armed with a single 12-pounder on the fo'c'sle head and an Oerlikon gun on a gun-platform aft, the latter always being kept loaded and ready for action. For months it had been *Stella Rigel*'s duty to systematically plod up and down the so-called 'War Channel' off the Essex coast, with sweeps out in a search for mines and with lookouts keeping a watch for enemy aircraft and E-boats. One cold, moonless night in February 1941, Spall ordered 'in sweeps' and after anchoring his vessel, told his tired men to go below and get some sleep. He himself stayed on deck close to the Oerlikon, and it was sometime later when he heard the drone of the engines of several low-flying aircraft. He had heard the sound many times before and recognised the aircraft as Heinkel bombers. He crossed swiftly over to the Oerlikon. Despite the darkness one of the aircraft must have seen the deeper blackness of the trawler's silhouette and, after circling, came into attack from aft. As Skipper Spall explained afterwards, he did not order 'Action Stations' for that would have meant running to the bridge and sounding the bell and there was no time for that. He fired at the approaching aircraft and knew instinctively that he had scored some hits as he let go with all the ammunition in the pan. The Heinkel lost height as it came over the ship and blew up as it struck the sea. It was all over in a few seconds but by that time the crew had tumbled up on deck to bear witness to the destruction of the plane. Skipper Spall was awarded the DSC but said he did know what all the fuss was about. 'It was just a damn lucky do', he explained.

Another Skipper to be awarded the DSC was W T Ritchie of the trawler *Syringa*, for an incident which occurred when on a joint sweep with another trawler *Reboundo*. The two were attacked by a Junkers 87 which dropped several salvoes of bombs, one of which pierced *Syringa*'s engine-room casing. It landed on the platform near the engine but did not explode. As the aircraft again came in to attack it was shot down by *Syringa*'s low-angle gun. Skipper Ritchie then went down the engine-room to survey his ship's unwanted cargo. In his Official Report he wrote: 'With the assistance of Chief Engineman E C Clinton, I carried the bomb on deck and threw it overboard.' Clinton got the DSM, an award that also went to Stoker Petty Officer G H Wood who had remained at his post in the engine-room despite the presence of the bomb.

The patrol service lost more ships in the war than did any other arm of the Royal Navy. A total of 268 of the trawlers and drifters requisitioned by the Royal Navy were lost, and a further 90 of both types which were specifically built to Admiralty order for minesweeping purposes (before an official class of minesweeper began coming off the stocks) were also sunk. In all the patrol service lost in excess of 500 vessels.

One requisitioned trawler used in anti-submarine patrols was the *Lady Shirley*. In October 1941 whilst patrolling off Madeira, she sank *U-111* (Commander W Kleinschmidt). Two months later off Gibraltar, the trawler was herself sunk by *U-374*. Life in 'Harry Tate's Navy' was something of a balancing act.

It would be easy to forget that many fisherman carried on their normal calling during the war years, a hazardous calling made even more so by the dangers of war. During hostilities 116 fishing boats were lost and 58 damaged from attacks by submarines, E-boats, and aircraft, and of course, from striking mines. During 1940 and 1941, Able Seaman Sam Gibbs regularly corresponded with a Mrs M Baker, whom he had first heard of in relation to a parcel of woollen 'comforts' – balaclavas, socks, gloves, and the like – which she and a group of friends had knitted for the crew of his ship, HM Trawler *John Stephen*. In one of his letters Sam wrote the following passage. It was based on his knowledge of what his comrades who were still engaged in fishing were having to contend with:

It's when its blowing and freezing hard it tells on you and we seldom stop [fishing] for weather, sometimes it gets too bad, then we have to stop, or we should lose some men.

Engines broke down in blinding snowstorms, that's the time you think of home and wonder if you will ever see it again . . . and now on top of all such things the Jerries try to bomb and machine-gun the poor devils.

The men of the Royal Navy Patrol Service called themselves 'Sparrows'. Their monument is in Belle Vue Park, Lowestoft, the famous fishing port on the coast of Suffolk which many of them came from. The monument is known as the 'Sparrow's Nest' and it commemorates the 13,890 men of the service who lost their lives, including 2385 who have no grave but the sea.

CHAPTER 3

One Came Home

Frederick Tenow had arrived in Britain in the early years of the century to escape the upheaval in his native Estonia. He joined the Merchant Navy and served throughout the First World War. In April 1918 he married a girl from Newport, South Wales, the port which he had made his home town. Mr and Mrs Tenow could not have children of their own so in 1930 they adopted a baby girl at birth and named her Pat. It was a close-knit family despite Fred's calling, and he adored his daughter, a fondness that was returned with interest. Pat Phillips (née Tenow) says, 'He was a dear gentle man; he cut my hair and mended all our shoes and was always immaculately turned out. His working dungarees were well scrubbed and he looked a "gentleman"'.

The 5th of August 1940 was a warm and sunny day in Newport, the weather auguring well for the marriage of the daughter of the Tenows' next-door neighbour, a ceremony at which Pat was to be a bridesmaid. Fred, who had recently signed-on as Fireman/Trimmer aboard the SS *Anglo Saxon* (Captain P R L Flynn) down at Newport docks, was dead set on seeing his daughter in her bridesmaid's dress. Though the ship was due to sail the following day he obtained special permission to spend a few hours at home. It was a brief but happy interlude and afterwards Fred strode off down the road towards the docks, turning more than once to wave to his wife and daughter as he went. The last they ever saw of him was as he gave a final wave before disappearing around a corner.

The minds of members of other families in Newport and adjacent ports of South Wales were also on *Anglo Saxon* that day, for a third of its 38-man crew came from those parts. Cynthia Widdicombe, whose husband, twenty-one year-old Roy, was an Able Seaman on board, was one; she lived within a few minutes walk of the Tenow home. Twenty year-old Leslie Morgan, the Assistant Cook, was also from the town, whilst two brothers called Williams came from nearby Barry.

The remainder of the crew came from all over the British Isles. Captain P R Lympany Flynn was from Plymouth (he was related to Moura Lympany, the concert pianist), and Chief Officer B Denny came from London. Second Radio Officer R H Pilcher was a Durham man and Able Seaman Roy Tapscott, aged nineteen, came from Bristol. The ship carried one DEMS gunner, a Royal Marine aged forty-four, Francis Penny from Mortimer in Berkshire. Third Engineer Leslie Hawkes, aged twenty-three, was from Dudley.

Anglo Saxon, a 5500-ton freighter built in 1929 and owned by Nitrate Producers Steamship Company of London (known as the Anglo Line), had seen better days. There was a war on, and it showed in her rust-streaked and dirty appearance. On top of that she was loading a cargo of coal for Bahia Blanca, for trade had to go on even in wartime. *Anglo Saxon* was typical of the kind of ship that made up the bulk of the British merchant fleet of the time and, scruffy as she and her many sisters were, they were crucial to the war in which Britain in 1940 was losing more ships to enemy action than she could afford.

The ship sailed on the 6th and on the following day at Milford Haven joined a slow North American convoy. She would stay with it until it was deemed safe enough for her to detach and make her own plodding way to Argentina, for she was the only ship in the convoy making for South America. On 13 August the time came, and *Anglo Saxon* left the convoy and headed southward.

By the 21st she had reached a point some 200 miles north of the Tropic of Cancer and crew members were basking in the knowledge that they were now well south of the known U-boat danger areas. They would have been less complacent had they known they had entered the patrol area of the German raider *Widder*. Commanded by Lieutenant-Commander Helmuth von Rucktenschell, the raider had sunk seven ships over the past ten days totalling well over 40,000 tons. One of the seven was the Finnish barque *Killoran*, the only sailing ship to be sunk by a raider in the Second World War. Now, a little after 2000 hours on that dark, clear night, she had *Anglo Saxon* in her gunsights.

Without warning four shells tore into the ship. Raiders often fired on sight as they could not afford the luxury of a warning shot across the bows; any such delay could be utilised by the victim to send off wireless messages. One shell killed many men in the fo'c'sle and another hit the gun-platform aft, causing the ammunition there to explode. *Widder* then closed her victim, raking the decks with cannon and machine-gun fire which destroyed both lifeboats. She also jammed the airwaves, preventing the transmission of signals. The bridge and wireless room were hit, killing Captain Flynn, who was busy dumping the ship's papers overboard. Another shell pierced the starboard side in way of the engine-room, causing the main boiler to explode. By that time there were few men left alive, and in the fire and chaos that was the maindeck, Chief Officer Denny ordered the survivors into the only remaining serviceable boat, an 18-foot jolly boat, much smaller than a lifeboat and never intended to be used as one.

Only seven men made it, including Denny himself. Able Seaman Robert Tapscott had been in the fo'c'sle when the attack began and in a bid to escape the mayhem there had been blown in the air, losing consciousness in the process. With shrapnel wounds in his back he came to just in time to reach the boat. Roy Widdicombe, who had been at the wheel but had escaped unscathed, rushed from the wheelhouse, passing on the way the body of the captain which was slumped against a bulwark. Off-duty Third Engineer Leslie Hawkes also made it. The other three, like Tapscott, were wounded. They were Second Radio Officer Roy Pilcher, Gunner Francis Penny, and Assistant Cook Leslie Morgan.

Tapscott, together with Widdicombe who had injured his hand whilst lowering the boat, fended it off the ship's side and away from the still-turning propeller, which was cleared only by inches. As the boat pulled away from the blazing ship, the sea and swell carried it across the raider's bows, and any second the men in it expected a burst of tracer to come their way. Water was slopping around their feet, and although some of it was coming in over the side, there was more in the boat than from that source alone. As two men rowed and others began baling out, Chief Officer Denny groped around the bottom and discovered that the drainage plug was half out. He drove it home with an axe.

All of a sudden, between the boat and the burning ship, lights were seen which were taken to be from life-rafts perhaps containing other survivors. Denny ordered the oarsmen to pull in that direction, at the same time signalling briefly with his torch, but stopping when he realised the flashes might be seen from the raider. A stream of tracer bullets from the raider then tore towards the lights and from the top of the next crest the men in the boat saw the lights had disappeared. The rafts, if indeed that was what had been sighted, together with any men who might have been on them, had gone. Denny, who began to keep a log on the reverse side of some radio operational time-sheets brought aboard by Pilcher in his 'emergency' attaché-case, recorded of this incident 'the raider . . . fired tracer bullets into two life-rafts launched from the vessel'. It should be noted that not only was it dark at the time (in those latitudes it would have been dark by about 1900 hours), but also that the boat was probably not close enough for its occupants to have been certain what the lights were or where they were coming from.

It was nine o'clock by Denny's watch when an explosion occurred aboard *Anglo Saxon* which he took to be the main magazine going up. In fact, according to *Widder*'s log, it was caused by a torpedo. The freighter then sank. Denny wrote up the sinking in his log:

> Vessel sank stern first . . . Raider headed off to the eastward. Assumed that Germans wanted no members of the crew left alive and were fortunate in this boat's crew escaping observation.

At dawn the following morning, with nothing in sight, Denny decided to sail west; to have sailed east would have meant sailing against the prevailing wind and current. Apart from the boat compass there were no navigation instruments on board and he told the men that a westerly course would take them across trade routes frequented by neutral ships, and that if one of those did not pick them up, and even should they somehow pass through the outer Leeward Islands without sighting land,

behind those islands lay the whole Caribbean. They were bound to fall in
with something, he told them. The dipping lug sail was raised and course
set WSW. There was a good easterly breeze behind them.

Roy Pilcher, who had taken his turn at the oars without demur during the
night, was found to be more seriously wounded than he had let on. Shrapnel
had shattered his left foot reducing it to a pulpy mass. His companions
wondered how he had been able to row but Pilcher, a good-looking young
man of twenty-one, played it all down saying he had felt no pain.

It was shrapnel which had caused most of the other wounds in the boat.
Francis Penny had a deep tear across the hip in addition to a bullet
wound in his right forearm. Assistant Cook Leslie Morgan was nursing a
jagged cut above his right ankle. Robert Tapscott had three pieces of
metal embedded in various parts of his body. Denny did what he could to
clean and dress the wounds using the inadequate facilities of the boat's
first-aid kit. He noted in the log, 'Medical treatment given', which was
rather overstating what the contents of the kit allowed him to do.

An inventory was taken of the equipment on board. In addition to the
sail there was a small sea-anchor, a boathook, some oars, an axe, a rope
painter, the boat's canvas cover, the compass, an oil lamp, and some red
flares and matches in watertight containers. As for food supplies, there
were eleven tins of condensed milk, three tins of boiled mutton, and a
thirty-two-pound tin of ship's biscuit. The Mate carried a clasp knife, and
Pilcher's attaché-case, from which the paper used for the boat's log had
come, also contained tins of tobacco and a book of bible quotations, which
was to prove useful for making cigarette-papers. Apart from the first-aid
kit, that was it, except of course, for the most important item of all, the
water breaker. This was a small keg sitting in a cradle, complete with two
dippers for scooping the water out. It should have held about seven
gallons but to everyone's dismay, it was little more than half full. Denny
set each man's water ration at half a dipper twice a day, which amounted
to something less than half a pint, not much liquid in ordinary circumstances, let alone in an open boat under a strong sun.

During the second night after the sinking the silhouette of a blacked-
out ship was seen against the skyline. Denny set off a flare and immediately regretted it. It might be the raider returning, and even thirst was
preferable to being shot at. The mystery ship must have seen the flare for
it turned and made towards them in a wide circle. Denny ordered down
sail and the men in the boat, catching his apprehension, crouched low.
After some minutes the stranger turned and made off northward. It was a
great let-down, but one experienced so close to the day of the sinking,
when hopes of rescue were still high, that they soon got over it.

As the days passed, each marked by Denny with a notch cut in the
gunwale, it was the failing condition of Roy Pilcher which provided
the greatest concern, apart from the ever-reducing level of the water in the
breaker. 'Sparks' was bearing the agony of his wound with remarkable
courage, but already it was showing signs of gangrene.

It was a Sunday when the Chief Officer announced there would be mutton for dinner that day. The men watched eagerly as he cut half the contents of a tin into seven portions and doled them out. They chewed slowly, savouring every scrap and for the remainder of that day were in high spirits, with only the sickly smell of gangrene hanging in the air to spoil matters.

The following day brought calms and no headway was made under a burning sun. Thirst now really took hold and when Denny dished out the remainder of the mutton from the previous day, no one had the stomach for it without water. After that Denny, assisted by Tapscott, set about the unpleasant task of dressing Pilcher's foot, now swollen to twice its normal size and of a green-black colour. It smelt horribly as they bathed it in salt water before binding it with the last of the bandages. During the process, which he bore with stoicism, Pilcher kept apologising for causing so much trouble. The wounds to Morgan's ankle and Penny's thigh were also found not to be responding to the only treatment available.

Until the supply ran out each man had the daily luxury of rolling a cigarette for himself from Pilcher's tobacco. However, lighting them ate into the small store of matches, matches that might be required later for lighting the oil lamp. The fittest amongst them bathed over the side occasionally, taking great care they did not swallow any sea water.

There was not much talking now, for it was painful to converse with a parched mouth. All were aware, too, that the simple task of changing watch-keeping positions was becoming ever more difficult. There was a tendency to lose one's footing. In an effort to raise morale Denny organised a lottery based on the date they would be picked up. It was a success, and created some humour especially when Pilcher declared emphatically that something told him he was holding the winning date. Daily the stench of gangrene increased, for now Penny's wound had turned green as well. Pilcher spent most of the time apologising for the smell he was creating. At one point he actually agreed to have the offending member lopped off with the axe, but when it came to it, neither Denny nor anyone else aboard had the stomach for the task. On the tenth day 'Sparks' passed away peacefully having refused his last water ration in the knowledge that at that stage it could not help him much. Denny wrote: 'W/T operator passed peacefully away. Committed his body to the deep with silent prayer.' For the rest of that day the boat remained silent, all thoughts on the passing of a courageous young man.

On 2 September, Chief Officer Denny, the one real symbol of authority and discipline in the boat, made what was to be his final entry in the log. It was a straightforward record of the boat's heading and of the food and water issue. After that he lay down in the bottom in a semi-coma between bouts of retching. On the following day he could not rise to his feet. Controversy then broke out over who was to take command. Third Engineer Hawkes, as an officer, knew the right was his, but Able Seamen Widdicombe objected to that on the basis that Hawkes knew nothing about sailing a boat. Hawkes at first stood his ground and Widdicombe lost his temper, telling him 'to sail the bloody boat yourself then'. A compromise was then agreed to; Widdicombe would take charge of sailing the boat, and Hawkes would write up the log and issue rations. Apparently the agreement did not last long. At Widdicombe's behest the water ration was increased despite the breaker being nearly empty, and the log entry for the 3rd was in the seaman's handwriting.

However, on the following day it was Third Engineer Hawkes who wrote the log entry which included a note on the suicide of Gunner Penny. 'The Mate is going fast now. 1.30 p.m. Sunday, Penny very much weaker slipped overboard.' Hawkes then reiterated details of the sinking, stating that the raider had 'evidently intended to smash all the life-boat gear to kill all inquiry'. That was to be his farewell message.

On the day after that Denny was well enough to take a stint at the tiller and it was as he did so that the rudder carried away in the heavy swell. He dropped the now useless tiller, lay down, and closed his eyes, the loss of the rudder apparently being the last straw for him. As Tapscott and Widdicombe shipped the steering oar in place of the rudder, Hawkes stretched himself out alongside Denny. Some hours later Denny opened his eyes, croaked he was 'going over', and asked who was going with him. Only Hawkes agreed to do so.

A short time after that the Chief Officer rose to his feet and handed Widdicombe his signet ring with the instruction that it was to go to his mother if the seaman survived. 'Keep going west, no more south', was his last order. He and the Engineer then shook hands and jumped, and the last the three men remaining in the boat saw of them was as they floated away holding on to each other. The log entry for that day was again in Widdicombe's hand: 'Chief Mate and 3rd Engineer go over the side. No water.'

On 9 September he wrote, '2nd Cook goes mad dies. Two of us left.' On two occasions after that Widdicombe and Tapscott decided to end their own lives but changed their minds after going over the side. One day they made themselves drunk by imbibing the alcohol in which the compass card floated in its bowl, and both slept well that night. Only three more log entries were made after that, those made on the 12th and 20th reporting that it had rained and that they had managed to collect water. On the 24th, thirty-four days after the sinking of the ship, a short entry noted that all water and biscuits had gone but they were still hoping to make land. Had the two men known then that they were not even half-way through their ordeal there can be little doubt that they would have ended it somehow. But they did not know, and the will to survive was still there.

Now they found themselves sailing through patches of seaweed and they ate it together with any small crustaceans attached to it. Sometimes they caught crabs, and one night a flying fish landed aboard. With no log being kept and no date-notching of the gunwale after the 24th day, they had lost track of time, every day simply melting into the next. They thought it must have been about 8 October when a ship was sighted about half a mile away, but it passed by apparently without seeing them. This was taken in their stride, for by then they were automatons, creatures of habit locked into a rhythm of trying to stay alive. A few days later a storm blew up and they fought it for two days. Small things began to give extreme annoyance, Tapscott being especially angry whenever Widdicombe called him 'Bobby', a name he detested. Once the two men actually fought.

It was dawn on the 70th day when Widdicombe spotted land, though at first neither of them could believe their eyes. As they drew nearer they saw the line of a breaking reef. They found a small channel through it and soon after that the bow of the boat grounded on a white beach. The two, looking more like skeletons than men, scrambled out and staggered up the beach to fall into the shade of a bush. The date was 30 October. They had landed on the island of Eleuthera in the Bahamas after travelling some 2500 nautical miles in one of the epic survival voyages of history. They were soon found by islanders and taken to an official government residence. The following day they were flown to Nassau by order of the Duke of Windsor, who was Governor of the Bahamas, and there hospitalised.

Roy Widdicombe recovered faster than Tapscott. He left the Bahamas in January 1941 for New York to find himself something of a celebrity there. In that port he joined the *Siamese Prince* for home, but on 18th February, the day before the ship was due to reach England, she was sunk by *U-69* and everyone aboard was lost. Robert Tapscott stayed in the Bahamas until May 1941 when he was shipped to Canada. He enlisted in the Canadian Army. He eventually arrived home, the only one of *Anglo Saxon*'s crew to make it back. After the war he married and he and his wife Norma had a daughter, Diane. He died in 1963 at the age of forty-two, no doubt the ordeals of 1940 having much to do with his early death.

In 1990, Ted Milburn, the son of the *Anglo Saxon*'s Chief Engineer, began a search for the ship's jolly-boat. The boat had been auctioned in the Bahamas in December 1940 and had eventually ended up as an exhibit at the Mystic Seaport Museum in Connecticut, and that is where it was tracked down. By arrangement with Mystic, in early 1998 it became the centre-piece of the first-ever Merchant Navy exhibition at the Imperial War Museum in London. One can still see the notches on the gunwale, and one can marvel how it was that a craft of such small size could have travelled over half an ocean bringing two brave men to safety.

Captain von Rucktenschell of the *Widder* was brought to trial in 1947 as a war criminal, indicted on five separate counts, each dealing with a different ship. One of the counts was to the effect that he had fired on the *Anglo Saxon*'s lifeboats and had failed to ensure the survival of men in them. This indictment was based solely on information contained in an affidavit sworn by Robert Tapscott. Rucktenschell was found guilty on three of the five counts, including the *Anglo Saxon* one, and sentenced to ten years' imprisonment.

We have seen that both Chief Officer Denny and Third Engineer Hawkes recorded that *Widder* had fired on men aboard life-rafts, but a question must hang over whether what they recorded was actually true. No doubt they thought it was true, but were they close enough to be sure? The life-rafts, if that is indeed what the men in the boat had seen, may have been torn adrift by the shelling, and raft lights are self-activated when floating in water. Perhaps there was no one on the rafts. On the strength of the evidence used, the verdict of the War Crimes Tribunal, in regard to the *Anglo Saxon* incident anyway, may have been unsound. On the other hand von Rucktenschell was known as the most ruthless, as well as being one of the most efficient, of German raider captains. Furthermore, had the Tribunal had in evidence the diary of James Lawrence, the Chief Officer of *British Petrol* which *Widder* had sunk some two months earlier than *Anglo Saxon*, and who was a prisoner on board the raider, it might have made the verdict reached a safer one, even though the evidence was circumstantial. Lawrence recorded *Widder*'s victims chronologically, noting the names of the ships and whenever survivors were picked up, which was on most occasions. However, the note for 21 August 1940 merely stated:

> Aug. 21st. raider sighted vessel during daylight and attacked soon after dark at 2000 hours. No survivors were picked up and we could obtain no information re the vessel.

It could it be that von Rucktenschell had something to cover up and so forbade any talk of this incident among his crew who had previously been only too pleased to boast of their ship's triumphs to their captive audience. We will never know the truth now for Captain von Rucktenschell died in prison in 1948 at the age of fifty-eight.

CHAPTER 4

The Automedon Affair

The Blue Funnel steamship *Automedon* sailed from Liverpool for the Far East on 24 September 1940. She was loaded with general cargo including military equipment, frozen meat, whisky, and cigarettes. Her strong-room was packed with bags of mail, some of them lead-weighted and marked 'Safe Hands of British Master Only', indicating that their contents were secret. The master, Captain W B Ewan, had not been surprised when he was asked to sign personally for those mailbags. Although his coal-burning ship dated from 1922, she was capable of 14.5 knots, well above the average speed of ships at that time, and faster merchant vessels were often used as couriers when no naval ship could be spared for the purpose.

Captain Ewan was a man who kept himself to himself yet was still able to contrive to be popular with his crew. In his early fifties and of medium height with greying hair, he had been a Company man for many years. He had, as they say, been around, and there was not much left that would have surprised him. Nevertheless, the visit he received shortly before sailing by a rather reticent official specially sent up from a government office in London must, at the very least, have provided him with food for thought.

The official handed Captain Ewan a sealed package marked 'Top Secret'. It was addressed to Air Chief Marshal Sir Robert Brooke-Popham, Britain's Commander-in Chief in the Far East, based at Singapore. Ewan had to sign for that too, before placing it in the weighted green canvas bag also handed over by the official. He was instructed that in the event of the ship being attacked the bag must be jettisoned at all costs. This instruction was over and above those already received for jettisoning the weighted mail bags and the standing instructions given to all shipmasters over the disposal of secret codebooks and routing charts that were always carried in their own weighted bags. (To ensure they sank rapidly, ships' codebooks and other secret material had lead inserts in their covers.)

As with all Blue Funnel ships, *Automedon*'s home port was Liverpool, and many of the crew therefore hailed from Merseyside. Amongst them was Fourth Engineer Sam Harper. This was his first voyage on this ship, although he had been with the shipping line since joining the Merchant Navy in the spring of 1939. Shortish and burly-looking, Sam, like many Liverpool seamen, was, and still is, a man of decided opinions and never slow to express them. He was tough and fit and, as we shall see, those characteristics were to stand him in good stead in the coming months. Sam also possessed the local sense of humour and that, too, was to be a useful attribute in the trials that lay ahead. Another of the Liverpudlians on board was Able Seaman Stanley Hugill, an experienced seamen then in his mid-thirties who, as a teenager, had sailed round the Horn in the German barque *Gustav*. Yet another was Second Officer Donald Stewart, thirty-four, who was to display a high degree of common sense and courage during the voyage and its aftermath. The youngest crew member was sixteen year-old Deck Boy Frank Walker from New Brighton, the seaside resort which lies in the shadow of Birkenhead on the other side of the Mersey. Another youngster on board was Alex Parsons, a seventeen year-old steward.

The majority of the crew of sixty or so were from mainland Britain but one seaman came from Malta and the stokers and trimmers were Hong Kong Chinese. There was one foreigner on board, the ship's doctor. He was from Eastern Europe and his name was Sperber. It was unusual for a freighter to carry a doctor and Dr Sperber was probably there because his foreign medical degree did not permit him to practise in Britain.

On this voyage the ship carried six passengers, three of them ladies. Mrs Ferguson was travelling to Singapore with her husband, who was a marine engineer going out to join a ship of the Straits Steamship Company, a sister company of Blue Funnel. One of the other ladies was a nurse. Sam Harper, who to this day has a sailor's eye for such things, remembers her as 'a good-looking bird'. The third lady was an American.

The voyage down the Atlantic, which was partly in convoy, was uneventful, and after a bunkering stop at Durban *Automedon* set out on her own to cross the Indian Ocean. War with Japan was still a year away, and although German submarines and surface raiders were known to be operating in the Indian Ocean, it was considered that the ship's speed and the standard routine of making frequent changes of course to throw the enemy off would be sufficient to keep her clear of danger. She set course for the northern end of the Malacca Strait and Penang, which was to be her next port of call.

Captain Ewan had received no special warnings from the Naval Control Office at Durban about possible dangers along the route. Nevertheless, being a prudent seaman, he made sure that a vigilant lookout was kept at all times and that the wireless-room was manned continuously by the two radio officers working watch and watch about. Twice during the next few days the radio officers intercepted messages concerning suspicious-looking ships, but apparently the shore authorities took these to be false alarms. *Automedon* herself maintained radio silence as instructed by the Naval Control Officer at Durban, which was, again, standard routine.

Unbeknown to Captain Ewan a particular menace was lurking along his ship's route in the form of the German raider *Atlantis*, under Captain Bernhard Rogge, which had entered the Indian Ocean from the Atlantic in August. Since leaving Germany *Atlantis* had sunk or captured twelve British and Allied ships. She was now looking for an unlucky thirteenth victim. *Atlantis* was a ship of several disguises and quite a few names. She had begun life as Hansa Line's *Goldenfels*, and gained her new name after conversion to an armed merchant cruiser at Bremen. On the way down the Atlantic she variously disguised herself as the Russian *Kim* or the Japanese *Kasii Maru*. The German Navy code-named her *Schiff 16*, whilst the British Admiralty knew her as *Raider C*. Capable of 18 knots and fitted with six 5.9-inch guns, four torpedo tubes, a miscellany of lighter weapons, mines, two aircraft, and a crew of 347 officers and men, she would have posed a danger to any naval ship smaller than a cruiser that happened across her path, let alone any merchant ship.

It was soon after daybreak on 11 November, and when *Automedon* was still some 250 miles south-west of Achin Head, the north-western tip of the island of Sumatra, Donald Stewart, who was officer-of-watch, spotted a ship about three points on the port bow. The stranger was hull down and some miles off, but in keeping with standing instructions Stewart called the captain.

Second Officer Stewart and Captain Ewan were soon joined on the bridge by other officers, and all looked long and earnestly through their binoculars at the still-distant ship. It became apparent that the stranger was proceeding on a similar course to their own, but was slower, and that *Automedon* was overtaking her to port. Donald Stewart later reported that the mystery ship was taken to be one of the Dutch ships that regularly plied between India and the Dutch East Indies, for she had all the look of one of that breed. Captain Ewan made the decision to maintain course and speed, at the same time ordering the bridge party to keep their glasses trained on the ship they were slowly closing.

Aboard the ship of many names, Captain Rogge's second-in-command, Lieutenant Ulrich Mohr, was himself gazing through binoculars towards the 'huge volume of funnel smoke' coming from the approaching ship. He was to say later that as he did so, his thoughts were partly on the significance of that day's date. 'It was the 11th November . . . the anniversary of the Day of Armistice,' was the way he put it.

At 0820 hours the ships were less than 1000 yards apart and, behind various screens that served not only to disguise her true outline but also to hide her armaments, *Atlantis*'s crew were at action stations. 'If we'd waited much longer [to fire a warning shot],' Mohr reported, 'we would have had to make a deviation in order to avoid a collision'. As Captain Rogge ordered the warning shot fired, Mohr hoped the victim would not use her wireless. 'If she uses her radio now, it will be suicide,' he thought.

Within seconds of the shot *Atlantis*'s radio operators picked up the first part of an RRR signal from *Automedon*, informing all ships and stations within radio range that she was under attack by an enemy raider. 'It was brave, it was futile, it was suicide,' Mohr wrote. He went on, 'And into that elderly steamer with her long antique stack, poured the shells.'

Donald Stewart, who has been described as a short, pleasant bloke with a pushed-in face, had been relieved of the watch at 0800 hours and was shaving in his cabin when the warning shot came. Rushing to the porthole he saw the strange ship was now flying the swastika. He made a run for the bridge. 'The next instant,' he wrote in his post-war report, 'all hell was let loose.' Sam Harper was on duty in the engine-room. 'Suddenly,' he says, 'there was a God Almighty bang followed by the screaming hiss of escaping steam because the second shot from the raider hit the base of the funnel.' Eight or nine shells poured into the ship at close range and it was all over in less than three minutes. 'At 0822 I got the order to stop engines, and I carried the order out,' says Sam.

On the wrecked bridge Stan Hugill, who had been at the wheel, scrambled from what remained of the wheelhouse. He was bleeding from the nose and from a wound in his back, and was surprised to be still alive. 'The captain was killed. Two mates were killed. There were about five or six killed around me', he recorded. Donald Stewart, who had reached the bridge in time to be knocked senseless by the blast, came to after a minute or so to find himself lying between the dead bodies of Captain Ewan and Third Mate Whitaker. Stewart, who had been hit in the head by shrapnel, a piece of which was to remain lodged in his forehead until his dying day, staggered from the bridge, his mind set on jettisoning the ship's code-books and confidential documents which he knew were kept in the safe in the captain's accommodation. He found Chief Officer Peter Evans lying badly wounded and unconscious near the door of the wreck which had once been the captain's day-room, and guessed that Evans had gone there with the same idea as himself. Stewart was still groping among the debris, trying to find the key to the safe, when he was found by members of the German boarding party.

It was Lieutenant Mohr who led the boarders aboard. 'I had seen some of them looking pretty bad,' he wrote, 'but *Automedon* was the worst of the lot. My first impression as I swung over her side was one of astonishment, incredulity even, at the degree of havoc our shells had wreaked . . . her wireless cabin lay like a heap of wood shavings.'

Passengers and surviving crew members were ferried across to the raider, the last to go being the most seriously injured. Amongst the latter was Steward Alex Parsons whose hip had a huge hole in it gouged out by shrapnel, and he had other shrapnel wounds to his face, chest and arms. A Chinese member of the crew had his penis shot off and later committed suicide aboard *Atlantis* by the extraordinary method of swallowing his own signet ring. Whilst the transfer was taking place Mohr led a search of *Automedon*, taking with him as guide the slightly-wounded Stewart, the only deck officer still able to walk. On reaching the strongroom Stewart, who knew about the bags of secret mail, passed it off as the Bosun's store and was mightily relieved when Mohr accepted that.

Then came the mischance. One of the ladies who had been sent over to the raider requested that her baggage, which was stored in the baggage room adjacent to the strong-room, be retrieved. Captain Rogge, being something of a ladies' man, acquiesced and signalled the order to Mohr, who demanded that Stewart show him where the trunks were stowed. Stewart tried to bluff but failed and after that the Germans blew the doors off both compartments and discovered the mailbags. They also blew the ship's safe and retrieved the contents of the weighted bag there. That was not all. During a search of the wrecked bridge the Germans found the green bag containing the secret communication to Air Chief Marshal Brooke-Popham, a bag that Stewart had known nothing about.

Working as fast as possible because of the partial signal *Automedon* had managed to get off and which might have been picked up by any British warship in the vicinity, the Germans transferred a quantity of frozen meat, whisky and cigarettes to Atlantis as welcome replenishments to the ship's stores. After that *Automedon* was scuttled and the raider raced from the scene to make for a rendezvous with two Norwegian tankers she had previously captured and which had prize-crews aboard.

Automedon's signal had indeed been picked up. The radio station at Colombo heard the message but there was no British warship in the vicinity to relay it to. The nearest ship to the actual incident was *Helenus*, also Blue Funnel Line. She relayed the message home to the company's Head Office in Liverpool, and things moved fast there. In 1945, after having spent nearly four years in a German prisoner-of-war camp, Deck Boy Frank Walker discovered that within fifteen days of the signal, the allotment of ten shillings a month he had made to his mother (one-fifth of his monthly wage packet) had been stopped in accordance with the rules then in force about the ending of Articles of Agreement (see Introduction). One can imagine the extra distress this allotment cessation caused Mrs. Walker, who did not learn until months later that her sixteen year-old son had survived and was in fact in a prison camp.

Aboard *Atlantis* Rogge and Mohr went through the captured haul of intelligence material with ever-increasing excitement. It is small wonder, for the haul was sensational, providing what was probably the single most important capture of *documentary* intelligence material – as opposed to signals intelligence material such as that from the well-known Enigma source – of the war. *Atlantis* had captured copies of Admiralty deciphering tables Nos. 7, 8 and 9, new fleet ciphers, Merchant Navy codes, details of minefields, Admiralty Sailing Instructions, and British Intelligence Summaries dating from September. On top of that, one of the mailbags contained coded communications to British Secret Intelligence Service officers (later in the war SIS came to be called MI6) throughout the Far East. But Rogge, who was a highly intelligent man, quickly realised the most important document of all was the letter to the British C-in-C, Far East. More will be said about this document below.

One of the two Norwegian tankers captured a day or two earlier by Rogge was the *Ole Jacob*, and with a prize crew aboard in addition to its Norwegian crew she was pressed into service as a courier vessel and sent on a circuitous route to Kobe in Japan. In addition to her valuable cargo of aviation fuel, which could be sold in Japan and so add to Germany's war coffers, she carried a trunk containing all the secret material. The Norwegian crew had been promised release in Japan in return for their co-operation, to be followed by repatriation to their homeland across Russia via the Trans-Siberian Railway (Russia, like Japan, being still neutral at that time). Donald Stewart managed to slip a letter addressed to Blue Funnel Head Office to one of the Norwegian officers before *Ole Jacob* set out on the voyage. The exact contents of Stewart's letter are unknown, but he must have reported the fact that much secret material had fallen into German hands, though, it must be stressed, he knew nothing of the green bag document. It is known that this letter reached England in early January 1941, via Shanghai where Blue Funnel had an office. (The content of the letter is likely to have been signalled to London somewhat earlier than that date.) As Shanghai was a base for several British Intelligence organisations, and as Blue Funnel, as we shall see, had close connections with those organisations, the letter was probably handed over to the British authorities there.

The raider was now crowded with the survivors of several other ships in addition to those from *Automedon*. So when five weeks later she rendezvoused with the tanker *Storstadt*, Captain Rogge transferred most of his Merchant Navy prisoners to her for the long voyage back to Bordeaux and captivity, leaving only those on board who were still being treated in his ship's sickbay. One of the stay-behinds was Alex Parsons, and he was still aboard when the raider sailed deep into the Antarctic to store at an island whaling station there. Later he was transferred to the supply ship-cum-blockade runner *Tannenfels*, to eventually end up at *Milag*, the camp for Merchant Navy prisoners of war in Germany.

With over 500 prisoners on board, conditions aboard *Storstadt*, which Sam Harper describes as a prison ship, were pretty appalling, though it must be said that the same conditions were being 'enjoyed' by its German crew. Some 80 junior officer prisoners, for example, were accommodated in the fo'c'sle, each man having only nine square feet of deck space. Sanitary arrangements were primitive and what little food was available was awful. Sam Harper pays considerable tribute to Second Mate Donald Stewart, who took on the job of superintending a fair distribution of food and water. On top of everything else, the first part of the voyage was through bitterly cold waters, for to avoid British patrols the tanker sailed 600 miles south of the Cape of Good Hope. It was so cold that one seaman died of pneumonia. Christmas came and went in those southern latitudes, the day being marked only by the issue of a bottle of beer to each man. During that voyage *Storstadt* rendezvoused with and refuelled several German ships including the pocket-battleship *Admiral Scheer*, which in November 1940 had sunk the British armed cruiser *Jervis Bay* in the latter's epic effort to protect convoy HX84.

An escape committee was formed by the more junior officers, and Sam Harper was a member of it. The idea was to take over the ship if the opportunity arose. When senior officers heard of the plan 'they became quite hostile and advised us to leave such matters to older and, one supposes, wiser heads', says Sam. Members of the committee decided to keep watches anyway and the deadlights over some of the portholes were forced. Second Officer Buchan from the *Port Wellington* somehow manufactured a signal lamp with the idea of using it should the occasion arise. Buchan also plotted the ship's course to such good effect that his prediction at the end of seven weeks at sea of the ship's arrival at Bordeaux was only a few hours out.

The final part of the run to Bordeaux was made by keeping to neutral Spanish waters At the French port the prisoners were taken to a camp known as *Front-Stalag 21*, arriving there on 5 February 1941. They were told they were considered civilian rather than military prisoners and as such, under international law, the Germans were not obliged to feed them but only to see they had shelter and fresh water. In the event, as few of the prisoners had any money, the Germans relented a little and did supply some food. Sam Harper, by then dead set on escape, begun to save some of his ration.

It was five weeks later when all the prisoners were marched out of the camp and down to a railway station about two miles away. They were told that a seven-day rail journey lay ahead to a camp in Germany. Sam's heart dropped. Somehow he must get off the train within twenty-four hours for, he estimated, after that the train would be too far north of the border between Unoccupied and Occupied France for any escape attempt to succeed.

Over forty armed German guards manned the train and not only did they dismount and patrol the platform of any station the train stopped at but, whenever it slowed down for whatever reason, some would lean far out of the windows to watch for anyone jumping off. By that time Sam Harper's resolve to escape had spread to three other engineers, Ernest Howlett and Ross Dunshea, respectively Fourth and Fifth Engineers of the *Maimoa*, and Robert Bellew, Fifth Engineer of the *Nowshera*, who could speak a little French. Each took it in turns to stand by the door to watch for a suitable opportunity to leap from the train.

Let Sam himself take up the story.

Midnight found us still standing by the door, and our companions were beginning to pull our legs unmercifully, which did not make us any more pleased with ourselves. One o'clock came and everyone was asleep; just about half past one I felt the train slacken speed, apparently to take a bend. I gave Howlett, whose head was out of the window, a nudge, and said 'Now or never'. He just said 'OK', opened the door and dived out. I jumped next and the others followed. The train was travelling about 35 miles an hour when we jumped and we landed on a track of broken stones.

Sam was badly shaken up, although the parcel of food and clothing he carried broke his fall to some extent. He picked himself up and soon the four men stood together watching with relief as the rear light of the train disappeared round a bend. Each of them was badly battered, but miraculously there were no broken bones. They began to walk east.

They reached a main road, crossed it, and made for a wood where they intended to rest awhile, only to find they had blundered into a German military encampment. Crawling back to the road, they made along it. Later on they were spotted by two German guards outside a house, although they were allowed to pass unchallenged. 'We were very lucky indeed,' says Sam, 'for afterwards we learned that a curfew was in force between 10pm and 6am.'

After some forty-eight hours of adventures, including being wished 'a kindly goodnight' by a German officer as they walked past him in the town of Bloise, and being helped on their way towards the frontier town of St Aignan by first of all, a friendly French peasant, and then by two French gendarmes who asked for their autographs before sending them in the right direction, they came to the river marking the border between the two Frances. They stole a punt and in it reached the comparative safety of the other side at 4am on 15 March.

By that time all four were bordering on collapse, so it was decided to throw themselves on the mercy of the owner of the next farm they came across. That farmer, says Sam, 'was one of nature's gentlemen'. He gave them breakfast and 'a good stiff tot of brandy' and then took them to the village of Orbigny where he introduced them to Madame Gervais, the Mayoress. The farmer knew what he was doing, for Madame Gervais's husband and son had been taken prisoner by the Germans and so she bore the occupiers of half her country considerable ill-will. She did not have much English herself but called in a lawyer called Aubier, who did. He had previously held a high position in the French Colonial Ministry and had much influence with the local authorities. He began to pull strings on the escapees' behalf.

Aubier took them to the nearby village of Montressor, where the local populace made a big fuss of the Britons. Between drinks in a local cafe they were entertained to a concert of English songs from the Great War era followed by a moving rendition of the Marseillaise. The Britons responded with 'an unmusical but hearty rendering of God Save the King accompanied by one of the Frenchmen on a cornet'. Then the villagers had a whip-round and handed over 400 francs.

Early the following morning Aubier took them to the town of Lockes and introduced them to an officer in the French Intelligence Service. The officer gave them train tickets, ration cards and 80 francs each, and put them on the train south to Marseilles after getting them to promise to present themselves to the French Military HQ there when they arrived. They reached the port-city on the 18th and duly presented themselves to the HQ Commandant, who received them most sympathetically and gave them the right of freedom within the city limits. They made their way down to the docks and found the Seamen's Mission, which despite the war was still being run by the Reverend Donald Caskie of the Church of

Scotland. A small, thin man, Caskie possessed a personality out of all proportion to his size and it was said that he could control the toughest crowd of sailors. He had no trouble with his new charges and took them under his wing.

At the mission they were introduced to a man who could get them across the border into Spain, but it was not until 9 April that they heard that the next stage of their adventure was on but that it could be for only two of them. They drew lots, and Sam Harper and Ross Dunshea were the lucky ones to board a train for a town in the Pyrenees. A guide met them there and late that night they set out, marching first through the cork trees of the foothills before beginning the mountain climb. They were soon joined by a party of smugglers and by four British soldiers who had been hiding in the woods for some days.

It was not long before Sam was exceedingly pleased he had kept himself in fighting trim during the stay at the mission. The climb was steep and went on through the night. At dawn they slept in a pigsty sited in a wind-swept valley. It was bitterly cold, and had it not been for the protection offered by the low building, some of the Britons, Sam reckons, might have died from exposure. They were off again in the late afternoon and once again marched through the night. The pace set by the guide was a gruelling one and by 6am everyone was dog-tired, though by then they were going downhill. Sometime during the night they had crossed the border into neutral Spain, having climbed to a height of 4000 feet in crossing the mountains. This time they slept in a shed.

Early the following morning they reached the town of Figuares, and after instructing the British party to take a train for Barcelona the guide, his job now over, left the escapees to their own devices. They found the station but no sooner had they entered it than they were arrested by the Guardia Civil. None too gently, they were taken to a jail which already held over twenty other escapees, most of them Poles, Belgians and Dutchmen. Two days later all the prisoners were put on a train which went via Barcelona to Ciberici, where there was an internment camp. At Barcelona station Sam Harper bribed a Spaniard to take a note to the British Consul, who hurried down with money and cigarettes.

After fifteen days at Ciberici, fifty prisoners, Sam Harper and Ross Dunshea amongst them, were transferred to another camp at Miranda de Ebro on the other side of the country, south of Bilbao. From there Sam managed to send a telegram to Captain A H Hillgarth, the British Naval Attaché in Madrid, who sent money and a message promising that he would see what could be done about getting the merchant seamen released. Miranda Camp was a hell-hole. The weather was cold with incessant rain; many of the internees were put to hard labour and all suffered severe hardship. 'We suffered in body and spirit from the brutality of the Spanish soldiers,' said Sam in his report. Apart from the hope engendered by Captain Hillgarth's message, the only bright spot there for Sam was the friendship he and Ross struck up with two Dutchmen. One of these was Baron Pierre-Louis d'Aulnis de Bourouille, who had spirited himself out of German-occupied Holland in March with a companion, Cees Fortuyn.

On 29 May the British Embassy in Madrid effected the release of Sam Harper and Ross Dunshea. They were taken to Madrid and housed in the Embassy for a night, but not before undergoing a thorough delousing process. Then they were sent south to Gibraltar, crossing the border into British territory on the last day of the month.

Sam Harper and Ross Dunshea arrived back in Britain on 27 June 1941 after what had been the most adventurous and dangerous months of their young lives. Similar escapes were often rewarded with medals, but that was not the case for these merchant seamen. To have given Sam a medal, however well deserved, might have brought out the fact that he had served aboard *Automedon*. In view of the loss of the secret papers and the blanket of secrecy immediately thrown over the incident by British authorities, publicity of any sort was not what was wanted. Sam Harper was invited to dine at shipowner Lawrence Holt's home in Ullet Road after he arrived back in Liverpool, the only other guest being a naval officer 'with rings up to his elbow'. After that Sam was kept out of public view. He has written of his return home, 'Holt's management [Alfred Holt Limited were the owners of Blue Funnel] did keep me under wraps.'

Sam brought home with him a letter to the exiled Dutch Government in London from Baron Pierre-Louis, and in consequence the Baron and his compatriot eventually arrived in Britain themselves. Both joined the Special Operations Executive (SOE) and both were later dropped by parachute into Holland. The Baron earned the DSO for his exploits behind German lines, but Cees Fortuyn was captured and died in the infamous Auchswitz concentration camp.

But what of the letter in the green bag? After the *Ole Jacob* reached Kobe, the trunk of secret material was despatched to Germany via the Trans-Siberian Railway, but a copy of the green bag document was handed to the Japanese. The German Naval Attaché in Tokyo, Admiral Wenneker, reported that it was received 'with extraordinary interest'. Wenneker went on to report that on that very evening he was summoned to see Admiral Kondo, the Japanese Vice Chief of Naval Staff, who thanked him repeatedly. From that moment Japan's already strong resolve to move south against the French, British and Dutch colonies in South-east Asia was cemented. The information in the document confirmed what they already knew from their intelligence services, that they could prepare for a southward advance and expect little or no opposition from the Royal Navy, thus permitting the main strength of the Imperial Japanese Navy to be concentrated against the United States Pacific Fleet, and exactly when and where it suited them. Eleven months later it suited the Japanese to make their initial attack at Pearl Harbor.

For the document in the green bag was a copy of the minutes of the deliberations of the British War Cabinet of 15 August 1940. It summarised Britain's strategic policy in the Far East, stating that Britain did not at that time have the wherewithal to meet any Japanese aggression in the area and that open clashes must therefore be avoided, and specifically stated that Britain would put up with a Japanese attack on Thailand or French Indo-China without going to war. It outlined what can only be called a policy of appeasement, one not too dissimilar in principle to that agreed at Munich by Chamberlain in 1938. There was much else besides in the document, including details of the deployment and equipment of the Royal Navy and Royal Air Force in the Far East and details of Singapore's fortifications. It cannot be said, as some people have suggested, that the receipt of the document resulted in the fall of Singapore, for many more important and more proximate occurrences which did lead to that event were to come during the intervening twelve months; the combined action of the United States, Britain and Holland in cutting off Japanese access to all oil supplies was just one such occurrence. The green-bag document was merely confirmation, albeit welcome confirmation, of what Japan already knew from other sources about the weakness of British forces in the Far East towards the end of 1940.

Sam Harper has a theory, one which is shared by several people who have written about the *Automedon* affair, based on why such an important document as the one in the green bag was sent out in a merchant ship. Put in its simplest form the theory is that the document was sent out that way so that it *would* fall into enemy hands and eventually bring Japan into the war, an event which might realise Churchill's dream of getting the United States into the war on the British side. There has even been an attempt to show that the Germans knew of the secret mail on board and were deliberately out hunting for *Automedon*. There are many difficulties with these theories, not least amongst them being, as Sam Harper's shipmate Stanley Hugill pointed out before he died, how it could be guaranteed that *Automedon* fell in with a surface raider. For had she met with a submarine instead, it is almost certain she would have gone to the bottom of the sea, green bag and all. Furthermore, had Captain Ewan not been killed, the green bag would likely have ended up at the bottom anyway. And surely, had those aboard *Atlantis* known of the secret mail on board *Automedon*, (a) they would not have risked the interception operation by capturing two ships over the previous three days, either of whom could have sent out warning distress messages, and (b) they would not have battered *Automedon* into what Lieutenant Mohr said was the worst state of any of the raider's victims, for had her ammunition locker been struck, she might have sunk with no chance of a visit by a German boarding party. Furthermore, Mohr would surely have mentioned any such foreknowledge in the book he was later to write.

Assuming that its loss was not by design, then the fact that secret material fell into enemy hands in this way was an Intelligence disaster of gigantic proportions and it can be argued that such an important document as the one in the green bag should never have been placed aboard a vulnerable merchantman. However, it has to be said that *Automedon* was not by any means a slow ship, and that given the much shorter fuel range of a warship, which would have meant more frequent bunkering calls than a merchantman needed, it is doubtful if the overall voyage time would have been much less had a warship been used. Furthermore, not only would it have been difficult to spare a warship in late 1940 for such a task, it was not necessary. Although the document was important, *its contents were not of an urgent nature*. A.C.M. Brooke-Popham was already aware of most of the information it contained, for he had been told before he left England, and for him (as with the Japanese) it was of a confirmatory nature and its quick arrival would not have made one iota of difference to his military situation.

We have seen how the letter in the green bag aided the Japanese in their decision-making, but what of the other captured documents? In his *Price of Admiralty*, Professor John Chapman states that one of the codes seized from *Automedon* was used with good effect in the successful air ambush of the Royal Navy's Force H in the Mediterranean on 10 January 1941, in which the carrier HMS *Illustrious* was severely damaged and the cruiser HMS *Southampton* sunk. By that time, in view of *Automedon*'s loss and the news of it which had got back to London through the medium of Second Officer Stewart's letter, the Royal Navy would have been well into the process of changing their codes. However, any such change takes time with a far-flung fleet, and unless *all* ships begin using the new code at the same time any messages sent out in both the old and new versions present cryptographers with an opportunity to use a process they aptly call 'cribbing'. As for the other material seized, the MI6 documents were in code and probably not addressed to named operatives. It is possible, therefore, that they did not help the Axis much in discovering the names of British agents in the Far East. Anyway, the British intelligence effort in the area can be described as being rather amateur, and A.C.M. Brooke-Popham himself was to complain during the following year that it was generally known in the area who the MI6 agents were.

They included Commander Charles Drage and Kenneth Millar in Hong Kong, Gerald Wilkinson in Manila, Harry Steptoe in Shanghai, and Captain Frank Liot Hill, in Peking. The long-serving China hand 'Hilly' Hill, a Canadian veteran of the First World War who was married to an American lady called Clyde, had files of secrets dating back to the 1920s, and he loved them. If he ever heard of the loss of the *Automedon* papers it is likely that the gap in his filing system would have worried him almost as much as the lapse in security involved. So fond of his files was he that when a month or two before the Japanese entered the war he received instructions from London to destroy them all immediately, he did not do so until literally the very last moment. As with his colleague Steptoe in Shanghai, whom he disliked intensely, Hill carried out his secret work under the guise of being a consul.

Blue Funnel had its own Intelligence Service. Almost from its inception in the early 1800s, the company relied heavily on information supplied from the string of offices it set up worldwide. Most of the information was of a commercial nature, of course, and was used by the company to ensure that one of their ships was first in to pick up an available cargo. Over the years, however, much valuable non-commercial information came to hand and this was passed on to British Naval Intelligence, especially after the Managing Director Lawrence Holt took the company's Intelligence Service under his wing in the late 1930s. He served on several important wartime Government Committees and was a friend of Churchill, who himself had a deep interest in all matters concerning Intelligence.

Lawrence Holt was thus close to the centre of power, and this was to pay off. Within a few days of Germany's surrender on 8 May 1945, a group of Blue Funnel deck and engineering officers, including Sam Harper, were flown to Germany by Dakota aircraft and landed near Kiel. In that port was a ship called *Hansa* which before the war had been *Glengarry* of Glen Line, one of Blue Funnel's sister companies. Launched at Copenhagen just before the Germans invaded Denmark on 7 April 1940, she had fallen into enemy hands. Ten days after the group's arrival at Kiel, *Glengarry* sailed to rejoin Britain's merchant fleet, probably the first captured vessel to do so.

What of the later career of *Atlantis*? After *Automedon*, she sank three more vessels in the Indian Ocean before making back into the South Atlantic in March 1941. In April she sank her seventeenth victim in an incident that could have precipitated the United States into the war some eight months before Pearl Harbor. The incident, concerned a ship called *Zamzam*, and it was reminiscent of the sinking of the *Lusitania* in the First World War which helped bring America into that conflict.

The Egyptian liner *Zamzam* was on a voyage from New York to Cape Town and Egypt. Of her 340 passengers, many were Americans, including missionary families, priests, and volunteer ambulance drivers, the latter travelling to Africa to work with the Free French Forces. The ship made calls at Port of Spain and Recife before setting off across the Atlantic on the voyage to the Cape. She was more than halfway there when before dawn on 17 April 1941 she fell in with the German raider. The liner was steaming blacked out, a practice not normally adopted by ships of neutral nations. Moreover, as an ex-Bibby Line vessel – she was the old *Leicestershire* – she had a similar profile to ships that were serving as either British troopships or auxiliary merchant cruisers. *Atlantis* opened fire without warning and the mortally-wounded *Zamzam* began to sink.

Ordering cease fire, Captain Rogge closed the stricken victim, and as dawn came up was horrified to see women and children, many in their nightclothes, congregating at the ship's rails. The first lifeboats from the ship to reach the raider contained mostly panicky Egyptian crewmen, and one of them was first aboard *Atlantis* when a rope was thrown down, despite there being passengers in the boat. This so enraged Rogge that he ordered his seamen to get the Egyptian out of sight or he would shoot him. The Germans boarded the sinking vessel and, after assisting the last of the passengers and crew off, set demolition charges to hasten the ship to the bottom.

Eleven passengers had been wounded by the shelling, two of the most seriously injured being Americans – one of them, 'Uncle' Ned Laughing-house, a well-known figure in the tobacco industry, was later to die of his wounds – and Rogge knew he had got himself into an international incident. He told the British master of the ship, Captain William Gray Smith, that had the ship displayed lights as required under International Law for neutral ships, he would not have opened fire. Some time later it emerged that Captain Smith had been ordered by the British Admiralty not to light his ship, something that has been construed by some writers to have been part of a dark British plot to get America into the war. On top of the American factor, Rogge was confronted by a petition from some of *Zamzam*'s Egyptian officers demanding to know why he had sunk the ship. (Egypt's neutral status is arguable for, whether her citizens liked it or not, Egypt was a base for British troops. On top of that, in the particular case of *Zamzam*, her cargo included oil and a hundred American trucks destined for the British 8th Army.)

Zamzam's passengers and crew were transferred to the German blockade-runner *Dresden*, aboard which they eventually reached a port in Occupied France. From there the Americans were repatriated whilst Captain Smith and his men ended up at *Milag*. The sinking of the ship did not bring America into the war but it certainly had an anti-German effect on some public opinion there. A month after the sinking and before anyone apart from the immediate participants knew exactly what had happened, American newspapers headlined the missing ship. The *New York World-Telegram* for 19 May carried the banner '196 AMERICANS FEARED LOST WITH EGYPTIAN MERCY SHIP'. Underneath that, '*Zamzam* Missing a Month; "Enemy" action blamed'. The word 'Enemy' was in inverted commas but the fact that it was used at all must have gladdened the hearts of the diplomats in the British Embassy in Washington.

Two of the *Zamzam*'s passengers were David Scherman, a staff photographer for *Life* magazine, and the editor of *Fortune*, Charles Murphy. Scherman not only managed to take many pictures of the incident but was also able to hide some of his films from the Germans, including one which contained a photo of *Atlantis* itself. The remainder of his films, amounting to some 1500 shots, were at first confiscated, but after examination were handed back to him. Scherman's photograph of *Atlantis* was subsequently circulated to every British warship.

Atlantis met her fate on 22 November 1941 while posing as the Blue Funnel ship *Polyphemus* off the Brazilian coast, and David Scherman's photograph helped to identify her to the British cruiser HMS *Devonshire* which sank her. In a year and nine months of operations *Atlantis* had sunk or captured twenty-two merchantmen totalling 135,697 tons, and the Admiralty must have breathed a corporate sigh of relief at her demise. As there were U-boats in the area *Devonshire* made no attempt to pick up the *Atlantis* survivors, but they were soon rescued by *U-126*, and all but seven were saved and taken back to Germany. Later in the war Captain Rogge was again to meet many survivors from the ships he had sunk, when he was placed in command of *Milag* camp.

About a year after the sinking of *Zamzam*, David Scherman was in London on an assignment for *Life* magazine. During a session photographing the British Foreign Minister Anthony Eden, the discussion got round to the sinking. Afterwards Scherman reported something which has been construed by some as adding to the allegation that the sinking of the ship was all part of a cynical British ploy. 'You chaps on the *Zamzam*', Eden remarked, 'were quite a disappointment to us. We expected that incident to bring America into the war.'

CHAPTER 5

The Blockade Run to Sweden

Ball-bearings were of special strategic importance to all combatant nations during the Second World War. They formed vital components of tanks and other military vehicles and, even more importantly, were needed in the construction of aircraft frames. So vital were they to the British war effort that the Government created a post called Controller of Bearings, the appointee being responsible for rationing the scarce supplies amongst those industries in need of them. According to the Controller's figures, one hundred tons of ball-bearings were enough to complete nine hundred Lancaster and nearly a thousand Mosquito aircraft. In the early years of the war, before Britain expanded its own production and before imports from America increased, three-quarters of the ball-bearing requirement for British airframe manufacture was obtainable only from neutral Sweden, the world's No.1 producer. William Casey, who after the war became head of America's Central Intelligence Agency, once wrote with regard to Sweden during the war, 'the name of the game was ball-bearings'. Sweden also manufactured special steels and tubes together with machine tools essential for making weaponry. Before the war Britain recognised that steps must be taken to ensure that the supply of these commodities did not dry up if and when Germany occupied the countries surrounding Sweden. A corollary to that was the prevention of similar shipments reaching the Axis if at all possible.

In October 1939, a month after the war began, Sweden sought to bolster her neutral status by signing two very similar War Trade Agreements, one with Britain and the other with Germany, both of them limiting the volume of exports to the two combatant nations to the levels that pertained in 1938. In that same month, British Iron and Steel Control, one of the many 'front' organisations of the Ministry of Economic Warfare (MEW) whose job, as its name implies, was to wage economic warfare upon the Axis, took into its employ a man called George Binney. Two months later he was flown to Sweden with the remit to cultivate contacts within the Swedish steel industry, expedite the completion of existing export contracts, and to report any intelligence he picked up in the process of doing so.

A one-time arctic explorer, forty-year-old Binney was a man of buccaneering character with a highly developed sense of adventure. Not without good reason, he rather fancied himself as a sort of latter-day Sir Francis Drake, who was one of his heroes. After leaving university Binney had worked in the fur trade of the Hudson Bay Company and

later took a job with United Steel, an appointment which gave him a
great deal of experience in the steel industry. His character and expertise made him a good choice for the war job in hand though his unor-
thodox methods were to make him a thorn in the side of the conservative
and staid British diplomats stationed in Stockholm. On the other hand,
that other man of buccaneering spirit, Winston Churchill, thought
highly of him.

As 1940 progressed, with nation after nation falling to the German
juggernaut, Sweden became an oasis of neutrality surrounded by Axis
conquests and in consequence was very much isolated from Britain. At
that time Britain was still striving to bring her industries to a full wartime
footing and was not yet able to produce sufficient ball-bearings and machine tools itself or get them from the USA. In June Binney was sent a
communication from London telling him it was of paramount importance
that all the Swedish materials on order must be loaded aboard Allied
ships or stored in dockside warehouses pending shipment, and that he
'must, repeat must, at all costs get them to England'.

Binney decided to try to run ships through the Skagerrak, the waterway
between Norway and Denmark through which all ships to and from
Sweden must travel and which was blockaded by German naval and air
patrols. By that time Britain's highly secret Special Operations Executive
(SOE), whose role was defined as sabotage, subversion, and the formation
of secret armies in occupied countries, had been formed as an integral
part of MEW. In consequence, each of the three plans Binney was to
develop over the coming months was given an SOE operational code-
name. They were 'Rubble', 'Performance', and 'Bridford'.

When Norway fell to the Germans some two dozen Norwegian ships
found themselves stranded in Swedish ports. Immediately requisitioned
by the exiled Norwegian government in London, they technically belonged to the Allies, and the Swedes, in keeping with the rules of neutrality, refused a German request for the ships to be transferred back to
Norwegian ports. It was some of these ships which Binney chose for
running the blockade in Operation 'Rubble'. In the meantime, and while
he planned the breakout, the ships were to be used as floating warehouses
for the British orders as they came off the production line, this having the
added advantage that should Germany attack Sweden, which was more
than once on the cards, the ships could be scuttled to prevent their
cargoes falling into enemy hands.

Despite the rather luke-warm reception his plans received from some
London officials and the considerable hostility of Victor Mallet, the British Minister in Stockholm, who foresaw trouble for the Swedes from the
Germans if such a breakout was made, Binney pressed on. He settled on
five ships for the blockade-running attempt, the cargo ships *Elizabeth
Bakke, John Bakke, Tai Shan* and *Taurus*, and the tanker *Ranja*. Though he
had decided on the ships, he had yet to persuade the Norwegian crews to
attempt the run, and this proved to be his biggest problem, for many of

the sailors looked upon the attempt as a suicide mission. However, with the help of the exiled Norwegian government in London he was able to get some volunteers from all five ships, though none of the captains agreed to sail. Fortunately two of the first mates were eager to give it a go, and as both held master's tickets that solved the problem for the two Wilhelmsen Line ships, *Tai Shan* and *Taurus*. For the other captains and additional crew members Binney had perforce to look elsewhere.

When the Germans had taken the Norwegian port of Narvik in April 1940 four British iron ore carriers found themselves trapped there. They were the *Blythmoor, Romanby, Mersington Court*, and *Riverton*, and their crews, together with survivors from the destroyers HMS *Hardy* and *Hunter*, had, after a long march and many an adventure, reached Sweden. Since then they had occupied a detention camp at Halsingmo about 250 kilometers north of Stockholm as guests of the Swedish state. Binney travelled to the camp only to be greeted by the same lack of enthusiasm for his plan from many of the seamen there as had been shown by the Norwegians, and for much the same reason; the first twenty-four hours of any breakout attempt would be spent negotiating waters entirely controlled by the German navy and air force and, not only that, both sides had laid minefields in the area. Binney made no attempt to minimise the dangers and told them that only after that danger area had been crossed would a rendezvous be made with British naval and air units. None of the British masters volunteered, but two of the mates did. They were Andrew Henry, aged sixty-four, a torpedoed veteran of the First World War who was an ex-shipmaster called back out of retirement in 1939, and the much younger Bill Escudier who held a master's ticket but had no previous command experience. Binney was mightily impressed by both these men, but more especially with Henry who had been First Mate of Ropner Lines' *Romanby* at Narvik and who, Binney discovered by talking with others in the camp, had been largely responsible for keeping up the morale of the entire British escape party during the earlier arduous trek across Norway. The command problem for the other two freighters was therefore solved after Binney had obtained the approval of the Norwegian government in London to use British masters on them. To Captain Henry, the most experienced of the small band of masters, went command of the fastest of the five vessels, *Elizabeth Bakke*, Binney reasoning that the fastest ship had the best chance of getting through and that if anyone could milk the last fraction of a knot out of the ship's engineers, that man was Henry.

After further meetings in the British camp Binney obtained more officer volunteers, including all four radio operators, and other crew members, including some of the Royal Navy personnel. Then, using his not inconsiderable powers of persuasion, he managed to get one of the captains, a Shetlander called J Nicolson, to change his mind and take command of the tanker *Ranja*, the largest of the five ships. By using a handsome bonus inducement Binney then recruited some neutral Swedes to make up the numbers. Altogether fifty-eight Britons, including George

Binney, who 'signed on' as supernumerary but acted as fleet commodore aboard *Tai Shan*, the same number of Norwegians, one woman amongst them, thirty-one Swedes and a Latvian made up the final crews.

It was necessary to ensure that if any one of the ships was intercepted by the Germans it could be effectively scuttled. Binney had no explosives available so, with expertise supplied by the Lloyd's surveyor in Gothenburg, a man normally associated with practices to keep ships afloat rather than sinking them, a method was devised to sink the ships if and when the occasion demanded. A series of holes were bored in each hull and fitted with valves with remote-control levers, the levers themselves capable of being jettisoned as soon as the job was done.

So many crew members and shore officials were aware of what was going on that Binney was concerned lest German agents attempt to sabotage the ships. A Swedish ex-shipmaster with strong pro-British leanings, Captain Ivar Blucker, who was now in charge of the Gothenburg harbour police, proved invaluable. Not only did he organise round-the-clock guards on the ships, he warned Binney about the activities of certain German agents in the area and also that he could expect no co-operation from the Swedish Navy, which had been severely antagonised earlier in the war by the actions of the Royal Navy when four old destroyers that Sweden had purchased from Italy had been temporarily impounded in Britain.

It was close to the end of December 1940 before the crew arrangements and the loading and refuelling of the ships had been completed. Binney decided that the breakout from Swedish territorial waters would begin from Brofjord, a haven north of Gothenburg which opens directly on to the Skagerrak. So the ships made their various passages there, keeping as close to the Swedish coast as possible. Safely at Brofjord, the little fleet then awaited the right sort of weather for the escape run.

Aboard the 17-knot *Elizabeth Bakke*, Captain Henry called his crew together. Included among them were thirteen men from his last ship *Romanby*, who were prepared to follow him anywhere. He told them that as the fastest ship with the best chance of reaching England they had a special responsibility to get through and that he expected the highest standards of professionalism from everyone. He was to get it, for Andrew Henry was of that rare breed, a born leader. He had more trouble in persuading the ship's Norwegian Chief Engineer that for once economy of fuel consumption, together with that inbred caution all marine engineers have over misuse of their beloved machinery, had no part to play in the forthcoming venture; caution had to be thrown to the winds and the ship must steam faster than she had ever done before. In the end the Chief Engineer was won over, and later Henry was pleased to see him going into a long huddle with his Second and Third Engineers to discuss the best way of milking the last fraction of horsepower from the engines.

The right weather conditions for the run were of paramount importance. The cover of snowstorms was required if there was to be any hope of eluding German patrol ships and others waiting in Danish and

Norwegian ports, to say nothing of the *Luftwaffe*. It was late afternoon on 23 January 1941 before those conditions came along, and Swedish pilots arranged by Captain Blucker, who himself piloted *Tai Shan*, boarded to take them out as far as the three-mile limit. The slowest vessel, the tanker *Ranja* under Captain Nicolson, sailed first. She was in ballast and was to act as a decoy for any enemy warship waiting outside; better to lose a vessel in ballast than one with a precious cargo. *John Bakke*, Captain Bill Escudier commanding, sailed next followed by *Taurus*, Captain Carl Jensen. Fourth in line was Captain Andrew Henry on *Elizabeth Bakke*. *Tai Shan* under Captain Einar Isachsen, and with George Binney on board, was the last to sail. At the three-mile limit, and before Blucker clambered down the ladder into the pilot boat, he told Binney that he had taken steps to ensure that the local telecommunications system had 'broken down' and would not be operative again until morning; no messages reporting the sailings could be sent till then, so if the ships avoided being sighted by German naval patrols they would have a twelve-hour lead over any major warship sent after them. This remarkable Swede had earlier sent a message to the British Naval Attaché in Stockholm, to be copied to the Admiralty in London, that the breakout was on, and that the Royal Navy escort should make for the rendezvous point.

No one had been able to give Binney much guidance on the minefields, and anyway, mined or not, it was necessary for the flotilla to keep to the comparatively deep waters along the Norwegian side of the waterway. In fact, Binney was not so much worried about mines as the fleet left the sanctuary of Swedish waters as he was about the weather, for by then the snow was coming down less thickly, increasing the chances of detection. On the plus side the improved visibility provided an occasional opportunity to take bearings of the navigation lights along the Norwegian coast which, rather to his astonishment, he found still burning.

The tension aboard the ships was almost palpable. Aboard each it seemed that everyone except the engineers, who were down below tending their charges, was up on deck and joining in the search of the surrounding gloom for signs of the enemy. Stewards were kept busy supplying a continuous run of hot drinks, but minding the chore not at all, for it distracted their minds from other matters.

It was around midnight when *Taurus* and then *Tai Shan* passed first the slow *Ranja* and then *John Bakke*, the second-slowest ship. By that time the fastest of them all, *Elizabeth Bakke*, was out of sight. She was rattling along at a speed which had not even been achieved at her initial builder's trials, and was so far ahead that Binney had no idea where she was. By daylight the three ships at the centre of the tiny and now far-flung fleet were clear of the southern tip of Norway and making north-westward towards the rendezvous point some sixty miles ahead. Aboard *Tai Shan*, the middle ship of the three, Binney could make out the ship ahead and the one astern and also the Norwegian coast some thirty miles away. He was both elated and apprehensive. They had survived the night, but could they survive the next few hours unless the weather closed in again? He was unaware that German patrol craft in the Skaggerak had other matters to occupy them, having been ordered to cover the impending breakout from Kiel of the warships *Scharnhorst* and *Gneisenau*. So, entirely fortuitously, Binney's timing for the run had been perfect.

Meanwhile, two British naval squadrons were out searching for the Operation 'Rubble' ships and at 1000 hours the cruiser HMS *Naiad* fell in with *Elizabeth Bakke*. With a nominal maximum speed of 17 knots, she flashed a signal that she was doing 19, adding that the other four ships were somewhere astern. Captain Henry made no attempt to reduce speed as his vessel sped past the warship and so fast was she going that Rear-Admiral King aboard *Naiad*, a sailor who knew a good thing when he saw one, decided not to interfere and ordered Henry to proceed independently to Kirkwall in the Orkneys.

Aboard *Tai Shan*, on which tension was rising by the minute, Binney was concerned that so far there had been no sign of the expected British air protection. He was surprised too, at the non-appearance of the *Luftwaffe* and surmised it was due to snow affecting the Norwegian air bases, and perhaps also to the breakdown in communications that had been organised by Blucker. Aboard *John Bakke*, the second-slowest ship, the tension was even more unbearable. In the effort to get maximum speed from the engines an exhaust valve had burnt out and Bill Escudier had been forced to heave-to for repairs, a job which took two hours; two hours of continuous eye-aching search of sky and horizon for signs of the enemy. By the time the ship got underway again, the lumbering *Ranja* had almost caught up.

Just before midday *Taurus* sighted the *Naiad* and her consort HMS *Aurora* and within half an hour *Tai Shan* also hove into sight of the British warships. However, Binney was given little time to enjoy the successful rendezvous before a German reconnaissance plane arrived and began to shadow the two merchantmen and the attendant cruisers. Then, out of the western sky, two Bristol Blenheims from a Scottish airfield roared in to drive the intruder away.

Over towards the Norwegian coast an RAF Hudson reconnaissance aircraft spotted the two rearmost vessels, both of which were heading for the rendezvous point but at a speed of only 10 knots. At that date RAF aircraft and RN warships did not use the same radio wavelengths and it was necessary for the Hudson to fly within Aldis signal-lamp range of *Naiad* to report his find. However, by the time it arrived on the scene the cruisers' guns and the Blenheims were busy fighting off the attentions of three German fighter-bombers, and the Hudson had to wait in nearby cloud cover before an opportunity came to relay the report.

Arriving almost as if on cue, a second British naval squadron consisting of two cruisers and three destroyers raced up to take over the close escort whilst Admiral King turned his own cruisers to speed south-eastwards towards the reported position of the laggards. First *John Bakke* was sighted and then *Ranja*, both of them now being shadowed by German aircraft who, strangely, had made no effort to attack. Rather, according to Captain Bill Escudier's report, it was as if the German aircraft had decided to act as escorts to the ships, both of which were flying the Norwegian flag. Admiral King ordered *Aurora* to protect *John Bakke* whilst he raced for the tanker in *Naiad*. For the first time the Germans seemed to realise what the whole thing was about, and dive-bombers and seaplanes roared in to attack *Ranja*. Sticks of bombs straddled her, causing superficial damage and then a seaplane came in low and machine-gunned the bridge, severely wounding the Swedish First Mate. Suddenly, for reasons known only to themselves, the Germans then gave up the attacks and reverted to shadowing the ships until dusk fell.

Throughout the night the 'Rubble' ships made for Kirkwall Roads at their best speeds and they arrived one by one the following day to a series of triumphant receptions. Their cargoes proved invaluable and the ships themselves became much needed additions to the Allied merchant fleet. George Binney was showered with plaudits of one sort or another. Admiral Tom Phillips, Vice-Chief of the Naval Staff, who in December of that same year was to go down with HMS *Prince of Wales* off the Malayan coast, pleased Binney greatly by sending a signal asking why he had not bothered to sink *Scharnhorst* and *Gneisenau* while he was about it. Binney was recommended for a CBE but Winston Churchill raised the recommendation to a knighthood. All five of the captains, including the redoubtable Andrew Henry, were awarded OBEs and there were awards for other crew members. The only casualty of the entire operation, First Mate Nils Rydberg of the *Ranja*, unfortunately died in hospital from his wounds. Captain Ivar Blucker, whose actions back in Sweden had played such a significant part in the breakout, was presented with a pair of King George VI's personal cufflinks, it being considered that to honour him in a more formal manner would have offended the Swedish Government. As it was, Captain Blucker found himself dismissed from his official post in the port of Gothenburg due to German pressure.

Important as they were, the 'Rubble' cargoes only temporarily filled Britain's needs for these strategic commodities, and in April 1941 Sir George Binney was again flown to Sweden with instructions to secure further shipments together with more shipping tonnage for the Allies by running the blockade again. Binney flew over in an unarmed RAF bomber manned by BOAC aircrew, one of several such engaged in running the German air blockade of Sweden. These aircraft often flew back with their bomb-bays crammed with cases of ball-bearings, but these cargoes were necessarily small.

Once again Binney planned to use Norwegian ships lying in Swedish ports for his venture, codenamed Operation 'Performance'. He set his sights higher this time, choosing no fewer than ten vessels – five tankers, four cargo vessels and a whale-factory ship. Under pressure from the Germans, who had seen Swedish connivance as a major contributory factor in the success of the first breakout, the Swedish Government now placed legal obstacles in Binney's way. They even altered several rules of the game of neutrality as they went along in an endeavour to placate the Germans who, after all, were far nearer their doorstep than were the British, who at that time appeared to be losing the war anyway. As part of the Allied response to this, the Royal Norwegian Government in exile chartered out the ships on bare-boat terms to the British Government, which meant that once British shipmasters had been appointed to them they could enjoy certain immunities from German-instigated legal actions in the Swedish courts.

The British masters at the camp in Halsingmo who had not volunteered for Operation 'Rubble' were now prepared to take command of three of the vessels, as was a first mate who held a master's ticket. To make up the required numbers, six British masters were flown in from Britain, making hazardous flights over northerly routes to avoid German air patrols. Crew members for the ships comprised volunteers from their original crews, other Norwegians in exile in Sweden, and more Britons from the Halsingmo camp, together with others who had fought in the British contingent in Finland during the Russo-Finnish war of 1939-1940 and who over the intervening months had managed to make their way to neutral territory. Sir George Binney was never one to forget past friends, so the unemployed Captain Ivar Blucker was employed as the shore-based marine superintendent for the operation.

German-inspired legal wrangling in the Swedish courts went on for the remainder of 1941 and into 1942. The ships were prevented from sailing by the Swedish refusal to issue port clearance documents, without which they were unable to leave territorial waters. In the background, the British Minister in Stockholm, once again none too happy about the proposed breakout for fear of its effect upon the host country, also made life difficult for Binney. Meanwhile, the ten ships were armed with Lewis guns and other weapons that had been smuggled in by the air courier service from Scotland, along with explosives for precautionary scuttling charges. These weapons and explosives arrived in crates under diplomatic seal, and more than once the British Minister registered his concern with London that his legation was being turned into an arsenal.

On the evening of 31 March 1942, the legal obstacles at last overcome, Binney's fleet sailed from Gothenburg. He himself was aboard *Dicto*, a 5000-ton freighter and at 14 knots one of the fastest of the ships. Before sailing, each master was ordered to proceed independently as soon as his ship was able to clear territorial waters, and for security reasons to maintain radio silence. Binney was aware the Germans were ready for him this time; intelligence sources indicated that their naval units were in considerable force off the coast, and that in order to prevent a possible British invasion of Norway, the Germans had strengthened their air force in that country and in Denmark to the south. As if all that was not enough, Blucker informed Binney that not only could he expect no co-operation from the Swedish Navy; they were likely to make things extremely difficult.

Binney had a major additional worry. This time the Royal Navy would not be providing cruisers in close support once the blockade runners had reached the rendezvous point. The RN had suffered severe losses during 1941, and since January 1942 had been involved in the huge extra task of escorting Arctic convoys to Russia. It was also necessary to keep warships on standby in case the battleship *Tirpitz* and other heavy German ships broke out from their base at Trondheim. He would be far more on his own in Operation 'Performance' than he had been in Operation 'Rubble'.

The fleet headed north, hugging the Swedish coast as closely as safe navigation permitted. Though weather forecasts had predicted fog under which they could run for safety, there was no sign of it at first and the night sky was brightly moonlit, no doubt silhouetting them against the land for the benefit of watchful eyes aboard patrol vessels. The foremost ships soon ran into drift ice, forcing them seaward towards the edge of the three-mile limit, and the fleet began to scatter, some continuing to head north at reduced speed through the ice, others making off in various directions in endeavours to avoid enemy patrols. Some of the sternmost ships found themselves forced outside the three-mile limit by Swedish naval units which had followed them out of port.

At 0200 hours *Dicto* was fired upon by an armed German trawler and altered course to head back into Swedish waters and the comparative safety of the ice. Now, there are several basic rules for navigating in ice, in addition to the golden one which is never to enter it in the first place unless there is no alternative. Once a ship is navigating in ice and a large floe cannot be avoided, the rule is to strike it directly with the stem, as a glancing blow can cause damage to the hull plating. Another rule is never to proceed in pack ice at night without good searchlights. But Binney and *Dicto*'s master, Captain D J Nicholas, had no recourse but to break all the rules, for even rigging a light might have brought German shells down upon the ship. So on went the ship, blindly grinding a way through ice of unknown thickness and therefore unknown hardness. It was not long before the price was paid, for soundings of the bilges showed the ship to be making water in way of No. 1 hold after a floe had grated heavily along the side. The ship pressed on, endeavouring to get as far away from the trawler as possible, and hoping that the forecast fog would come and enable an escape seaward to be made under its cover. By 0400 hours, instead of fog it was snowing, though the meteorological officer on board was of the opinion it did not extend very far out to sea. The ship had to stay inshore. Finally at 0600 hours the promised fog arrived all along the coast, but it was only patchy. Nevertheless, it was enough to make some of the captains decide to risk all and head out into international waters. Almost immediately two of them sighted German patrol craft and had to head back in again.

At about the same time the British chief engineer on board the whale factory-ship *Skytteren*, an outspoken Geordie named Thompson, reported to the bridge that 'some bloody quisling had shoved a hammer through the telemotor piping', so sabotaging the ship's main steering gear. Her master, Captain Wilson, used emergency steering gear to head back towards the coast. Two other ships, *Lionel* and *Buccaneer*, suddenly found themselves in close encounter with a German patrol vessel and they too turned back, with the German giving chase. Two of the tankers, *Storsten*, Captain Reeve, and *B P Newton*, Captain Calvert, had both been forced to leave territorial waters under the guns of Swedish warships, but somehow, and no thanks to the Swedes, both managed to slip through the German picket line without sighting or being sighted by any enemy patrol.

Aboard *Buccaneer*, Captain G D Smail, on loan to Binney from the Ellerman Wilson Line, realised there was no escaping the chasing German vessel and decided to scuttle. He ordered abandon ship but the Germans, guessing his intent, began machine-gunning the boat-deck. Smail blew the explosive charges anyway and the Germans stopped firing as the ship began to settle and as the boats were lowered. Captain Smail, in the best tradition of the sea, was the last man to leave but, in the first tragedy of Operation 'Performance', slipped and fell and broke his neck on the gunwale of a boat. He was the first but far from the last to die.

Another German armed trawler closed with *Skytteren* as she made back towards the coast under emergency steering and fired on her, the shell passing right through the bosun's cabin. Captain Wilson ordered his crew to abandon ship before throwing the levers which controlled the scuttling charges. The resulting explosion killed a stoker and badly burned several other crew members, but the survivors managed to get away in four lifeboats to be picked up later by the Germans. They spent the remainder of the war in captivity, some of the Britons amongst them finally ending up in *Milag*. The Norwegian crew members were treated as traitors by the Germans and were badly treated, most not surviving the war.

When dawn came *Dicto* was lying off Hallo Island awaiting updated weather information, with Binney having no knowledge of the night's catastrophes. When the forecast came it was the worst sort possible, for it indicated a return to clear weather. He broke radio silence to send a coded message to the other ships saying the weather was now unfavourable and that each master was free to act entirely at his own discretion. He expected no acknowledgement of the signal and therefore did not know it had been sent out on a wrong wavelength so that none of his ships received it. In any event, by then the masters of the remaining ships were already acting on their own initiative. *Dicto* was now making water heavily, and Binney made the sickening decision to return to Gothenburg. Aboard *Lionel*, Captain Kershaw, an Ellerman Wilson man who knew these waters well, read the weather signs for himself. He, too, decided to head back to port.

The number of ships still attempting to break out was now down to six and the fates had not finished with them, not by a long chalk. The next to go was *Charente*, under the command of Captain James Donald. She fell in with two armed trawlers, one of which put a shot across her bows. Donald heaved-to, lowered the boats, and as a German boarding party neared, detonated the scuttling charges. So now there were five.

Storsten, one of the first ships to head out to sea, had some initial luck. Two German patrol vessels were sighted, both of which opened fire but missed, and as a fog bank closed in, the ship managed to elude them by steaming at her maximum 11 knots. She first headed south-westward but later altered course for the rendezvous point, and as the morning progressed with no further signs of German activity a mood of optimism arose in the crew. They should have taken more note of the date, for it was April Fool's Day. At 1400 hours they were spotted by a German bomber, but it was not the aircraft that did the damage. With a giant explosion that tore a wide hole in the starboard side, *Storsten* struck a mine. Then the bomber roared in to attack just as a German patrol vessel was seen racing up from the south. *Storsten* lowered three boats and the crew scrambled down into them as the scuttling charges were blown. Under cover of a fog bank the lifeboats made good their escape, their crews electing to make for the rendezvous with the British warships. The fleet was now down to four.

Largest and most important of those left was *B P Newton*. She was an oil-tanker, but on this voyage her tanks were loaded with over 5000 tons of special steels and ball-bearings. Twice she received the attentions of armed German trawlers which shelled and machine-gunned her, but her speed of 14 knots carried her clear of further trouble until late that afternoon, when a succession of bombers attacked her. To great cheering, one of the attackers was shot down by Lewis gun fire, and that probably threw the other bombers off their aim. There were several near-misses, one of which caused the electric steering gear fuses to blow, but the ship sustained no direct hits. She sped on at maximum revs, her crew praying for darkness to fall early that night.

The small steamship *Gudvang*, Captain H Nicholson, almost made it to the safety of the night. With only a few minutes of daylight left she was sighted by armed trawlers who lit up the area with starshell. As the trawlers opened up with more lethal ammunition, Nicholson ordered his men into the boats before pulling the scuttling charge levers. Nicholson, whose previous ship *Romanby* had been captured at Narvik, and his crew were picked up and taken to Germany as prisoners-or-war. One wonders how often during his long captivity Captain Nicholson rued the day he had not volunteered along with his First Mate Andrew Henry to join the previous operation.

As night descended after what to the crews seemed to have been the longest day of their lives, the three surviving ships, *B P Newton*, *Rigmore* and *Lind*, with well over a hundred miles separating the first from the last, were each heading for the rendezvous point, hoping to get some protection from the RAF when morning came. Beaufighters had indeed been up and about that very day but air operations were hindered by bad visibility. One RAF plane had sighted the sinking *Storsten* and its three lifeboats making westward, the pilot reporting that the men in the boats were waving Norwegian flags as he flew low over them.

Throughout the night the ships ploughed through a rough sea and a Force 6 westerly in the knowledge that every precious nautical mile sailed brought them closer to safety. Way behind them the three *Storsten* lifeboats were also pushing westward but much, much more slowly, the two without engines being towed by the only one with a motor and with all hands engaged in baling out. At dawn the motor-boat's engine failed and the smaller of the sailboats was abandoned, its crew being divided between the other craft. Now the position was reversed with the motor-boat being towed by the one with a sail. Blessedly, the wind turned and began to blow from the east, and the spirits of the men in the boats rose as they were pushed along at between 3 and 4 knots.

At dawn *B P Newton* sighted three British destroyers. Although of First World War vintage, they made a magnificent sight as they raced up to be greeted by cheers, waves, and the blowing of the ship's siren to which they responded with their klaxons. Soon a Beaufighter appeared overhead, and with it and one of the destroyers as escort, the tanker made for Methil on the Firth of Forth. The remaining destroyers, soon joined by three others of equal age, raced east in search of any possible stragglers. Two hours later the tanker *Rigmore* was sighted by Beaufighters, but a long way astern the much smaller tanker *Lind*, making a bare 8 knots, had yet to be sighted by anyone, friend or foe alike.

Rigmore was sighted again in mid-morning, this time by two RAF Blenheims. While one of the aircraft stayed with the ship as escort, the other flew back towards the British destroyers to signal the sighting. At noon the escorting Blenheim was short of fuel and signalled that she must return to base, so *Rigmore* was on her own again. That situation did not last, for less than half an hour later a German bomber came on the scene to be quickly followed by two more. The tanker's gunners put up a fight before two bombs blew holes in her hull. An SOS was radioed as the order was given to abandon ship, and then from grandstand seats in the boats the tanker's crew witnessed the unfolding drama. German torpedo-carrying seaplanes arrived to loose their armoury on *Rigmore* which received another blow but still would not sink. Suddenly, puffs of smoke were seen exploding near the aircraft as five British destroyers raced up in line abreast. As her fellows fought off the planes, HMS *Eskimo* made a lee for the tanker's boats and took the survivors aboard. After a discussion with the crew the decision was made to take *Rigmore* in tow, and with volunteers from *Eskimo* the crew attempted to reboard, only to find that the weather and the ship's list made it impossible. German air reinforcements were arriving on the scene by then so it was decided *Rigmore* must be sunk. The gallant ship, its Norwegian flag still flying proudly from the gaff, was sent to the bottom by gunfire from HMS *Faulknor*.

With *B P Newton* now well on the way to safety, only the tiny 461-ton *Lind* remained to be saved, except for *Storsten*'s crew still heading west in their lifeboats. As *Lind* plodded slowly westward it seemed to Captain Nicol and his crew that his ship had been forgotten by everyone and they were not sure whether that was a good or a bad thing. British aircraft out looking for stragglers probably missed her because of her smallness, just like the Germans had done. At long last however, she was sighted by a Hudson out of Kinloss and was subsequently taken under the wing of a destroyer. When she finally arrived at Methil she received a heroes welcome out of all proportion to her size, having spent over eighty hours negotiating one of the most dangerous and war-torn stretches of water in the world.

At dawn on 3 April the *Storsten*'s boats decided to separate. The motor-boat's crew elected to keep heading west towards England under oars, while the crew of the overloaded sailboat decided to head north for the Norwegian coast. After hours of toil the sailboat eventually reached land with its crew. At about 0800 hours the following morning the westward-heading motor-boat was sighted by a Hudson aircraft but later searches that went on all that day until the weather closed in failed to relocate her. The boat and its occupants were never seen again and what happened to her and her gallant crew is one of the many unsolved mysteries of the sea.

Though the cargoes of the two surviving ships were of immense value to the war effort, Operation 'Performance' had come very close to total disaster with so many ships sunk, lives lost, and men captured that Sir George Binney came under considerable criticism. Pundits said it had been too late in the season for the breakout to have had any reasonable chance of success and that the Germans had been given plenty of time to arrange reception committees. Binney himself placed a great deal of the blame on the hostility displayed by the Swedish navy. At the end of Operation 'Performance' Binney made the dangerous flight back to Britain to face the music. Never a man to break under criticism, although it hurt dreadfully, he was soon ready to bounce back.

Towards the end of 1942 the Swedish Government came under threat by Britain and America, especially the latter who by then had joined in the air side of the ball-bearing run with Dakota aircraft, that unless Sweden came up with some concessions, the Allies would see to it that all trade then being carried out by neutral Swedish vessels would be brought to an immediate end. The senior American official at the talks held in Stockholm took the threat even further. Stanton Griffis, who in peacetime had been President of Paramount Films, was now a sort of roving ambassador in Europe. He was sent into Sweden in the belly of an American bomber by Bill Donovan, Chief of the US Office of Strategic Services. Griffis, who had no doubt learnt to be tough in his dealings with temperamental film actors, was not about to take any nonsense from the Swedes. Unless concessions were forthcoming, he said, steps would be taken to make Sweden a pariah amongst nations in the event of an Allied victory.

Later he added the threat that America would consider bombing the SKF ball-bearing works in Gothenburg unless the Swedes fell into line. The attitude of the Swedes changed rapidly; concessions were made and a few restrictions lifted, though some proved to be transitory. Clearance certificates were issued to *Dicto* and *Lionel*, who had both safely returned to Gothenburg after Operation 'Performance', and they were permitted to sail north within territorial waters to Brofjord in mid-January 1943. However, still playing both ends against the middle, the Swedes informed the Germans what they were doing.

In February 1943 an Admiralty plan to break out the two ships never got off the ground in the face of further Swedish non-cooperation. That plan envisaged using three fast motor gunboats (MGBs) as close escorts for the escaping ships, and it was this which gave Binney and his advisers the idea for a series of blockade runs, to be called Operation 'Bridford'. The operation was planned against the background of a warning issued in March by the Controller of Bearings that the shortage of some types of ball-bearings was still critical, and that the supply being ferried in from Sweden by the air courier service was insufficient to fill the gap as each aircraft could carry no more than a ton at most.

Binney's plan was to use fast MGBs, not for close escort, but as blockade-runners themselves. They were to be manned by Merchant Navy crews and fly the Red Ensign, so getting around the International Convention which limited warships to stays of only twenty-four hours in a neutral port; staying longer meant being detained for the duration of the war. Five 117-foot MGBs underwent major conversion for the operation, each being gutted to provide cargo-carrying compartments capable of loading between 40 and 50 tons of cargo. Over these compartments folding derricks were fitted. The heavier guns were removed, twin Oerlikons and twin Vickers machine-guns being shipped in their place. Magnetic compasses were removed – they would have been useless in such small vessels when in close proximity to a cargo of steel – and replaced by gyro-compasses. The engines, a set of three originally designed to give a speed of 28 knots, were governed-down because of the heavy cargoes to be carried, to give a cruising speed of 20 knots with a maximum of 23 in an emergency. The engines were to give nothing but trouble throughout the six months that Operation 'Bridford' lasted, and it may have been this interference with their original capabilities that caused the trouble.

The fleet's home port was Hull, though Immingham across the river was also used as a base because from there the ships could proceed to sea at all states of the tide. Binney, who was given the rank of Commander RNVR and made commodore of the fleet, named the five boats *Nonsuch*, *Gay Viking*, *Gay Corsair*, *Hopewell* and *Master Standfast*. To command and man the craft he turned once more to Ellerman Wilson Line, and did not turn that way in vain. So many were the volunteers that he was able to select exactly the type of man he wanted; young, adventurous, and adaptable enough to put up with the cramped conditions on board. One reason for the more than ample number of volunteers may have been the carrot of a special bonus to be paid for every successful trip, a bonus over and above the standard monthly War Risk Money paid to every merchant seafarer. 'For each trip that was successful', wrote Lawrie Kohler, bosun aboard *Gay Corsair*, 'we received a month's pay!' Each craft was crewed by between eighteen and twenty men. Binney dubbed them 'Merchant Navy Commandos', a term taken up in reports made by the various British ministries involved in the operation and even by Churchill himself.

Each boat carried two wireless operators, so that a continuous radio watch could be kept. They also carried a designated Chief Officer in addition to a First Mate. The First Mates were the actual seconds-in-command, for the Chief Officers were SOE appointees from the Army or RNVR, who had the overt task of looking after gunnery and scuttling procedures. Their covert purpose, however, was to deal with all security arrangements in an attempt to keep the operation as secret as possible. One suspects that secrecy in such a close-knit shipping community as Hull was next to impossible to maintain. Bosun Kohler learnt about the purpose of the ships, which he said was supposed to be 'the best kept secret of the war', from shore-based firewatchers before he had even put a foot aboard.

There followed many weeks of fitting out, training, gunnery courses, shakedown cruises including runs under fully laden conditions, and fleet manoeuvres, the latter something completely alien to Merchant Navy officers unless they had served in the naval reserve. All the boats experienced engine breakdowns, an ominous foretaste of what was to come. The Humberside bases were set up and equipped to carry out maintenance. In addition, some personnel and equipment was sent to Sweden by air, where *Dicto* was to become the flotilla's depot ship at that end as well as serving as a floating warehouse. The blockade runs were to be made during the northern winter, the season of longest nights, and at times when there was no moon and plenty of cloud cover. Exact weather forecasts were therefore of paramount importance, and an experienced meteorological officer was appointed to *Dicto*.

At long last the great day arrived and the five ships left port on 26 October 1943 in the first attempt to run the blockade, a run that was to provide plenty of the ill-luck that dogged the entire six month operation. George Binney sailed on *Hopewell* commanded by Captain David Stokes, whom Binney described as a 'red-haired, blue-eyed individual with an infectious laugh'. It was also said of 'Ginger' Stokes that he had the voice of a town crier, and of a northern town at that. With Flamborough Head as its departure point the flotilla passed through the British minefields and shaped course for the Skagerrak. Early on the following morning, close to the Dogger Bank, a Danish fishing fleet was sighted operating without lights and course was altered to avoid them. As soon as the flotilla had passed the fishermen switched on their lights and Captain Stokes was convinced that the subsequent interception of the flotilla by an aircraft was caused by radioed information from the fishermen, who almost certainly carried German observers aboard.

During the night *Gay Viking* signalled she had engine trouble, and by dawn was nowhere in sight. Later that morning the other vessels were strafed by a German seaplane which was finally driven off by accurate Oerlikon fire. Binney radioed Coastal Command for air assistance, but was later to discover that the message had not been received. After that the flotilla altered course several times in case the message had been intercepted by the enemy. It was during this evasion period that all the craft developed engine problems, so that by dusk the flotilla was well short of the position they should have reached by then. They closed in around the flagship and the decision was made to abandon the run as engine problems made increasing speed to compensate out of the question. They arrived back at Hull on the 30th expecting to find *Gay Viking* already there.

But *Gay Viking* was not there, for after making repairs and the flotilla being then nowhere in sight, Captain Harry Whitfield decided to press on independently. No one who knew Whitfield would have been surprised at this decision. A short, hooked-nose man with sallow skin, he was the type who reached decisions after plenty of consideration and then stuck to them come what may. Unaware that the run had been officially aborted, *Viking* sailed on in lonely if rather anxious splendour. At noon on the 27th she was spotted by a Dornier aircraft which circled the fierce-looking little craft at a respectful distance. Whitfield ordered a German naval ensign hoisted and the aircraft flew off. As course was altered towards the north another aircraft was seen flying very low, but due to low cloud cover and generally poor visibility they were apparently not spotted. At dusk Whitfield rang down for full speed on all three engines and course was set for a fast run through the Skagerrak. With all hands tensed at action stations the ship raced through the night, lookouts clinging to every vantage point and with the radar operator's eyes glued to his set as he watched for tell-tale blips. The last part of the run called for some extremely tricky night-navigation through a chain of islands and rocks known locally as the *skargar*. That was not the only danger, for British naval intelligence had reported that the Germans were maintaining a special patrol in the area. It was with great relief that the ship finally arrived safely off Hallo Island from where she steamed slowly up to the port of Lysekil.

No need now for a German flag, and *Gay Viking* entered port in broad daylight sporting one of the huge Red Ensigns which Binney had supplied specially for such an event. 'Chugging to Lysekil in the morning light', wrote Whitfield later, 'gave us a wonderful thrill. We had an oversize Red Ensign aft, a small one at the gaff, the Wilson house flags were flying, and the whole ship's company was bursting with pride. We passed [some] fishing boats and the occupants stood up . . . waving and cheering.'

News of the ship's pending arrival had been relayed from the lookout station on Hallo Island and the first British merchantman to visit Lysekil since the war began found herself greeted by what seemed to be most of the town's population lining the quayside. She tied up at a wharf right under the nose of the German consul who had an office opposite, and there 'Bridford' shore staff came aboard. Only then did Whitfield learn that his was the only ship to get through. Later that day *Gay Viking* moved a few miles up the coast to Brofjord where she tied up alongside *Dicto*, transhipped her inward cargo of oil and equipment and loaded 40 tons of ball-bearings. She also took on board some Norwegian 'passengers', for throughout the Bridford operation the ships were to carry passengers in both directions. Sometimes they were secret agents.

The ship sailed at dusk the following day, but not before receiving a warning from the harbourmaster that a fleet of three trawlers flying the Danish flag had been sighted cruising off Hallo Island and that they were suspected of being Germans. Showing no lights and with engines at full speed, *Gay Viking* sped through the night and by dawn was 85 miles clear of the Skagerrak where she was met by two RAF Beaufighters. Twenty-four hours later she was back in the Humber, having completed the first successful 'Bridford' run.

When Churchill received a memorandum informing him of the success of *Gay Viking*'s solo effort together with an assurance that the operation would continue as weather and other circumstances permitted, the great man's answer came back in a word of one syllable – 'Good!'.

At dusk on the day of *Gay Viking*'s return, *Hopewell*, with Binney once again on board and in consort with *Master Standfast*, set out to make the second run. *Standfast* was under the command of Captain George Holdsworth in lieu of the sick Captain Goodman. The thirty-five year-old Holdsworth sailed off in the knowledge that if all went well he would be back in less than a week. That was important, for his wife was expecting a baby.

After a fast run made despite worsening weather conditions the two vessels were in sight of Swedish shore lights at 0230 hours on 1 November. With *Hopewell* in the lead they had begun the run shorewards when lookouts aboard the flagship reported that *Master Standfast* seemed to be having difficulties keeping station. Reassured that her consort was still there by a blip showing on the rudimentary radar screen, *Hopewell* pressed on. Captain Stokes was in the middle of an intricate set of coastal manoeuvres designed to avoid a known German patrol area when suddenly the radar blip taken to be *Master Standfast* was seen moving rapidly as if making for an outer passage *through* the patrol area. There was nothing *Hopewell* could do about it, and she arrived at Lysekil at dawn. There was no sign of Holdsworth's command in the port. It was a day or two later when reports came in that *Master Standfast* had been intercepted by an armed German trawler and that there had been casualties on board before she had been taken under escort to Frederikshavn in Denmark. It was to be almost six months before full details of the vessel's loss became known in England.

When Holdsworth first sighted the German trawler he had attempted to make off at speed but the trawler opened fire scoring hits on the bridge,

hits that wounded Holdsworth, the mate, the chief officer, and both radio
officers. Either there had been no time to blow the scuttling charges or,
because all those on the bridge had been injured, no order was made to
that effect, before a German boarding party had stormed aboard and
captured the vessel. Captain Holdsworth's wounds were fatal and he died
after being landed at Frederikshavn. The remainder of the crew were to
languish for the rest of the war in *Milag*.

Meanwhile *Hopewell* had moved round to Brofjord where she took on
board 40 tons of ball-bearings from the depot ships and six Norwegian
passengers. Whilst awaiting the right weather conditions for the return
run the ship's engines were given an overhaul. 'Ginger' Stokes spent some
time befriending a Swede who told him about a rarely-used passage between rocks at the entrance to the fjord which, with care and navigational
skill, could provide a short cut to safety.

The ship sailed on 16 November and Stokes had successfully negotiated the recommended passage when the trouble began. A strong wind
suddenly blew up creating a mountainous sea and at about the same time
one of the gearboxes seized up. There was no option but to turn round and
make back for calmer waters. Stokes said afterwards of the return run
through the passage, 'If the sea was boiling when we came out, it was
indescribable for the return. All . . . was foam and breaking water.' The
only way to make the passage back in those conditions and to avoid being
thrown against the rocks was to go in at full speed. 'Give her all she's got!',
he instructed the engineer, and on two engines he flung the craft through
the gap to reach calmer water, suffering only minor damage to the bow.
Back at Lysekil a coded message was sent to London asking for a new
gearbox to be flown out and it arrived at Gothenburg a few days later in a
Dakota aircraft from Leuchers in Scotland.

Under Swedish naval escort *Hopewell* made for Gothenburg for repairs.
Her adventures were far from over, for despite the presence of the escort,
she found herself being fired on by one of the forts guarding the entrance
to that port, one shell passing so low over the bridge that it made Captain
Stokes and everyone else there duck hastily. Only frantic signals from the
escort prevented what might have been a permanent end to *Hopewell*'s
career as a blockade-runner. Despite the incident, dockyard workers lined
the docks to cheer the MGB alongside. 'It was a triumph,' Binney
reported.

After repairs *Hopewell* made back to Brofjord, from where it was intended to make a second attempt to break out, but it was 30 November
before weather conditions seemed right. As dusk closed in the vessel
slipped out of harbour, this time relying on caution rather than speed,
and crept slowly through the night until well clear of the Swedish coast.
Only then did Stokes order full speed. To gain full advantage of the tidal
stream he decided to make through the Skagerrak on a course close to the
northern side of the channel even though this would take them rather
closer to the naval base at Kristiansand than he would have liked. At first

they were lucky, for off that port they picked up the radar echo of a destroyer but apparently were not seen themselves. Then some of their luck ran out when the big-end bearing on the centre engine seized up.

With considerable trepidation they pressed on at a modest 15 knots, and at first light Captain Stokes and George Binney on the bridge together, let out a combined sigh of relief when two Coastal Command Beaufighters came out of the clouds. However, the engine jinx had not finished with them yet, for suddenly the port engine gave out altogether, and for the rest of that day and the following night the ship wallowed through a rough sea on one engine, a wallowing that made even the most hardy seamen amongst them seasick. When she finally arrived at Hull there was only enough fuel left onboard for a few more hours steaming.

The marine side of the ball-bearing runs continued until March 1944. Not all of the runs were successful, for bad weather, groundings in fog, but most of all, engine unreliability, caused many of the trips to be aborted. Nevertheless, during the period of operations and for the loss of one of the five ships and one life, they brought back 347 tons of ball-bearings, special metals and machinery and 67 passengers. The concomitant air operation, involving the best part of 200 flights and in which 4 aircraft and 23 lives were lost, managed only 90 tons due to the low loading factor of the aircraft.

A Government Press Handout issued well after the end of Operation 'Bridford' described it as 'one of the boldest achievements of the British Merchant Navy'. Conversely, and true perhaps to the Merchant Navy tradition of rarely making a fuss about any accomplishment, Bosun Lawrie Kohler wrote, 'I believe that the whole operation . . . was puffed up out of all proportion'. He went on, 'It is true that we were penetrating the enemy's defence line, though we were a very small target and had the advantage of speed if we were spotted'. Perhaps Kohler was not fully aware of the importance of what may have seemed to him to be the small tonnages of cargo the MTBs carried in comparison to the thousands of tons of cargo carried by a standard merchantship. Furthermore, in view of the special dangers he and his shipmates had to face he was being over-modest when he wrote that the 'Bridford' crews were mollycoddled in comparison with merchant seamen elsewhere, citing that while awaiting suitable weather or phases of the moon they could spend much time at home with their families. The authorities placed great importance on the operation. One DSO, seven OBEs, nine MBEs, four DSCs, nineteen BEMs, and three Commendations were awarded to 'Bridford' crew members. The citation in the *London Gazette* for these awards was a simple one designed not to breach wartime secrecy rules. 'For gallantry and initiative in hazardous circumstances', it read. One of the BEMs was earned by the modest Lawrie Kohler.

Late in 1944 the SOE decided to use three of the 'Bridford' boats for running couriers and supplies to Sweden for underground resistance fighters in Norway, Denmark and the Low Countries. A number of the original crew members were available for this new operation, codenamed 'Moonshine'. In mid-January 1945, again flying the over-sized Red Ensigns that Binney had ordered (though he was not involved in this new operation), *Gay Viking, Nonsuch*, and *Hopewell* arrived in Lysekil after having transferred the most important items of their secret cargoes to a waiting Danish schooner in neutral waters. By that time it was obvious to all Swedes that the Allies were close to winning the war and the three 'Grey Ladies' as the Swedish press dubbed them, received the sort of welcome usually associated with the homecoming of victorious local heroes.

On 5 February, during the run home and sailing in line-ahead with *Nonsuch* in the lead, they ran into thick weather at night and the two sternmost ships closed up in order to see the wake of the craft in front. It was not long before Captain Stokes, now in command of *Gay Viking* and acting as tail-end-Charlie, realised they were off course and were running into danger. He was about to alter course and proceed on alone, when *Hopewell* ahead of him began signalling with a lamp, a forbidden practice when negotiating the Skagerrak. Aboard *Gay Viking* Stokes could read the signal even though he could see nothing of the outline of the ship it was coming from. *Hopewell* reported that she had lost sight of the lead ship *Nonsuch*, and in addition her gyro-compass was out of action. After that the lamp winked again, 'Please take the lead'. Captain Stokes, in accordance with standing instructions, did not signal back and, assuming his movements would be seen by *Hopewell*, altered course. Then disaster struck as *Hopewell*'s bow wave appeared out of the fog, heading straight for them. Such was her speed there was no way collision could be avoided and she smashed into *Gay Viking*'s side, dealing a mortal wound.

Stokes ordered abandon ship before jettisoning all secret papers and codebooks in a weighted bag. Scuttling charges were then set, and as the crew pulled away in rubber rafts the charges went off with a roar, the men pausing to watch as the boat sank. Captain Jackson aboard *Hopewell* broke standing instructions again by placing his own vessel in jeopardy as he searched the murky darkness for survivors. Even as the rescue operation proceeded two unidentified craft appeared on the scene, though they made no attempt to interfere.

All *Gay Viking*'s crew members were picked up, but as *Hopewell* had herself been badly damaged in the collision and was making water rapidly, it was decided there was no question of crossing the North Sea in that condition. They must return to Sweden. Daylight found the ship sailing slowly through enemy waters with radar echoes from ships seemingly coming from every side. Captain Jackson wrote 'that we all look like wearing a patch on our arses', a reference to the way Germans distinguished prisoners of war. But somehow they sailed on unchallenged until a German destroyer appeared and headed for them at top speed. Fortunately by then the 'grey lady' was close to neutral waters which she managed to reach only just ahead of the destroyer.

Nonsuch had reached home safely without her consorts, and a few weeks later she was followed by *Hopewell*, which had been patched up in Gothenburg. Both vessels later sailed for Dartmouth to be handed back to the Royal Navy, their days of sailing under the Red Ensign over for good.

Sir George Binney died in 1972. The only present-day survivor among the 'Bridford' commanders is Captain David Stokes OBE. He had a distinguished post-war career with Ellerman Wilson Line and became a Younger Brethren of Trinity House. Despite his years, the Merchant Navy Commando still has the blue eyes and infectious laugh that Binney wrote of all those years ago. Captain Andrew Henry OBE, the intrepid master of *Elizabeth Bakke* during Operation 'Rubble', went on to successive command of *Empire Spray*, *Fort Richelieu*, and *Empire Prospect*, but had no more noteworthy adventures. He retired, for the second time, on 19 May 1947. He was then in his seventy-first year.

CHAPTER 6

One Captain's Wartime Summer

The area of the Atlantic between the easternmost point of South America and the bulge of West Africa was one of the favourite haunts of U-boats. Allied ships and convoys making to and from South America and the Cape of Good Hope had to traverse the area, and although the gap between the two continents covers some 20 degrees of longitude, the need for ships to bunker at such places as Freetown, the main port of Sierra Leone, in the east, and Aruba and Curaçao in the west, created bottlenecks. The worst bottleneck of all was between Freetown itself and the Cape Verde Islands. According to the report of the Chaplain to the Missions to Seamen at Freetown, a man at the centre of looking after the welfare of seamen, up to 200 ships could frequently be seen at that port at any one time, and the approaches to Freetown therefore became a particularly happy hunting-ground for U-boat captains.

The spring and summer of 1941 was a period of his life that Captain E Gough of the *Clan Ogilvy* (British & South American Steam Navigation Company) was never to forget. His official report for the six months beginning in March of that year is typical of most of those produced by shipmasters during the war; it was a factual and undramatised account with a touch of humour here and there, and which largely underplayed both the horrors and the bravery involved.

On 12 March 1941 *Clan Ogilvy* sailed from Freetown as part of the homeward-bound convoy SL68. For the first three days all went well, but unbeknownst to anyone in the convoy it had been sighted by *U-105* (Lieutenant-Commander Oesten) operating in tandem with *U-106* (Lieutenant-Commander Schewe). Taking it in turns to attack and maintain contact, the two U-boats shadowed the convoy for a week, during which seven ships totalling 38,000 tons were sent to the bottom. On the 19th *U-106* also torpedoed the old British battleship HMS *Malaya*, which was helping to escort the convoy, although she managed to limp to safety.

Clan Ogilvy was the fifth victim to be torpedoed. She was struck at 2215 hours on the 20th, about half an hour after those on board had watched in horror as the fourth ship went down, and only twenty minutes before the U-boats claimed their sixth, Ben Line's *Benwyvis*.

Captain Gough reported:

It was near the end of the second alteration to starboard when we were struck on the port side, aft. The explosion blew the propeller off and a second explosion was caused when the magazine exploded. The deck aft and the steering-engine house collapsed amidst a raging fire. The gun's crew, including four naval ratings, along with the Chief Steward and Fifth Engineer, were killed, and also about twenty native sailors who were in the fo'c'sle. The remainder of the crew were ordered to stand by lifeboat stations, while the Chief Engineer and myself went aft to inspect the damage. In less than four minutes after the explosion the after deck was awash, the water in the engine-room having reached the middle platform.

Gough made the decision to abandon ship, which had to be done by the light of emergency oil lamps as the ship's dynamo had failed within seconds of the initial explosion. Due to the loss of personnel only three boats were launched, the Chief Officer's, the Second Officer's, and then the Captain's. A total of twenty-five men had been killed and three wounded. 'All living souls were off the ship when I myself slipped down the lifeline into No.1 boat,' Gough reported. 'From the time of the torpedoing to casting-off from the vessel was about ten to twelve minutes.' He went on to commend the excellent discipline and conduct of the survivors during the boat-launching operation. From his position in the boat Captain Gough watched as the oil lights burning on the ship were suddenly extinguished; he knew then that his command had gone down.

As daylight approached on the 21st, Captain Gough ordered sail hoisted and made a circuit of the immediate area. The Second Officer's boat, with which he had made contact during the night, followed, but there was no sign of the Chief Officer's. Wreckage and rafts were sighted, and also a lifeboat under sail which was towing a raft laden with survivors. The boat and raft were from *Benwyvis*, Captain H J Small. The Ben lifeboat was overloaded with forty-three men, and there were another nine on the raft. Captain Gough took the men on the raft into his own boat, and ten from Captain Small's were transferred to his Second Officer's. The two captains then decided that the three boats should make for the Cape Verde Islands, about 200 miles to the south, sailing separately in sight of each other by day, but making a tow during the hours of darkness.

Over the coming days they were lucky with the weather. It had set fair with a favourable trade wind blowing fresh for most of the time. Captain Gough had a hand-log constructed from a piece of wood and some boat lacing and so was able to estimate their speed, which varied between 2 and 4 knots. From the very first day Gough ordered water to be rationed at the rate of a tablespoonful at 0600 hours and another at 1800 hours each day. On particularly warm days he allowed one dipper of water shared between six men at noon. On the second day a large can of corned beef was opened, half being eaten that night and the other half the following morning. Though there were other cans of the meat aboard, this was the only time the experiment was tried, for the Captain found 'it made the men so thirsty'. After that their diet consisted of a small amount of condensed milk spread over a biscuit. Gough noted that 'after three or four days one didn't feel like eating and one biscuit lasted two days'. He added that malted milk tablets distributed each evening were very palatable and sustaining.

Three days after the sinkings, during the night of Sunday the 23rd, when the boats were hove-to and heading into the wind, a dark object suddenly appeared on the starboard quarter, not more than 200 yards away. Gough fired a red flare and the captain of the submarine, for that is what it proved to be, must have been even more surprised at this mid-ocean meeting than the men in the lifeboats were, for he crash-dived. A few minutes later Gough sighted a flashing green light about a mile away, apparently from another submarine. Discretion being the better part of valour, the boats raised sail and made off southward.

On the morning of the eleventh day, 31 March, a conference was held. 'It was obvious,' said Captain Gough, 'that we had missed sighting the Cape Verde Islands and were too far south. We decided, owing to the shortage of water, to proceed at utmost speed on a course of East in order to cross the trade routes to South America, and agreed that the boat fortunate enough to be rescued should give the whereabouts of the others.'

The three boats set off and were soon separated. At noon the following day a neutral steamer was sighted from Gough's boat and distress signals were made, 'but although we were only about three miles off our signals were unanswered.' The spirits of the men in the boat plummeted, but help was not too long in coming. Just after nightfall on that same day a light was sighted on the port bow. A ship was closing on what appeared to be a collision course, for there was no alteration in the bearing as her lights grew closer. Gough was not about to let this one get away:

> We closed to within 200 yards under full sail – inner and outer jib, mainsail and jigger – before making our presence known. Red lights were then burnt and the crew of the lifeboat shouted, while torchlight was shown on the sails. The vessel immediately responded by giving a prolonged blast on the siren, and by 1930 all hands were rescued and were on board.
>
> When we landed on deck we found that our legs were more or less useless to us. I had to hold on to the bulwark rail to prevent myself from falling. It was at least seven days before I could walk the length of the forward deck and back without wanting to sit down.

The rescue vessel was the Spanish *Cabo Villano* of Seville, commanded by Captain Don Luis de Arsuage y Sagardui. Due to the extra sails Captain Gough's boat had carried, it was assumed that his boat was ahead of the others, and he discussed the situation with Captain Sagardui. Then there came one of those acts of courage that collectively fall under the expression 'camaraderie of the sea'. The Spanish captain, well aware that to do so was inviting the attentions of a submarine despite his ship being neutral (several neutral ships disappeared without trace during the war and were assumed to have been lost to submarine attacks), stopped his ship and with all lights burning, including arc-lamps rigged at the mast-head, lay hove-to for the rest of that night in the hope that the two remaining lifeboats would see them. When daylight came with nothing in sight the *Cabo Villano* got underway again. A good lookout was kept, but they saw no sign of the other boats. The ship was heading for Santos in Brazil, where they arrived on 14 April. Captain Gough was rightly ful-some in his praise for the Spanish sailors 'who extended great kindness and generosity to us in providing comforts and clothing'.

The Chief Officer's boat from *Clan Ogilvy* was never seen again. The other Clan boat commanded by the Second Officer was picked up the day after Captain Gough's own rescue by the British motor vessel *King Edgar*, and the survivors were landed at Freetown. The Ben lifeboat under Cap-tain Small, with thirty-three British and Chinese seamen aboard, was adrift in the Atlantic for twenty-seven days, during which all but one of the occupants died. The lone survivor was seventeen year-old Cadet John Ross. He was picked up on 17 April by the French ship *Ville de Rouen*, which put him ashore at its destination, Tamatave in Madagascar. (The submarine *U-105* was sunk off Dakar on 2 June 1943. *U-106* followed its fellow to the bottom exactly two months later on 2 August 1943 in the Bay of Biscay.)

On 6 May Captain Gough sailed from Santos as a passenger aboard Blue Star Line's *Rodney Star*, Captain S J C Phillips, together with seven other survivors from the original two ships. A fast cargo liner capable of 15 knots, *Rodney Star* sailed independently, bound for Freetown to join a convoy for home. It was an uneventful voyage until the morning of the 16th, by which time the ship was little more than a day short of her destination. Then a torpedo struck amidships and Captain Phillips or-dered abandon ship. Captain Gough must have reflected then, that this just was not his year.

There had been no casualties and all hands got away in four lifeboats. They set a course for Freetown. Gough wrote:

> As we drew away the ship appeared as if nothing had happened, and this apparently annoyed the submarine commander, because he surfaced and promptly commenced to shell her. When we were about three miles away from the ship, sail was lowered in order to see the effect of the gunnery, which appeared to be rather poor. Our sails were down only a couple of minutes when behold, a shell plopped right in the middle of the four boats, only about 150 feet away. Needless to say, sail was again hoisted. It was 1010 [hours] before the ship sank, after three torpedoes and about seventy rounds of ammunition had been expended on her.

This time Gough was only in a lifeboat for three days before being res-cued, and on 23 May he arrived safely in Takoradi.

But that mad summer was not yet over for him. Having come full circle he joined another ship at Freetown once more as a passenger, and on 9 July sailed in a convoy bound for England. 'Every second day during the

early part of the voyage,' he wrote, 'we had submarine scares.' He must
have been wondering when the third blow would fall and, as he had been
lucky on the two previous occasions, what the third one had in store for
him. However, during the first three weeks of the slow, plodding voyage,
submarines failed to penetrate the escort screen. On 3 August, when close
to the English Channel, the convoy was joined by additional escort ships.
It was also joined by a German aircraft which kept out of range before
flying off without making an attack. Captain Gough, his spirits rising,
was told that a corvette had put paid to a submarine which had been
trailing them, and later that same day that a destroyer had accounted for
another one just over the western horizon.

Let Captain Gough's story end with his own words:

At 0210 hours on the 4th our convoy was attacked by a submarine. The first
ship to be struck was on our port beam, and she was soon ablaze fore and aft
with flames leaping 200 feet high. By this time our escort had sent up star
shells, which lit up the sea like daylight. As the submarine was sneaking out
of the convoy, conning-tower awash, she was sighted by the gunners of one
the convoy, who immediately opened fire and made a direct hit on the
conning-tower. A corvette then dashed over and dropped depth-charges –
and so one more submarine the less.

Perhaps the remarkable Captain Gough, whose exploits had earned him
the OBE, felt partially avenged for his summer of mishaps, especially as it
had been a merchant-ship gunner who had paved the way for the demise
of that last submarine.

CHAPTER 7

Milag, the Merchant Navy Prison Camp

Prior to 1942 Merchant Navy prisoners of war held by the Germans were kept in camps scattered over the western countries of Occupied Europe. In February of that year two adjacent camps called *Marlag* and *Milag Nord* were opened at Westertimke near Bremen in northern Germany. The former was for Royal Navy personnel, *Marlag* standing for *Marine Lager*, and the latter was for the Merchant Navy, *Milag* standing for *Marine Internierten Lager*. *Milag* held seamen from many Allied nations, although the majority were British. At its peak the camp had some 3500 inmates. In 1943 the *Inder Lager* was constructed nearby for seamen of Asiatic origins. A British officer, Chief Officer Herbert Jones of *Dalesman*, volunteered to go with them as Confidence Officer. He spoke Hindi and from all accounts did an exceptional job in looking out for the well-being of the men in that camp.

Third Officer William Mutimer of the steamship *Harlesden* (J & C Harrison Ltd) reached *Milag* in February 1942, having already been a year in captivity by that date, some of it spent in the sickbays of German ships and the rest in a German military hospital ashore. His story began aboard *Harlesden* which he joined in 1940 immediately after passing for his Second Mate's certificate. He was then twenty-one years of age. He made several voyages in the ship before what turned out to be the final and fateful one in February 1941. The ship sailed from the Clyde that month on a voyage to Canada, and by the 22nd had reached a point some 500 miles east of Newfoundland. During Mutimer's 8 to 12 watch that morning, several radio messages were received from an Allied merchant vessel in the vicinity reporting that a suspicious ship had been sighted and was closing in rapidly. The final message indicated that the merchantman was being shelled. After that the airwaves were silent.

Bill was resting in his cabin when at about 1500 hours he came awake to an explosion. Rushing on deck he saw disturbed water close alongside where a bomb had fallen, and looking up he saw a plane coming in to attack again. A second bomb was another near miss. Shrapnel from the first explosion had seriously wounded the Second Officer who was lying unconscious on the deck. As Mutimer tried to drag his colleague to safety under a hail of bullets from the plane which was now busy strafing the ship, he felt a blow in the arm. 'It felt', he wrote later, 'like an iron bar hit me with an almighty force'. In fact the bullet had shattered his right humerus. With the aid of the ship's cook, for there was no doctor aboard, the bleeding was stopped and the arm splinted.

About six hours later *Harlesden* came under shell-fire from the ship from which the plane had been launched, which turned out to be the battlecruiser *Gneisenau*. There were several direct hits, and by the time Mutimer managed to reach the deck *Harlesden* was lit up by a powerful searchlight from the German ship. *Harlesden*'s funnel had been shot away, many fires were burning on deck, and she was sinking. One of the port lifeboats was being launched, and despite the handicap of his wound Mutimer was able to reach it. Then, as the only deck officer aboard, he took charge and gave the order to pull away from the ship's side. Several swimming men were plucked from the water before the boat's crew lay to and watched their ship turn on its beam ends before plunging to the depths. Others had got away on rafts but of the crew of forty-one, seven had been lost, including the Second Officer.

The survivors were taken aboard *Gneisenau* and the wounded carried below to the ship's sickbay. Mutimer was anaesthetised and woke up to find his arm in plaster. After five days aboard the battlecruiser, days he described as being very miserable, he was transferred to the supply ship *Ermland*. The rendezvous point, wherever it was, caused Mutimer to wonder 'where the hell is the British Navy?' The battlecruiser *Scharnhorst* was there, together with a second supply ship, the *Altmark*, and several U-boats.

He was well treated aboard *Ermland*, the ship's surgeon and his staff spending much of their time fighting the gangrene that had invaded his arm. A month almost to the day after his ship had been attacked, he was landed at the French port of La Rochelle and taken to a nearby military hospital. Gangrene was now biting deep and he grew weaker by the day and would certainly have died there had he not been 'adopted' by Sister Elizabeth, a nurse of the German Red Cross. On 15 April his arm was amputated and when he came to he gathered that he was not expected to live despite the operation. The fact that he did was due, he said, to the continued ministrations of the motherly nurse. So attentive was she that by August he was well enough to be taken to Bordeaux to be entrained for Germany. After a few months at a mixed camp he arrived at *Milag* in a 'consignment' of several lorry-loads of Merchant Navy personnel.

On arrival, the prisoners were assembled in a large unheated wooden hall where they were allocated to various barracks, really nothing more than huts, which had been constructed from timber that had been allowed to lie in the snow all winter; in consequence, the buildings were damp and so badly put together that the wind whistled through the gaps bringing snow in with it. For the remainder of that first winter the inmates were cold, miserable and hungry. Matters got a little better in the spring, especially after some Red Cross parcels arrived.

Over the coming weeks and months more Merchant Navy personnel, those newly captured and those taken earlier in the war and previously

held in other camps, arrived at *Milag* in batches. Amongst the latter was
Second Mate Donald Stewart, together with thirty-four fellow crew members from *Automedon* (see Chapter 4). Also brought in were men from
Skytterren, Buccaneer, Gudvang, and *Charente*, all of them sunk while unsuccessfully trying to run the German blockade of Swedish ports during
Operation 'Performance' (Chapter 5). Later in the year they were joined
by survivors from *Master Standfast*, which had been lost during the follow-
up Operation 'Bridford'.

One survivor from *Skyterren* was not a merchant seaman at all, but a
captain in the British Army. Captain Dick Tawell had been one of the
British volunteers serving with the Finns during their so-called 'Winter
War' with Russia. When Germany attacked Russia, bringing the latter
country into the world war on Britain's side, Tawell had crossed over into
neutral Sweden and later signed on as an engine-room supernumerary
aboard *Skytteren*. Tawell maintained his Merchant Navy identity for the
remainder of the war to prevent the Germans discovering who he really
was and perhaps making propaganda use of his earlier activities against
the Russians. There were other men in the camp who were not merchant
seamen, passengers on ships that had been sunk.

The internal administration of the camp was placed in the hands of an
elected management committee, although the most senior posts were held
by men appointed by the Germans. The German camp commandant
could and did change the appointees whenever he considered that the
present incumbents were not 'co-operating' properly with him. The main
concerns of the administration were sanitation, the hospital, the galley,
mail, and of course food distribution and Red Cross parcels. The quality
and quantity of the food supplied by the Germans was minimal and had it
not been for Red Cross parcels, which sometimes made up 80 per cent of a
week's food supply, it is likely that the ever-present hunger would have
turned to starvation. The meagre food supply was also augmented by
vegetables stolen from nearby farms by members of working parties, but
men caught in the act were severely punished.

The camp had its own hospital block – which catered for *Marlag* pa-
tients also – run by a British Army doctor, a Royal Navy surgeon, a
British ship's doctor called MacDiarmid, and also by Dr Karel Sperber
from *Automedon*. Sperber's Czech medical qualification may not have
been acceptable to the British Medical Association, but it was highly
valued in *Milag*. He was very much respected, not least for having overcome an outbreak of typhus in a previous camp with the minimum of
facilities and medicines. At *Milag*, using very basic methods, he had some
success against diptheria. Sperber was a Jew and hence not popular with
the Germans, and towards the end of 1942 was taken away to a concentration camp, but he managed to survive the war.

Though the hospital facilities were extremely basic, the doctors were
able to relieve some of the severe stump pains from which Bill Mutimer
suffered. He spent several painful periods under their care but came out

the better for them. The camp had two burial grounds, one Christian, the other Indian. Thirty-six British merchant seamen are known to have been buried in the former, and fourteen in the other. Most of the deaths were from TB, cancer, or heart attacks, but five were from typhus. After the war the bodies of the merchant seamen buried in the cemeteries at *Milag* were reinterred at Becklingen War Cemetery at Soltau, which is run by the Commonwealth War Graves Commission.

As the weather grew warmer in that first spring, the prisoners began to organise all manner of activities, some with the blessing of their German guards and others most definitely without. A theatre group was organised by a fairly well-known Shakespearean actor called Henry Mollison. A cousin-in-law of aviatrix Amy Johnson, Mollison had been unfortunate enough to be a passenger aboard a ship captured by the German raider *Thor*. Over the coming years, and drawing on the surprising amount of theatrical talent available in both camps (there were enough aspiring actors to form three companies), he put on many shows. Aside from the actors, other behind-the-scenes requirements provided purpose to the otherwise dreary lives of many.

When the troopship *Orama* (Orient Line) was sunk by *Admiral Hipper* off Norway on 9 June 1940, most of her crew of 280 were saved and they became the largest contingent from a single ship in the camp. (The ship was carrying no troops at the time of the sinking.) Among the survivors were the members of the liner's peacetime band, who had been retained on board to double as sick-bay attendants, stewards and gunlayers. Under their leader, Neil Block, they were to form the nucleus of the camp orchestra, which came to be called the 'Orama Band', and which not only provided music for Henry Mollison's productions, but also gave concerts and other entertainments. Other 'showbiz' outfits formed were the 'Skylarks', a trio made up of a trumpeter, guitarist and an accordionist, and the 'Plantation Choir', which was a guitar vocal quartet. Largest of all were the 'Chordites' at over forty strong. This was a male (of course) voice choir and, as might be expected, most of its members were Welsh.

Education was not neglected, especially professional education. Classes were held for those officers and ratings who intended to carry on in their chosen profession after the war. Text-books were obtained through the Red Cross, and senior officers held classes in navigation, compass correction, cargo-handling, ship's business, geometry, and algebra. Second Officer Donald Stewart from *Automedon* constructed a deviascope to assist those learning to adjust magnetic compasses, and made other school equipment too. Again through the Red Cross, Board of Trade examination papers were obtained and candidates sat for their professional examinations under the invigilation of German officers. In April 1944 over a hundred candidates took these examinations, the papers being returned to London via Geneva, and the pass rate turned out to be over 75 per cent.

Some internees enjoyed pursuits of a more private nature. Quartermaster Stan Hugill of *Automedon* took up painting to while away the time.

He also honed up his sea-shanty singing skills, once used in his Cape Horn sailing ship days.

A Canadian prisoner developed a sophisticated and highly popular totaliser system of 'horse race' betting, the game being played by moving models along a track to the throw of coloured dice. An Australian – who else – called Dick Barton acted as race commentator. A proportion of the winnings was set aside each race day for the Red Cross, and after the war that organisation received a cheque for £1391.

Among the sports organised in the camp were football, cricket, boxing, and, after a significant influx of American seamen, baseball. An artist inmate produced the certificates that were awarded to winning teams and individuals. A steep-sided reservoir which had been dug out behind the wash-block to hold water in case of fire came to be used as a swimming pool. Bill Mutimer, who had been a keen swimmer, was anxious to prove to himself that he could swim one-armed. After diving in, that indomitable young officer found he could cope well enough until it came to getting out. Fortunately there were willing hands around to help.

All the above amusements and activities met with German approval to some degree or other. Some of the other activities, did not. Alex Parsons, who had been injured when his ship *Automedon* had been captured, was housed in Barrack 4 after arriving from his previous camp, *Stalag 10b*. He reports that some of the inmates there constructed an elaborate still, producing a potent spirit from potatoes and sometimes from the dried fruit contained in Red Cross parcels. Some of the product, but by no means all, was used as an antiseptic in the camp hospital. Other prisoners engaged in brewing and wine-making, that part of the product not being imbibed by the brewers and vintners themselves being used for bartering purposes.

The most expert at bartering proved to be Egyptian seamen from the passenger ship *Zamzam*. The blood of Port Said bumboatmen must have run in their veins. So successful were they that during their repatriation in mid-1944 they were able to bribe station-masters all across Germany and Austria with English cigarettes in order to travel in style. It is reported that they enjoyed the facilities of the same first-class coach throughout the journey, no matter how many times they changed trains. A considerable amount of 'trading' went on with German guards. One ship's officer was to lose his life during such traffic. He was Radio Officer Walter Skett who was shot and killed on 13 May 1942. The perpetrator was never brought to trial.

Several illegal radio receivers were constructed in the camp. These were made by inmate radio operators from 'odds and ends and parts' obtained from German civilians in exchange for English cigarettes. The main man behind their construction was Radio Officer Frederick Warner who had formerly been a member of Marconi's development staff; towards the end of his internment he even constructed a radio transmitter. Some of the sets were discovered and those held responsible were severely punished. During one search Dr Sperber hid a radio under the legs of an

Indian patient in the hospital. He pinned an 'Infectious!' warning on the door and that, in addition to the German distaste for any contact with non-Aryans, saved it from being found. Despite the dangers involved, during most of the camp's existence items from the BBC news were in general circulation. Radio Officer Warner kept a detailed map of Allied advances, gleaned from the BBC, pinned to the back of a door. During searches the Germans always slammed the door open, never bothering to look behind it. But one German officer, called Henschel, did know about the map. He was anti-Hitler, and was as kind to the prisoners as he was allowed to be. It was reported that he did not believe the lies being issued by Nazi propaganda and regularly slipped into Warner's room to acquaint himself with the true situation.

The camp had its own escape committee, and over the months three escape tunnels were dug from various barracks and out under the barbed wire perimeter fence. Makeshift pit-props were made from bunk boards, and one of the tunnels even had electric light. About twenty men escaped through the tunnels, but all were recaptured. The only successful escape from *Milag*, and one made without the use of a tunnel, was that by Third Mate Arthur Bird and he probably owed the success of his 'run' to the fact that he spoke Swedish. Whereas ratings were obliged to join outside working parties, officers were not, so that when Bird volunteered to join one of the parties working on a nearby farm, some of his fellow officers labelled him a collaborator. In fact, it was all part of his plan to escape and the physical work on the farm and the comparatively good food he enjoyed there allowed him to build up his stamina for the task ahead.

One morning in August 1943, instead of heading for the farm, he slipped away and began the fifty-mile walk to the port of Harburg on the River Elbe. He reached it on the third day and introduced himself to some neutral Swedish sailors in a riverfront bar. The Swedes smuggled him aboard their ship, hiding him under a stack of dunnage, and eventually he arrived safely in Stockholm and there reported himself to the British Legation. Before the war Bird had become engaged to a girl in Norway and the representative of the secret British Special Operations Executive at the Legation contacted the Norwegian Underground about her. Shortly afterwards she was smuggled over the border into Sweden and the pair were married. A few months later they were flown to England by Dakota, but Arthur Bird MBE was soon back at sea again. Other prisoners were sent home in the several repatriation programmes which took place over the years. Twenty-four young cabin boys from *Milag* were exchanged in March 1943, at the Saudi port of Jeddah. Later, batches of older and the more severely wounded men were also sent home.

The Germans had set up a British Free Corps in the hope of recruiting captured Britons into its ranks. It was the brainchild of the renegade John Amery (son of Leopold Amery, a British cabinet minister), who was hanged for treason in 1946. It was known that four merchant seaman joined the Corps and drawings of the Tower of London with a plaque containing their names circulated in *Milag*. The four names were Minchin, Rowlands, Voysey and Berry.

Able Seaman Alfred Minchin left *Milag* in May 1943 after having heard the Corps advertised there. He became totally committed to its cause and was promoted to non-commissioned rank. He returned to *Milag* several times, resplendent in the uniform of the Corps, in an attempt to recruit others. He had success only with Rowlands and Voysey, and that only after both men had been on the receiving end of some 'softening up' by German security officers in the camp. Herbert Rowlands was an oiler from *Orama* and Ronald Voysey, who had been born Ronald Barker in Goulburn, New South Wales, was a cabin boy on *British Advocate*. After the war, at their trials for 'assisting the enemy' it was probably the fact that they had been to some extent coerced into joining that resulted in Rowlands and Voysey being sentenced to only two years hard labour, whereas Minchin received seven years.

Kenneth Berry was treated more leniently by the British. Only fourteen when he was captured aboard the tanker *Cymbeline* in September 1940, the Germans allowed him to live in Paris in the care of a paroled English woman. In 1943, now seventeen, he was first interned and then introduced to John Amery, who fed the lad a lot of propaganda which resulted in him joining the Corps. It was not long before he realised he had made a mistake, but was unable to extricate himself. Berry received a sentence of nine months' hard labour in 1946. All four of these sentences were low compared with those meted out to members of the armed services for similar offences.

In war it is bad enough when a combatant suffers serious injury. For a non-combatant it is probably worse, if for no other reason than while being on the receiving end during the battle in which the injury was sustained he had little chance of hitting back. Young Bill Mutimer could have been forgiven, therefore, for feeling bitter over the loss of his arm, a loss which he knew had put paid for good any chance of him carrying on in his chosen profession. Yet the memoir he wrote of his experiences contains not a trace of bitterness or self-pity.

He was repatriated in October 1943 along with other seriously wounded prisoners and 'protected personnel', including padres and some civilians. They journeyed to Rostock; from there a German ferryboat took them to Treleborg in Sweden where they were given a good welcome by the Swedes. The official 'exchange' with German prisoners brought in on *Empress of Russia* took place at Gothenburg. Bill was never to forget the strange experience of being aboard that liner in the Skagerrak under escort of a German destroyer.

Back in Britain, Bill took up employment with the British Legion. After the war he tried to trace Sister Elizabeth, the lady who had saved his life in the military hospital, but to his infinite regret was never able to find her. He married a lady called Winifred and they had two daughters who presented them with grandchildren. For a time he worked with the War Graves Commission, before once again taking up employment with the British Legion. He ended his working career as Personnel Manager at that organisation's Poppy Factory at Richmond in Surrey. This gallant, self-effacing man, died in 1997.

At least two of the *Automedon* survivors at *Milag* changed their careers after the war. Stanley Hugill, who had a talent for languages, was sent to London University by Blue Funnel, where he obtained a degree in Oriental Languages. The company had intended to employ him in one of their agencies in the Far East, but instead he became an instructor at the famous Outward Bound School at Aberdovey. On the side he became famous as 'The Shantyman', singing at many festivals and producing books on that genre of music and other nautical topics. Stan died in 1992 at the age of eighty-five.

Another to make a career change was Steward Alex Parsons. The wounds he received on *Automedon* were serious enough to prevent him returning to the Merchant Navy after the war, and that is something he regrets to this day, for his heart had been set on a career at sea. However, Blue Funnel, one shipping line which has always looked after its staff, enabled him to work closely with ships for the rest of his working career. He was employed in one of their shore-gangs, which work on ship's husbandry whilst a vessel is in port. He was not on the sea, but from where he worked he could still smell it.

Second Officer Donald Stewart did not change his career. He was mentioned in despatches on 20 November 1945. The London Gazette for that date says it was awarded 'for distinguished service'. It was awarded for his 'school work' at *Milag*. Stewart later rose to be a master with Blue Funnel. In 1966-67 he was asked to take part in a French television version of *This is Your Life* in honour of Captain Bernhard Rogge of *Atlantis*, but he was unwilling to do so. He died, aged eighty-five, in 1991.

CHAPTER 8

All in the Same Boat

Anchor Line's passenger cargo vessel *Britannia*, 8799 tons, sailed from Liverpool bound for Bombay via Freetown on 11 March 1941. With a crew of 203, which included a fair proportion of Lascars, she was under the command of Captain A Collie. The ship carried a full cargo of war materials together with 281 passengers. The passengers were mostly service personnel, with a few naval nurses amongst them. About 50 Indians, half of them itinerant Sikh pedlars who were now on their way back home, filled the third-class accommodation.

The Royal Navy personnel among the passengers, both officers and ratings, were allocated shipboard duties. These included acting as extra lookouts and helping to man the ship's single 4-inch gun, the Lewis guns and a pair of Holman projectors. The latter weapons must have given these professional warriors something to think about. The Holman was basically a steel tube linked to the ship's deck steam supply (which normally provided power for the windlass and winches). The idea was to build up steam pressure to the maximum, drop in a hand-grenade, and release the steam pressure, which would, hopefully, blow the grenade clear of the ship, and even more hopefully, destroy any *very* low-flying enemy aircraft. The device was a menace, not so much to enemy aircraft but to the crew of the ship it was fired from. It was tested by firing potatoes, as much to protect the lives of the crew as it was to conserve the small stock of grenades supplied with it.

That description of the workings of the Holman projector is based on that given by Captain S F Nicolson in his memoir in the archives at the Imperial War Museum, London. Sam Nicolson also describes another equally crew-unfriendly device, the PAC (parachute and cable-carrying) rocket. When fired the rocket trailed a long wire, its descent then being delayed by a parachute. 'Hopefully this would become entangled again with a *very* low flying aircraft. It was not uncommon for these to be set off accidently at night in convoy by somebody tripping over the control wires . . . this brought verbal rockets from the Commodore.'

Three men on board who were to play major roles in the forthcoming voyage of one of the ship's lifeboats were *Britannia*'s Third Officer William McVicar and two of the naval passengers, Lieutenant Frank West RNVR and Sub-Lieutenant Ian McIntosh RN. Bill McVicar was twenty-six and the son of a Church of Scotland clergyman from Southend, Mull of Kintyre. A born seaman, he had joined Anchor Line as a cadet at the age of seventeen. Before joining *Britannia* he had seen action aboard the company's *Transylvania* which, as a converted AMC, took part in the Northern Patrol, whose purpose was to prevent German merchant ships from reaching home via the Baltic. *Transylvania* had been torpedoed and sunk (by *U-56*, Lieutenant Harms) on 10 August 1940.

Frank West, aged thirty, had a love for the sea but was no seaman. After leaving public school in England he had gone to New Zealand to train as a farmer. He was travelling now to take up a post involving airfield defence at a Royal Naval Air Station in Egypt.

Ian McIntosh was twenty. An Australian from Melbourne, he had entered the Royal Navy as a cadet two years earlier. Like McVicar he was a born seaman, with the added advantage of having had considerable experience in handling small boats.

The first ten days or so of *Britannia*'s voyage were spent in convoy with four other merchantmen, three destroyers and an AMC, and they passed peacefully enough. In fact, with the lady nurses on board, the voyage took on something of the character of a peacetime cruise. But by the 25th the ship was sailing on her own on a southerly course about 720 miles west-north-west of Freetown. Sometime that day Captain Collie would have to order the ship round on an easterly course to make the approach to Freetown, an order of some import for the area of ocean to be crossed was a favourite haunt of U-boats. As it turned out Captain Collie never had to issue the order for a little after dawn his ship fell in with the German raider *Thor*.

Thor, 3862 tons, commanded by Captain Otto Kahler, and known to the British Admiralty as *Raider E*, had sailed from Kiel in June 1940 and over the intervening period had sunk eight Allied vessels. On top of that, with her six 5.9-inch guns she had in separate battles got the better of two British AMCs, *Alcantara* and *Carnarvon Castle*. The coming engagement with *Britannia* was therefore no great contest.

A few minutes before 0800 hours that day, *Thor* opened fire. *Britannia* returned fire, took evasive action and dropped smoke floats, but all to no avail. A shell from the raider exploded immediately above the ship's gun, putting it out of action, with the men around it going down like ninepins. Hits and near-misses alike caused heavy casualties, and the ship's lady surgeon, Doctor Miller, had her work cut out even with the help given by the naval nurses. A shell struck a fuel tank situated on the after end of the boatdeck and started a fire. At 0920 hours Captain Collie struck his colours and ordered abandon ship. That did not stop the shelling and there were at least five more direct hits. Everywhere the decks were a shambles with dead and wounded lying all over the place, bulkheads crushed, and some lifeboats hanging damaged and useless from their davits.

At last the raider ceased firing and the evacuation of the ship began in earnest, and up to a point it was carried out in an orderly fashion. However, after Lifeboat No. 7, Bill McVicar's charge, had been lowered into the water, some Indian passengers swarmed down into it via a rope ladder and knotted life-lines. There was nothing wrong with that except that they came complete with suitcases, brown paper parcels and even suits on clothes hangers, strapped to various parts of their bodies. In the face of howls of protest from their owners the packaged encumbrances were thrown over the side to make room for other bodies. All the while, McVicar aided by Ian McIntosh, fought to keep the craft in position yet clear of the ship's counter, which kept threatening to bear down on the boat as the ship moved in the seaway. When the boat at last pulled away it already had far more people aboard than the fifty-six it was designed to carry. Four other boats, those not too damaged to use, also got away, likewise crammed with people. Other survivors used rafts, wooden doors, and anything else that would float. The last craft to leave was Captain Collie's No.1 boat, which was damaged enough to quickly become waterlogged.

As the survivors drew clear of *Britannia* the raider fired several rounds into the fore part of the ship from close range. The men in the boats watched as the stricken ship's bows began to dip, and soon she was standing almost vertical with her stern high in the air. She seemed to hang like that for a moment or two before sliding, slowly at first and then more quickly, beneath the waves. After watching the demise of her ninth victim *Thor* made off to the north-east in search of the tenth, but not before picking up one *Britannia* survivor whose raft had drifted across her path; the sailor on the raft arrived at *Milag* PoW camp in Germany many months later and was the ship's sole representative there. (*Thor* found her tenth victim that very same day in the shape of the Norwegian *Trolleholm*, 5047 tons. Ten days later she engaged the British AMC *Voltaire*, at 13,250 tons much larger than *Thor* but less well-armed. After a fierce two-hour battle *Voltaire* sank, taking 75 of her complement with her. Captain J A P Blackburn and 194 others were taken prisoner.)

Boat No.7 had been holed in several places during the action and water was coming in so fast that the freeboard of the overloaded craft was soon down to a few inches. Those not engaged in stepping the mast and raising the fore-sail, an extremely difficult task because of the overcrowding, were set to baling. One Sikh passenger at first refused to join in until McVicar left him in no doubt what would happen to him if he refused to follow orders. Three rafts with survivors aboard were taken in tow and, with the rafts acting as a drogue, No.7 lay-to under the fore-sail with the idea of remaining as close to the point of sinking as possible in case a rescue ship turned up in answer to *Britannia*'s SOS signals. It also provided time to take stock of the situation and see what water and food was aboard.

At midday, by which time the other lifeboats were out of sight, the rafts were pulled in and their six occupants taken off, raising the number in the boat to eighty-two, nearly 50 per cent over the designed capacity of the 28-foot craft. Two of the rafts broke away during the first night and next day the third raft was cut adrift after the only thing of value on it, a stretch of rope, had been retrieved.

The officer contingent aboard the boat consisted of Bill McVicar and Seventh Engineer Liddell of *Britannia*, and eight naval officers including two holders of warrant rank. Apart from Ian McIntosh the only other naval officer with much knowledge of seamanship was Lieutenant F Lyons RNR. He was about forty-five years of age and had spent many years in merchant ships. The senior among the naval officers was Lieutenant Frank West. Sub-Lieutenant K Harman was the only badly injured man on board, having lost one of his kneecaps during the shelling. There were two white passengers aboard, one of them a missionary named Cutler.

West kept a diary of the ensuing epic open-boat voyage and many years later published a book based on the diary. He wrote that on the second day an officers' conference was held to discuss what was to be done, as by then there had been no sign of any rescue craft and it was clear that it was up to the survivors to save themselves. The nearest point on the African coast was only 600 miles away but to reach it the boat would have to sail against the prevailing wind. About twice as far away, but in the path of the wind, lay Brazil. West reported that the decision was made to attempt to tack into the wind for a while and, if no progress was made, to turn about and head for Brazil.

It is difficult to understand why an experienced seaman like McVicar, let alone others like McIntosh and Lyon, agreed to try to sail a lifeboat close-hauled against the Force 4 to 5 prevailing wind; that type of boat is an ungainly sailer at the best of times, let alone when grossly overloaded. It seems therefore that the decision to make the attempt, which soon proved abortive, came as a result of combined decision-making. In a general statement concerning decision-making aboard the boat, West recorded, 'We evolved a workable arrangement which continued throughout. On all important matters, decisions were made at our daily conferences and I do not recall that we ever had any serious disagreement.' Maybe there was no serious disagreement, but command by committee is never a good thing and probably never less so than in an open lifeboat where each decision can be a life-or death-one.

This is not to say that there was anything intrinsically wrong in holding that first officers' conference; it was needed to assess the situation, allocate responsibilities based on individual expertise, and decide on the rationing of provisions. However, it must be said, albeit with the benefit of hindsight, that Bill McVicar who, as the senior *Britannia* officer on board was legally in charge of the boat, should have put his foot down and vetoed any attempt to sail against the wind. Furthermore, had he stamped his authority on the assembly then and there, some of the other unfortunate decisions that came out of the following series of such conferences might not have been made. As the only *Britannia* officer aboard apart from Seventh Engineer Liddell, perhaps McVicar was overly impressed by the number of naval officers in the boat and so allowed the situation to develop. In fact, a reading of some of what Frank West has written leaves one with the impression that in some respects at least *he* thought he was in command. Normally any list of the complement of a ship or boat is headed by the name of the person in command, yet when West listed the names and ranks of those in the boat, his name was at the top followed in order of seniority by all the other naval personnel and only after that was McVicar's name mentioned. A small point perhaps, but one that seems indicative of West's attitude of mind. One cannot help wondering whether his list would have taken on a different shape had Captain Collie been on board.

The next bad decision was to separate the boat's occupants into ethnic groups. Frank West wrote:

> Our next job was to move the people round so as to get them in their different groups. It was decided to put the Indian crew for'ard, the steerage passengers amidships and the Britishers aft. Davies [one of the Naval Warrant Officers] and I went for'ard to carry out this plan, which could only be done very slowly owing to the terrible over-crowding . . . and the need to keep the boat trimmed.

This segregation, the necessity for which West did not explain and which turned the boat into a sort of floating Alabama bus, and the implementation of which placed it in some jeopardy whilst men were moved around, was almost certainly at the root of some of the trouble that was to come. Had the 'Britishers', to use West's term, remained spread out amongst the crew, some of the practices which caused friction later on would probably not have taken place. It is doubtful whether the segregation idea came from Bill McVicar. He had served with Anchor Line for nearly ten years; the deck crews and stokers of company ships nearly always came from India, and he was trained to see to the well-being of these men. Indian crew members had, of course, their own separate accommodation space on board ship, but so would British ratings have had. Here, in a lifeboat, there was no real need for this separateness. On the contrary, as all were in the same boat, both literally and figuratively, discipline and hygiene arrangements, to say nothing of morale, would have been more easily controlled had figures of authority been scattered here and there instead of all being aft where only the 'skipper' and those others capable of handling the boat needed to be.

A careful analysis of Frank West's book leads one to suspect that the segregation policy might have originated with him. Apart from anything else, he was one of those who implemented the policy. In the preface to his book, after posing the question 'Why did so many Indians die?', he then wrote, 'I and those British who survived with me may possibly not be so well qualified to give the answer as are some of the politicians and others who talk and write with such hysteria and authority on the rights and responsibilities of coloured people.' He went on to say that no

Indians would have survived at all but for the presence of British officers and men. It is difficult not to judge this racial issue from the modern point of view. However, even considering it within the constraints of the mores and attitudes applicable in those days, it has to be said that the policy of segregation was wrong.

McVicar knew the approximate position of the ship's sinking and, with the aid of Lyons, who knew the South American coast well, and McIntosh a rough chart was drawn on scrap paper. After the short and abortive attempt to head for Africa, course was set for the Brazilian coast, a course based on the knowledge they possessed of the winds and currents in the area. It was estimated that a landfall would be made within twenty-four days and so rations of water and provisions were based on a twenty-eight day period, which provided a reasonable margin for error and for unforeseen circumstances.

The rations were not much. Water was issued at the rate of a third of a dipper per man a day and with that went a spoonful of condensed milk and, for so long as the supply lasted, a ship's biscuit. That was all, for although efforts were made to catch fish, for lack of proper equipment the attempts were unsuccessful. Rations were issued by the officers and there is no question that the distribution was anything but fair and even-handed. However, to have included one or two Indians in the process would have been good for morale, as equitableness would have been seen to be done. A suggestion put forward by one or two of the Britons at one of the later conferences, that the size of rations should be dependant upon the amount of work put in by individuals, was fortunately given short shift. West left no record of any attempt made to collect together any small 'luxuries' brought on board in order that they be shared by all, the usual procedure in such circumstances. Perhaps the lack of space obviated any attempt to do so. At one point he referred to the Indians as having more tobacco than the British.

The boat was made as seaworthy as possible by nailing 'tingles' fashioned out of tobacco tin lids over the outside of shrapnel holes in the boat's hull. This work was carried out by young McIntosh as men in the boat held on to his legs. This stopped some of the ingress of water but by no means all as some holes could not be reached from outside and the positioning of the buoyancy tanks prevented them being tackled from inside. Continuous baling was required throughout the voyage.

Two ships were sighted during the first three days and although every effort was made to attract their attention, on both occasions the ship sailed on obliviously. That was to happen several more times during the voyage.

In his diary entry for the third day Frank West noted that he had compiled 'a complete record of the names and addresses of the British, and have made a detailed count, with the aid of McVicar and Davies, of the Indians'. He went on, 'It proved an exhausting and difficult task to count the number in the boat.' The lack of any real attempt to make a 'complete record' of the Indians is hard to justify. There were sixty-three of them on board and only nineteen British, but even so and in spite of the overcrowding it was surely not beyond the ingenuity of someone to devise a way of compiling a full record of everyone. The job could have been delegated to one of the Sikhs, who appears to have been some sort of leader among that group. In such overcrowded conditions the fact that the 'Britishers' were treating themselves somewhat differently to the others would not have passed unnoticed. It was on the third day of the voyage that several Indians were seen augmenting their water ration with sea-water. They were warned of the likely consequences by McVicar but it is clear that some took no notice.

The discomfort caused by the overcrowding and the constant movement of the boat in the seaway was acute. Not only that, the overcrowding was such that when halyards carried away, as they often did, it was extremely difficult to repair them. West put it another way. It was difficult to work, he recorded, 'amongst a mass of black humanity, which, except for a few Lascar seamen, sat or stood absolutely dumb and unheeding'.

West, who acted in the capacity of medical officer, also reported that it was difficult to get the Indians to observe the most elementary rules of sanitation and that this 'made baling a particularly unpleasant task'. It can be argued that had some of the officers not required for the handling of the boat, West himself for example, been strategically placed around the boat instead of all aft, that situation might have been avoided, as might the drinking of seawater. As it was, hygiene gradually improved in the days that followed as bodies ceased to function normally.

Despite these tribulations, the wind driving from the quarter caused the boat to make excellent progress. Speed was estimated by throwing a handful of kapok from a life-belt into the water from the bows and noting the time it took to float the 28 feet to the stern. On the sixth day, having covered an estimated 300 miles in a WSW direction, a more southerly course was adopted to take full advantage of expected winds and currents. The Brazilian coast was then about 900 miles away.

The first fatality came during the early hours of the seventh day when an Indian cook who had been drinking seawater either jumped over the side or fell over. He could not be seen in the dark and with a strong breeze blowing from astern there was nothing to be done about it. On the eighth day West cleaned the only two guns on aboard, a Webley pistol and a Browning automatic with lamp oil, noting that, 'Neither was ever used or even carried and they remained safely in the ship's bag throughout the voyage. Perhaps in an extreme emergency they may have been useful, but while authority and discipline could be maintained by other means, they were best out of sight and out of mind.' Out of sight whilst being cleaned? The sight of the guns was hardly likely to please the majority of those on board.

Another Indian died from the effects of drinking seawater on the ninth day, the same day that McVicar had cause to take a knife from an Indian who was brandishing it about. Two days later some of the Indians cried out for extra water and West reported that some tried to bribe him. Later on he wrote:

> It was difficult to show much sympathy for them or even feel it – at least I found it so. It seemed to me to be no time or place for bickering and quarrels, for sullen laziness . . . Perhaps I lacked understanding, maybe I still do.

By the twelfth day the weather had become unbearably hot and two more Indians died. The injured Harman was now in a bad way as was another Briton, Beck, a naval rating who had been in poor health even before entering the boat. Both of them died the next day.

On 7 April, the fourteenth day in the boat, it rained heavily and about two gallons of water were collected using the sail as a chute. More might have been collected but for the overcrowding, which made it very much a case of each man for himself. Although refreshed by the rain, no one had much energy by then and even such relatively easy chores as working out the day's noon position tended to get postponed. Six Indians were found dead on the 8th. Later that day the wind got up, fortunately from the right direction, and the boat bowled along at a tremendous pace. A heavy curtain of rain was seen heading their way and the mainsail was lowered into position as a water catcher. Just before the rainstorm hit, a ship with the Japanese flag painted on its side was sighted, but either the sighting was not mutual or the men on her bridge took no notice. That night, despite all having drunk their fill in the storm, several more Indians and one Briton died. The death toll was mounting but it provided the benefit of making more space available for those who were left.

Bill McVicar afterwards wrote of those last few days in the boat:

> The mind was becoming a little immune to sorrow for the unlucky ones who died each day. The innate selfishness of mortal man was beginning to dominate them. Each man who died gave another ration of water for those who lived. Each man who died gave the boat more buoyancy and more room for those who survived. As long as one was alive it did not matter who died. They were all bordering on insanity.

On the seventeenth day the estimated position put the boat bang on the equator. 'No wonder it is so hot,' West wrote. By then those remaining had strength for baling, or for any other task, only in the early hours before the sun rose high. The following day brought heavy tropical downpours which gave enough water to see them through to the estimated date of arrival and also brought some relief from the heat. That day an oil tanker was sighted and during the night the lights of another ship, but still the boat went unseen.

On the twentieth day course was altered due west for the run in to the Brazilian coast. Over the next two days and even as hopes of making land rose, several more men died, including two Britons, one of them the missionary. McVicar's health now gave cause for concern; he had a bad foot infection which West could do very little about.

On Easter Monday, 14 April, a seagull hovered overhead and they knew that land was near. By the following morning the colour of the sea had changed from blue to green, and pieces of driftwood and other shore debris floated by. By midday what at first had appeared to be a long white cloud on the horizon had hardened into land and by late afternoon they were running north-west close in, looking for a gap in the heavy surf. The misery was not over yet for no gap had been sighted by the time night fell and they had to stand away from the coast until morning. On the morrow, back in close to land and with the expectation of being safe some time that day, Lieutenant Lyons died. In fact, it was not until fairly late on that at last a safe place was found to run in and beach the boat. Thirty-eight emaciated survivors then staggered up the beach; thirteen Britons and twenty-five Indians. They were found there and eventually taken under the care of the British vice-consul in the nearby port of Sao Luiz. As well as suffering from exposure, dehydration, and near-starvation, most had dysentery and beri-beri. The epic voyage hit the headlines in Brazil and elsewhere. Geoffrey Bryan, the British vice-consul at Sao Luiz, had Lifeboat No. 7 taken round to the port and there carried out an experiment. He tried fitting eighty-two men into the small craft but managed only seventy-four and that was with the mast unstepped. After their return to England, Bill McVicar, Frank West, and Ian McIntosh were awarded MBEs, and some BEMs went to other survivors.

Those aboard Lifeboat No.7 were not the only people saved from *Britannia*. Four days after the sinking, the Spanish ship *Cabo de Hornos* picked up first one boat load, then some from rafts, and finally men from two other boats, a total of seventy-seven souls. Another Spanish cargo vessel, the *Bachi*, rescued survivors from another boat, and a further sixty-seven were rescued by the British steamer *Raranga*. Among those saved were Captain Collie, Dr Miller, and the naval nurses. However, 122 crew members and 127 passengers were never seen again.

William McVicar went on to serve on the troopship *California* (Anchor Line) and was among the survivors when she was sunk by German bombers off the Portuguese coast on 11 July 1943. After the war he rose to become Anchor Line's senior master. He retired from the sea in 1976 and died on 9 August 1997 at the age of eighty-three. Ian McIntosh is now Vice-Admiral Sir Ian McIntosh DSO, MBE, DSC.

On 30 November 1942 the German raider *Thor*, now under the command of Captain G Gumprich, was laying alongside the supply tanker *Uckermark* in Yokohama harbour when the tanker blew up, taking the raider with her. Also destroyed in the explosion was the British ship *Nankin* which had been renamed *Leuthen* by the Germans after her capture by *Thor* on 10 May 1942. The ensuing fire, which at one time threatened to destroy the whole of Yokohama, was witnessed with much cheering by the crew of the British *Speybank* which had been captured by the raider *Atlantis* on 31 January 1941. *Speybank*, renamed *Doggerbank* by the Germans, subsequently made a successful blockade-run to Bordeaux with her original crew still on board as prisoners of war. They ended up in the *Milag* prisoner of war camp. *Doggerbank* was later torpedoed in error on 3 March 1943 by the German submarine *U-43*.

CHAPTER 9

The Malta Blockade-Runner

The fall of France in June 1940 resulted in the loss to the Allied cause of the greater part of the French fleet, and more importantly it altered the strategic situation in the Mediterranean, a situation made even graver for the Allies when in that same month Italy entered the war on the German side. Despite the fact that Britain still held Gibraltar at one end, and controlled Alexandria and the Suez Canal at the other, the Mediterranean was no longer dominated by the Royal Navy. Lying about halfway between the British-controlled ends of that sea lay the isolated outpost of Malta. The island's position made it of vital strategic importance, sitting almost astride the Axis supply routes to North Africa. From the British point of view the island had to be held at all costs; and ships carrying aircraft, munitions, oil, food, and everything else a beleaguered fortress needs had to get through.

Throughout the many months of the siege of Malta, during which the island became an exceedingly sharp thorn in what Churchill later called 'the soft under-belly of the Axis', getting those supplies through proved to be extremely difficult and hazardous. The 980-mile route from Gibraltar and the 820-mile one from Alexandria were within reach of German and Italian aircraft based either in Sardinia and Sicily to the north, or in Libya to the south, not to mention the forays that were made from the Italian island of Pantellaria, which was actually on the route from the west. Sections of the western route were also in range of motor torpedo-boats based at Cagliari, Sardinia and Augusta, Sicily, and as the military front in North Africa pushed first one way and then the other, torpedo-boats could from time to time also threaten the eastern route. On top of all that, in the background and so always to be taken into consideration by British naval planners, was the threat posed by the Italian Navy lurking in its homeland bases. It was all very well for British wartime propaganda to denigrate the Italians, but no one knew better than the Royal Navy's commander in the Mediterranean, Admiral Sir Andrew Cunningham, that the Italian fleet was equipped with faster battleships armed with longer-ranged 15-inch guns than the British.

The Royal Navy had its work cut out in keeping both routes open, especially the most important of the two, that from Gibraltar. (Supplies coming from the other direction had first to be sent round the Cape of Good Hope, adding weeks to the journey.) As the Axis increased their pressure and Malta's situation grew more and more perilous, the British tried every conceivable way to get supplies through, even resorting to sending in small quantities by submarine. Merchant ships in some of the most heavily protected convoys of the war, made the run. A famous convoy, code-named Operation 'Pedestal', in August 1942, included the saga of the tanker *Ohio* (an American ship but manned by Britons) which, on fire and seriously damaged and with Royal Navy ships lashed to port and starboard, managed to reach the island in its darkest hour. At other times single fast merchant ships were used to run the gauntlet, relying on speed and the very fact they were alone to get them through. Of much lesser renown was the attempt to reach the island made by a slow blockade-running steamer belonging to Stanhope Shipping Company. She was called the *Parracombe*.

Parracombe was built in Sunderland in 1928 and took her name from a pretty village on the edge of Exmoor in Devon. Maybe the ship had once been considered attractive-looking herself, but no one would have used any complimentary adjective to describe her appearance as she lay in Imperial Dock, Leith in April 1941. By then the better days of the 10.5-knot, 4700-ton coal-burning vessel had long since passed her by. Rusty and salt-streaked, she had recently returned from a winter voyage to St John's, Newfoundland, and there had not been time for much in the way of maintenance or for sprucing her up. On top of that, on 19 March she had sustained minor damage when a mine exploded close to her off Southend. She had bunkered recently and was covered in coal dust. All in all *Parracombe* looked expendable, though that was not the reason why she had been selected by the Admiralty to attempt the dangerous task ahead.

When the 'Parracombe Plan' was first mooted by the Admiralty earlier in the year, it was decided to co-opt shipowner Jack Billmeir as adviser to the project. If any shipowner of that era had swashbuckling characteristics, then Jack Albert Billmeir was the one. Born in 1900 and embarking on a shipbroking career at the age of fourteen, he was a shipowner by the age of twenty-eight and had formed Stanhope Shipping in 1934. He made a huge fortune during the Spanish Civil War by concentrating his fleet of ships on running the blockade which General Franco had thrown around the Spanish coast to prevent food and supplies reaching the lawfully-elected Republican Government and the other factions fighting against the Fascists. Written evidence seems to be lacking, but it is almost certain that some of his ships ran in consignments of arms for the anti-Franco forces, perhaps with the connivance of the British Government.

It was probably Billmeir himself who recommended the *Parracombe* for the blockade-running task to Malta, for the ship could easily be disguised as one of the rather old neutral ships still trading in Mediterranean waters despite the world war. At the time of the ship's selection, and up to 24 March 1941, *Parracombe*'s master was Captain David Edward Jones, who in Billmeir's *Stanwell* had run the Spanish blockade more than once; on a single day at Barcelona in 1938 his ship had suffered damage during three consecutive Fascist air-raids. As will be shown at the end of this story, personages high up in the British Admiralty apparently erred in thinking, because of the similarity in names, that the master they had got in the deal was another, even more expert blockade-runner, named Captain David *John* Jones, known famously as 'Potato' Jones. Of all the masters engaged in blockade-running during the Spanish war, 'Potato' Jones was by far the best known. So famous was he, and so open about his opposition to the Fascists, that Franco put a price on his head, dead or alive. It was the Royal Navy who gave him his nickname. In order that the captains of warships protecting British ships around the Spanish coast, and those engaged in the so-called Non-Intervention Patrol, could differentiate between the several Welsh blockade-running captains with the surname Jones, the Navy used nicknames for them even in official documents. 'Potato' got his from a cargo of potatoes he successfully ran in for the starving populace of Bilbao, and it was taken up by the world press who made something of a hero out of him, a rather ancient hero to be sure, for at the start of the Spanish conflict in 1936, Potato was already sixty-six years of age. (The Royal Navy nicknamed other Jones's after their cargoes – 'Corn Cob' Jones after a cargo of grain, and 'Ham-and-Eggs' Jones for one who ran in a general cargo.) All that having been said, Captain David *Edward* Jones was relieved of his command after the incident with the mine off Southend and his place was taken by Captain David Llewellyn Hook.

David Hook, a forty year-old Welshman from Lampeter in Cardiganshire, was also a veteran of Spanish blockade-running, having several times run ships into Alicante and Valencia. Captain Hook was quite proud of his new command; she might be old, slow and dirty, but for the coming voyage she was to sail under Royal Navy orders and had in effect become a naval auxiliary, although she only carried the usual guns for self-defence.

Whilst loading at Leith, Captain Hook found himself short of three sailors and after signing on a local man, Able Seaman Stanley Sutherland, asked him to snoop around the port to see if two more could be found. Stan found them easily enough, one of them being his stepbrother, Jimmy McIntyre. Hook advanced all three the sum of £5 which reportedly did not go very far when they went ashore on a spree that night.

The ship's cargo was solely military, and included twenty-one crated Hurricane aircraft urgently required in Malta, although except for Hook himself, the crew were as yet unaware of the ship's destination. The boom-defence equipment stowed on deck raised suspicions in some minds, but no one knew for sure. The crew were aware though, that the authorities attached no small degree of importance to the cargo, for as Stan reported, 'It was loaded and shifted around a few times by big nobs of the Army, Navy and Air Force.' Just before the ship sailed some of the crew were warned by dockers (a section of Britain's wartime working community which always seemed able to glean or deduce information no matter how secret) that they were going somewhere dangerous. It was not news designed to put anyone's mind at rest, especially as it was linked with the dire warning that should the ship go down, she would do so with a big bang, a reference perhaps to the ammunition in the cargo.

On completion of loading the ship steamed north about Scotland making for Oban, the gathering point for many outward convoys. At Oban a Spanish sea captain called Luis Diaz de Lassaga boarded the ship and when the news got about that he was to sail with them, there was much tongue-wagging. Diaz was one of a handful of Spanish captains who, finding themselves in British waters during the Spanish conflict and being opposed to the Fascists, elected to remain there. He had made his home in Belfast and was now forty-six years of age. Six RAF groundcrew also joined the ship. They 'signed on' as supernumerary deckhands at wages of a shilling a month.

Parracombe sailed from Oban as part of a large convoy, but a few days later was ordered to detach from it. With no fewer than three destroyers as escort, course was then set for the Straits of Gibraltar. A day or two later, still out of sight of the Rock, the escorts left and *Parracombe* sailed on alone. It was then that Hook assembled his crew and told them the ship's destination.That night, a cold one which made the job uncomfortable, the ship stopped, stages were rigged over the side and the Spanish flag and a Spanish name painted on each side of the hull. It was now easy to guess why Captain Diaz was aboard. The following morning, with a Spanish ensign flying at the gaff, the ship passed through the Strait keeping well south over towards the Spanish Moroccan side. With Captain Diaz conning the ship, *Parracombe* made steady progress eastward keeping well inside Spanish territorial waters and passing so close to the port of Ceuta and, on the following day, to Melilla that the crew were able to see clearly the details of ships in both harbours. On one occasion a signal lamp winked at them from the shore, but a flashed answer from Captain Diaz seemed to satisfy the shore signaller, whoever he might have been. The night before the ship entered the territorial waters of Vichy-French Algeria, the ship was stopped once more and the Spanish flags on the hull painted over with wartime grey. The next day, and now flying the French flag, she was buzzed by a large Italian aircraft, but the pilot flew off, apparently satisfied by the sight of the tricolour.

As the ship approached Cape Bon on 2 May, Hook explained the plan of action to his officers. After rounding the cape, course would be set south into the Gulf of Sirte to give the impression to any prying eyes that the ship was making for the Tunisian port of Sfax. Then, when night fell, the stokehold crew would be doubled, maximum steam raised, course altered to port, and the run made over the final 200 miles to Malta. Captain Hook was well aware of the chances being taken. Even flat out the ship's speed was nothing to write home about and, on top of that, the engines were old and unusual strain on them might cause something to blow. Of much greater concern to him, however, was the fact that the waters between Cape Bon and Sicily had been mined by both sides to such an extent that the area had the reputation of being among the most heavily mined in the world. Hook had charts to show him where the British mines were, but had only the barest information on the Axis ones, and for all he knew the French might have been at it as well.

All that was hypothetical, for *Parracombe* never reached Cape Bon. Suddenly, with a huge explosion, the ship struck a mine in a sea area where no mine was supposed to be. Stan Sutherland was working with other seamen on the deck when it happened, and after picking himself up ran with the others for the boat-deck. After reaching it, Stan looked towards the bows, and, all seeming well in that direction, made another run for the fo'c'sle to rescue some of his personal possessions. It was an act that probably saved his life. While he was still rummaging around the accommodation, there came a series of large explosions as some of the cargo blew up, just as those Leith dockers had warned it would. 'It tore the bottom out of her,' wrote Stan, 'and carried away the bridge and killed those left on the boat-deck.'

Debris was flying everywhere and Jimmy McIntyre saved his own life only by having the presence of mind to dive into a potato-locker until the worst was over. After that he threw himself over the side, not realising until later that one of his legs had been broken in three places and that he had lost two of his toes in the blast. In the fo'c'sle meanwhile, Stan and a few others were struggling to get out of the compartment as the sea flooded in. They made it at last and began making their way aft over a deck covered in wreckage and looking, as Stan described it, 'like a knacker's yard'. They were climbing uphill too, for by the time the group reached the stern it was high in the air. There was nothing for it but to jump, which Stan did. He went down so deep he thought he would never surface again. When at last he did, he swam away from the sinking ship as fast as he could. He paused to look round and saw the ship about to take the final plunge. 'She went down with a screaming crowd hanging on her starboard rail aft. Our appeals for them to jump were all in vain. They went down with her.'

Thirty officers and men went down with the ship, leaving eighteen survivors in the water, including both Captain Hook and Captain Diaz. There had been no time to launch boats, but two rafts must have broken loose as the ship went down, for they soon burst to the surface. As some of the survivors began climbing aboard, Stan noticed his brother was not amongst them. He yelled out, and hearing an answering shout, swam towards it and soon found Jimmy clinging to a piece of timber. With considerable effort Stan took the injured Jimmy in tow and made for a nearby boom-defence tank which had floated clear from the ship. The second mate, John Wilson, his right arm hanging off at the shoulder, and a gunner with an injured ankle, were already in it, and there was no room for four. After depositing Jimmy in the tank and telling the others he would swim over to one of the rafts and bring it back, Stan set off. 'I misjudged the distance,' he wrote later, 'and could feel a seizing in my heart. I slipped off my lifejacket, also my dungarees, and swam a bit easier.' When he finally reached the raft, he and the men already on it attempted to paddle across to the tank but found the current too strong. It was thirty hours before the survivors, all suffering from exposure and six of them, including Captain Diaz, suffering from injuries sustained on the ship, were picked up by Vichy-French seaplanes and flown to the naval base at Bizerta. There, except for one Arab seamen who died later, they recovered from their ordeal.

A few days after the loss of the ship London received the following communication from the American Embassy.

The American Charge d'Affaires presents his compliments to His Majesty's Principal Secretary of State for Foreign Affairs and, with reference to Mr. Winant's notes RBI-1059 and RBI-1122 of May 13, 1941, concerning the survivors of the ss *Parracombe*, has the honour to set forth below excerpts from a despatch dated May 8th, 1941, from the American Consulate at Tunis:

'On the 6th May the Consulate received information from the Residence General, Tunis, of the arrival at Bizerte of eighteen members of the crew of ss *Parracombe*, 4,710 tons, which struck a mine on the 2nd May, about 1pm and sank within two minutes. The Consulate was asked to send someone to Bizerte as the crew was British and several survivors needed financial aid.

Vice Consul L Pittman Springs, of this office, proceeded to Bizerte the following morning, where he learned the explosion took place about five miles from Cap Bon and immediately afterwards the French naval station at Bizerte sent out naval planes which succeeded in rescuing eighteen members of the crew. At first the French naval authorities thought the ship to be French as it was flying the French flag. However, it was subsequently stated by the crew that the ship was proceeding from a British port to the Eastern Mediterranean, with a British crew of forty-seven.' [Including Captain Diaz, it was forty-eight.]

The American message ended with a list of the survivors.

Churchill, who had been aware of the blockade-running plan from its inception, sent a strongly worded note to Admiral Sir Dudley Pound:

This is surely a pretty humble role for the Admiralty to play. I should like to know the reason why merchant seamen in a poor little tramp steamer carry out Hurricanes vitally needed by Malta, while the Royal Navy has to be kept far from these dangers. I never thought we should come to this.

Later he minuted, 'I was never an enthusiast for this project. I trust "Potato" Jones is saved.' One wonders what the great man said when he learned that Potato had not been involved in the project at all and that he, Churchill, had not been informed. ('Potato' Jones lived to be ninety-two, dying at his Swansea home in August 1962.)

After recovery in hospital the *Parracombe* survivors were shifted to Tunis. Stanley Sutherland says that he and his companions were marched barefoot through the town and were spat upon by Italians. They were lodged in a flea- and rat-infested jail and later sent inland to a fort at El Kef, where they spent many long and weary months under heavy guard. Of that period, Stan reported, 'the only cheery bit was the sing-songs, which the skipper led, as he had a good voice and was a regular guy and well liked.' As the months passed, the fort became crowded with other merchant seamen prisoners, so crowded that eventually all were moved to another and larger camp. They managed to get in touch with the Red Cross and it was that organisation's food parcels that kept them alive. A Scottish padre named Dunbar based in Tunis was allowed to visit the camp occasionally and he brought gifts of food and organised church services.

Stan Sutherland and some of his mates did not make model prisoners; in fact they went out of their way to give their gaolers as much aggravation as possible. On one occasion Stan and two fellow Scotsmen caused a riot and were punished by being sent to a special camp in the desert. The regime there was so hard they went on their best behaviour until they were sent back to join their mates. Soon after that all the prisoners were moved to Sfax, which being on the coast was a much more pleasant and healthy place in which to be interned. Later, as their Italian guards grew ever more jittery because of the push being made in their direction by the British Eighth Army, the seamen took over the camp. Some of them, including Stan and Jimmy, stole a train normally used to bring phosphate down to the port from an inland mine. They stayed at the railhead for a few days before making for Metloui which by then had been taken over by Free French sympathisers. Finally they made for Tebessa in Algeria, where they fell in with British troops who sent them on to Algiers. Some twenty months after losing their own ship, they joined up with the other survivors to board the troopship *Orontes* for home.

On arriving at Greenock the *Parracombe* survivors were met by the managing director of Stanhope Shipping, Jack Billmeir, who presented each with a new suit and ten pounds to get them home. At an investiture at Buckingham Palace on 9 February 1943 Captain David Hook and Second Officer John Wilson were decorated with the Distinguished Service Cross, and Stan Sutherland and Jimmy McIntyre with the Distinguished Service Medal. The awards were naval instead of civilian because *Parracombe* had been sailing under direct Admiralty orders. The relevant Lloyd's Confidential Sheet, a contemporary document covering the loss of Parracombe, is endorsed in red: 'SECRET. *Not* to be mentioned in any return.' It seems that by keeping the matter under wraps the Admiralty left the door open for other similar voyages. However, no other attempt to reach Malta with a lone, slow ship was ever made.

Jack Billmeir was not one to send men into danger he was not prepared to face himself, and on one occasion signed on as a supernumerary aboard one of his own ships which was part of an Arctic convoy. The Arctic also provided the venue for Billmeir's final involvement, albeit an indirect one, in a blockade-running operation. So urgent was the need for merchant and naval ships in the build-up to, and implementation of, Operation 'Torch', the Allied invasion of Vichy-French North Africa in early November 1942, that for a short period escorted convoys to Murmansk and Archangel were suspended. To help fill the gap the British Admiralty came up with a plan which can at best be described as misguided. It was to sail a series of single unescorted ships to and from the Russian Arctic ports, the plan being code-named Operation 'FB'. (A seaman who took part in the operation waggishly said that 'FB' must have been an abbreviation for 'Foolish Bastards'.) It was rightly considered a highly dangerous venture, and Jack Billmeir dug his hand in his pocket and offered a bonus to be paid in advance of £100 per officer and £50 per rating to any British seamen who volunteered to make such a voyage. The attrition rate was expected to be high, and so it turned out to be. Over half the ships involved, mainly British and American, but including some Russians, failed to get through, and many men lost their lives.

The crew of one of the British ships involved, *Chulmleigh* (Atlantic Shipping Company), probably suffered most of all. On the night of 5 November, in an attempt to evade German bombers, and in bad weather, the ship ran on to a reef off Spitzbergen Island. The crew under Captain D Williams, took to the boats, losing one man in the process, but reboarded later and tried unsuccessfully to refloat the ship. Spread between two boats and in bitterly cold weather, Williams and his crew then headed east for the mining settlement of Barentsburg. It was as well they left the ship, for soon afterwards it was bombed by five German aircraft. Some time later the boats separated, the second one never being seen again. Fighting against severe frostbite and debilitation, after a week of appalling misery and still short of Barentsburg, the boat containing Captain Williams and twenty-seven men was driven ashore. They set up residence in nearby empty seal-hunters' huts. During the next four days over a third of the survivors died from gangrene. Over the weeks that followed, weeks that brought more deaths from cold and hunger, several attempts were made to send small parties overland to the settlement, but all were forced back by the conditions of the terrain or by snow blizzards. It was not until 3 January 1943, almost two months since the ship's stranding, that Captain Williams and nine remaining survivors were found by a patrol of Norwegian soldiers out of Barentsburg. One more man was to die before the rest arrived back in Britain in mid-June. The bonus paid by Jack Billmeir was a lot of money in those days, but it is to be doubted whether Captain Williams and his men thought that the earning of it had been worthwhile.

CHAPTER 10

'They got it all, and they ain't too holy'

British seamen who found themselves without a ship in a foreign land, either from shipwreck or having landed there after being rescued, were called Distressed British Seamen (DBS) by Government Departments. In wartime there were many of them and all had a legal claim to living expenses and to be repatriated free. (Deserters, those who had 'jumped ship' as it was called, had no such legal claim.) There were also many survivors who landed on home shores, and they had to be looked after as well.

As the Government was only prepared to foot the bill for those matters falling within the existing rules and regulations, there was much scope for additional succouring work. Much of this, indeed most of it until 1942, was carried out by voluntary societies. Then, in that year, the British Government, in belated recognition of the fact that the attrition rate amongst merchant seaman had become dangerously high, brought in two measures to alleviate the situation; it established the Merchant Navy Training Board to train more seamen, and it appointed Welfare Officers to the main British ports and to New York (where most survivors who landed in the Americas ended up), to look after the interests of those already serving. However, even after 1942 many of the welfare needs of seamen were still the object of sterling work carried out by various kinds of Seamen's Missions and similar societies, and no book about the Merchant Navy at war would be complete without including some mention of them.

The best known of these societies was The Missions to Seamen, or 'Flying Angel' as it was called from the figure in white depicted against a blue background on its flag. The society had been officially formed in 1856 by John Ashley, although it had earlier origins in the Bristol Channel Mission. The primary aim of the Flying Angel was to extend the pastoral work of the Church to seamen and, as a means to that end, Institutes were set up in many ports. These provided a home-from-home for itinerant sailors of all nationalities and from all types of ships including warships, and by the 1930s there was a world-wide network of missions covering many major ports. An Anglican organisation, it was not alone in this work. The Roman Catholic Church had a similar set-up called the Apostleship of the Sea, or 'Stella Maris', and there were others, some of them individual societies which looked after the needs of seamen in a particular port. In New York, the forerunner of the present Seamen's Church Institute had been founded even before John Ashley began his work in England, and there was a Mission run along similar lines operating in Honolulu around 1850.

Having been in the business of catering for seamen's needs for over eighty years and with the necessary network of Institutes and staff in place, the Flying Angel was able quickly to adapt itself to looking after vastly increased numbers of seamen at the time of their greatest ordeal during the Second World War. Some Flying Angels overseas, those in strategically located ports, became key centres for rest and recreation. One of them was at Fremantle, Western Australia, where the Chaplain in charge kept in regular contact with his counterparts in such ports as Colombo and Durban, so that as ships arrived he and his team of volunteers from the local community were ready to provide for the needs of their crews, including finding billets ashore for them if that was required.

From time to time some Chaplains in charge of missions found themselves in the front-line. This happened at Dunkirk, where the Chaplain stayed on until the very last moment, helping both seamen and ordinary refugees to escape. It was a similar story at Rotterdam, where the Chaplain made arrangements for many to escape on a small ship which eventually reached Tilbury and safety. The Flying Angels at Kobe and Yokohama kept their doors open until mid-1941, just a few months before Japan entered the war, despite the many difficulties the Japanese imposed on all foreigners in their land after July 1940, when fifteen alleged British spies residing in that country were arrested. One of the alleged spies, Vincent O Peters, was arrested in Kobe and was sentenced to eight years' imprisonment for being a member of a spy ring which had been under police surveillance for some time. This, according to the police, followed suspicions aroused by activities actually centred on the Seaman's Mission there, with an unnamed Blue Funnel Line ship. which regularly called at that port, acting as the courier service to British Naval Intelligence in Hong Kong. Two of the other Britons arrested were brothers named Ringer who ran an old-established shipping agency at ports in western Japan. It should be noted that the Japanese did not arrest any of the staff of the Kobe Mission and did not close it down, so apparently there were no suspicions that the staff were in any way involved. (For fuller details see the author's *Far Eastern File*.)

There were two Chaplains attached to the Mission at Hong Kong, a large building right down on the waterfront. One of them, the Reverend Charles Strong, had been a Master Mariner prior to his ordination, and as the clouds of war gathered in the Far East, he was asked by the Royal Navy to take on the highly confidential work of Ship Routing Officer in addition to his Mission duties. The other was the Reverend Cyril Brown. Just before the Japanese attacked Hong Kong, both men were appointed Chaplains RNVR. As the fighting neared the waterfront, Reverend Brown made use of the Mission's launch *Dayspring* to convey women and children refugees from Kowloon to Victoria on Hong Kong Island, and made several such trips before the launch was sunk by Japanese gunfire. Both men became prisoners of war and did sterling work in the prison camps, the Reverend Strong being awarded the MBE after the war.

At Singapore, where the Flying Angel had no premises of its own, it shared the use of Connell House, the famous Institute near the waterfront which had been set up mainly with funds subscribed by the man after whom it was named. The Chaplain there was the Reverend A V Wardle. He remained at his post after getting his wife and children away before the Japanese took the city, but was eventually interned on the island of Sumatra. He held services at Palambang camp, where his special charges were the Merchant Navy internees there. Reverend Wardle almost made it through to the end of the war, but died of malaria and malnutrition in early 1945. One of his fellow internees said of him: 'He instilled new hope in us. As the days grew darker, his words of help and example . . . were an inspiration . . .'

Missions other than Flying Angels were also in the forefront of things. We have already seen how the Reverend Dr Donald Caskie, a priest of the Church of Scotland, who was in charge of the British and American Seamen's Mission at Marseilles, helped Fourth Engineer Sam Harper and his colleagues on their way after their escape from the Germans. That Mission, at 46 Rue de Forbin, became an escape route not only for Allied seamen, but for airmen too, until Dr Caskie was himself interned.

Men of the cloth of many denominations helped with the spiritual needs of seamen during the war. Outstanding among these was Brigadier Best of the Salvation Army who, travelling as a passenger on board a ship sunk by a German raider, found himself in *Milag* prisoner of war camp. Other ordained people in that camp were a group of missionaries who had also been unfortunate enough to be passengers on a captured ship.

In one or two places Seamen's Missions suffered under special local handicaps which were much accentuated by the increase in numbers of seamen as a result of the war. At Capetown, South Africa, the Flying Angel had the colour-bar to deal with, and the increase in the number of merchant seamen from India and some African countries made it necessary to develop special clubs for them adjacent to the one for European seaman. However, once inside the doors the colour-bar was never rigidly enforced, especially in chapel services where seamen of all races sat down together. Perhaps the busiest of all overseas postings for a Missions to Seamen Chaplain, was Freetown, the capital and largest port of Sierra Leone. Its strategic position on the bulge of Africa made it an important bunkering port on the convoy route to and from the Cape. There was no Institute there as such, but the Government requisitioned one of the local Grammar Schools as a hostel for torpedoed seamen, and the Missions Chaplain was asked to take charge of it. He set about improving the building with money subscribed by friends in South Africa. On one occasion there were 248 survivors being taken care of under its roof, and the total number of men to receive succour there during the war ran into several thousands.

Britain itself was in the front-line during the German bombing campaign. The London docks came in for special attention from the *Luftwaffe* in the autumn of 1940, in night after night of the Blitz. The Flying Angel at Tilbury was destroyed and the sailor's hostel near Victoria Docks had to be temporarily closed when a bomb fell on its roof. One of Flying Angel's launches, used to convey chaplains aboard ships, was sunk in the Thames near Woolwich. After an air attack on Bristol, the Mission carried on its work under a tarpaulin covering a huge bomb hole in its roof. At Cardiff, on the other side of the Bristol Channel, a bomb fell through the roof of the Institute but failed to go off. In January 1941, the Flying Angel at Swansea was destroyed in an air-raid. In all these cases, and many similar ones, buildings were either repaired or new ones soon found. All over Britain the staff of the Missions, both permanent and volunteer, had their work cut out to cope. Cope they did, but not without casualties. At Belfast five lady volunteers returning from the Mission in a car during the blackout, died when their vehicle took a wrong turning and plunged into the dock.

Not all Flying Angel establishments were of long standing. Some were created because of the war. The Mission at Methil, a small port on the northern shore of the Firth of Forth, was one of those. It was established because it was off this port that many convoys assembled and many survivors were landed there. It was built under the railway arches which ran close to the dockside, so close in fact, that the entrance to the Mission was virtually at the end of the gangway of any ship berthed alongside. It became famous as 'The Mission Under the Arches'. There, throughout six years of war, many hundreds of survivors, often wet, covered in oil, and owning nothing but the clothes they stood up in, were provided with hot meals and dry clothes by local volunteer ladies under the supervision of a most remarkable man, Lay Reader E Stanley Price. It was under those arches that survivors underwent the necessary examinations by Security Officers and Immigration and Port Health officials, together with the inevitable Customs formalities. There also, a representative of the Shipping Federation, a shipowners' organisation dating from 1890 when it had been set up to counter the work of sailors' unions, but now acting as a sort of agency of the Ministry of War Transport, gave out cash advances and issued railway warrants to take the men back to their home ports.

The Methil Mission was small, so small that when on one cold day in October 1940 it was suddenly confronted with the arrival of 266 survivors from eight ships sunk in the same North Atlantic convoy, Stanley Price had to think quickly about how to cope with accommodating so many. He recorded, not under his own name, but modestly under the pen-name 'Breakwater':

I shall never forget the almost miraculous flash-back to a scene in which I was a participant twenty-three years before. As I stood in the doorway of our Mission, surrounded by all these men, there flashed across my mind the picture of Halifax, Nova Scotia, after the terrible explosion of 1917, when the trains were shunted into the sidings for the homeless people.

In minutes he was on the phone to the Traffic Superintendent of the London North Eastern Railway, whose reaction was both positive and immediate. Very soon, coaches were being shunted into a nearby coal siding to provide a temporary addition to the Mission's facilities.

Although small, the Methil Mission managed to duplicate many of the facilities which were a feature of Flying Angels in larger ports. There are still seamen around who remember with affection the dances, concerts, film shows and whist drives which were held under a roof and inside walls that shivered and shook every time a train lumbered overhead. At least one seaman survivor met his future wife at one of those dances, their sparking apparently not at all affected by the noise.

Missions in general were to play a special part in the preparations for D-Day in 1944. So many were the merchant ships that took part in that operation that a special reserve pool of men was organised by the Ministry of War Transport to man some of the ships. For days prior to D-Day, these men were infiltrated secretly into many ports around Britain. They came, said the Reverend Denis Daley of the Glasgow Mission, in small groups, and:

> a liaison was established between the Merchant Navy Pool and ourselves in putting up groups of 10, 20, and 50 men, and then suddenly they would vanish. So closely was the secret guarded that when a man fell sick aboard his ship he was sent to an isolation hospital and kept there. I tried to see several men who had been ill, but could not for security reasons.

It was the same in many other ports. For days the Missions' staff worked flat-out, arranging accommodation and other comforts for many hundreds of men for the armadas of ships that clogged lochs, ports and rivers around the coast. Then, one morning in early June, they awoke to find the ships and men had disappeared.

During the war a system of 'comforts' for merchant seamen was developed. There must be more than a few senior citizen ladies still around who recall knitting sweaters, scarves, balaclava helmets and gloves for sailors. These were issued by an impersonal central authority but when, as often happened, one of the ladies enclosed a letter with the product of her labour, personal contacts were made, and individual sailors, even ships, found themselves 'adopted' by a group of industrious knitters.

It was mentioned above that one of the Ministry of War Transport's Welfare Officers was based in New York. This was the only overseas posting for these officers, and it was deemed necessary because of the large numbers of British and Allied seamen survivors who, one way or another, ended up at that port after being rescued. However, because of the great Christian kindness proffered by the Seamen's Church Institute of New York and to the funds collected by British resident organisations in America, it seems likely that the appointment was not really necessary.

The Seamen's Church Institute had its origins in the New York Port Society of 1818 and passed through various other forms before being incorporated as the SCI in 1844. During its early years and up to 1910, the Institute and its forbears owned successively one floating chapel and two floating churches. Then, in 1913, the Institute opened its giant premises at 25 South Street; a multi-storey building that from the outside looked much like a plush hotel, and one which could accommodate more than 800 men (at from 25c to $1 a night). It was open to seamen of all nations. It took a special interest in the welfare of apprentices aboard British, Scandinavian and German vessels (there was no equivalent rank in the American Merchant Marine), deeming these young men to be at special risk from the vices which abound on all waterfronts. In 1919 the so-called Apprentices' Room was redecorated and upgraded into 'a room out of an English country house, simple, beautiful, with a subtle air of welcome and home'.

The Institute was a centre that provided most of a sailor's secular needs as well as his spiritual ones. It even had its own Employment Bureau for finding ships for experienced seamen and also for new entrants into the industry. In 1925 Robert Uhl was a sixteen year-old lad who wanted badly to go to sea. He got to talking to an old shellback down on the Battery waterfront.

> 'Was I you, Kid,' said the sailor, 'I'd head for the Institute. You can eat there; sleep there; they'll stow your gear. It's cheap and it's clean. They got a job board – tell you what ships are lookin' for a crew. They got it all; and they ain't *too* holy.'

When the Second World War began in Europe in September 1939, the Superintendent of the Institute, the Reverend Harold H Kelley, initiated plans based on those used by a predecessor during the earlier global conflict, to house and look after the expected influx of survivors from ships sunk in the Atlantic. Reverend Kelley and his team did not have long to wait. On the sixth day of the war, 8 September, the British steamer *Winkleigh* (Tatem Steam Navigation Company), on a voyage with grain and timber from Vancouver to Manchester, was torpedoed by *U-48* 500 miles west of the Bishop Rock. The survivors were picked up by a westbound ship and landed at New York a week later. There they were most famously looked after, including being taken on an excursion to the World's Fair, until it was time to join other British ships. No need for so-called counsellors in those days; the Americans concerned in the Institute's operations just did what came naturally to a generous-spirited people.

We have seen (Chapter 1) how the crew of *Heronspool*, sunk on 13 October 1939, were picked up by the American liner *President Harding*

(American President Line). They too ended up at the Institute in New York, but not before suffering more hardship and adventure. According to Captain James Roberts of the *Harding*, after the rescue his ship ran into one of the worst storms in living memory, during which a giant wave towered over the bridge of the 14,000-ton ship before falling on her decks with tremendous force, injuring seventy-three people. Paul Johnson, a cabin boy, was swept overboard and lost, and the battered ship arrived in port flying its ensign at half-mast in the lad's honour. The thirty-six *Heronspool* survivors, under Captain Sidney Batson, were completely outfitted at the Institute and royally entertained. Two of the ship's apprentices, when asked to sign the Apprentices' Room Register, did so noting that they had 'Arrived from . . . Death's Door, Davy Jones's Locker'. Each man was fitted out with a suit and shoes paid for by the British Consul, and other British institutions in the port, including the St Andrew's Society, the St George's Society, Daughters of the British Empire, and the British War Veterans' Association, helped with funds and such comforts as cigarettes. Whilst the *Heronspool* people were at the Institute they met up with survivors from the French *Emile Miguet*, the tanker they had sighted being shelled by a U-boat prior to their own ship being sunk. The Frenchmen had been rescued by the American freighter *Black Hawk*.

Another group of survivors to arrive were from *Kafiristan* (Hindustan Steamship Company). Under the command of Captain John Busby, she had been torpedoed when about 300 miles south-west of Ireland, and the crew of thirty-five took to the boats, only for six of them to be lost when one lifeboat capsized. The German submarine concerned then surfaced and its commander offered to tow the remaining boats nearer land and send out an SOS, but as the preparations were being made, a British bomber arrived on the scene and sprayed the submarine with machine-gun fire before dropping two bombs which fell close alongside. The U-boat submerged and was not seen again. However, the survivors were picked up almost immediately by the US freighter *American Farmer*, whose master, Captain H A Pederson, had witnessed the aircraft attack.

By February 1940, six months after war began, the Seamen's Church Institute had cared for the crews of thirty-eight torpedoed ships, a figure that had risen to well over the one hundred mark by the war's end. And it was all done with compassion and understanding, something that is well illustrated by the treatment given to non-Christian seamen. Were they Muslims or Hindus, or of any other religion, scrupulous care was taken to see that the food supplied to these men was strictly in accordance with the rules of their religion. By no means all survivors who enjoyed the hospitality of the Institute were there as a result of war action. The British freighter *Sea Rambler* foundered in a storm off Halifax, Nova Scotia in April 1940. The crew were picked up by two Norwegian vessels and brought to New York. Another such victim was the British *Matakana* (Captain Evan Davis) which ran aground off the Bahamas in May 1940. Her crew were rescued from the cay on which they had landed, by boats from the American liner *Panama*, and brought to New York to get the full Institute treatment.

The Christian charity of the Institute was not directed solely at seamen. In mid-1940, 258 British child evacuees arrived in New York aboard the Cunarder *Samaria*. They came from bombed-out homes from cities all over Britain and stayed at the Institute until they could join their American foster-parents, a wait made longer by an epidemic of measles amongst them.

We saw in the chapter on Ropner's Navy how the captain and crew of that company's *Pikepool* placed themselves in dire peril whilst rescuing the crews of two torpedoed ships, the *Blairangus* (George Nisbet & Company), and Bank Line's *Elmbank*. The survivors were landed at St John's, Newfoundland. In November 1940 the crew of *Elmbank*, fourteen British officers and thirty-eight Lascars, arrived at the Institute to be cared for until ships were found for them. They were followed in December by the crew of *Blairangus*. Amongst the latter were two apprentices called Towers and Hardie. Despite their lack of years, for both were only eighteen, they were old hands at all this and were able to show their shipmates the ropes. For the two lads had been brought here a little over a year earlier with other survivors from the same company's *Blairlogie* after it had been torpedoed on 11 September 1939.

The indomitable duo, Towers and Hardie, once again enjoyed their stay at the Institute, especially a dance held in the Apprentices' Room. Young Hardie spotted a face he recognised from his previous visit, and made his way through the crowd towards an attractive girl. 'Pardon me, Miss,' he said. 'You may not remember me but I was here a year ago with *Blairlogie*'s crew and at the time you promised to teach me how to dance. I want to apologise for not coming to the dance but we had to ship out that afternoon. But I'm here now and anxious to learn, please.' So the young lady taught Hardie the foxtrot and the waltz.

One wonders whether Hardie told the young lady a story from the *Blairangus* sinking. The survivors were sliding down ropes into the boats in rough seas when suddenly the second mate remembered the ship's mascot, a grey and white cat, who had recently had five kittens. Without hesitation the Second Mate went below and amidst the burning wreckage found the cat and her offspring. At the ship's side he shouted down to another officer in a boat some thirty feet below, who held out his cap. Then, one by one, mother and kittens were tossed down to be safely caught in it.

Hardie could also have told the girl a story from the earlier *Blairlogie* sinking, of how the U-boat commander observed International Law to the letter and allowed the crew to get off in boats before sending the ship to the bottom. After that he handed over a bottle of schnapps and cigarettes and stayed with the boats until dawn, even firing red rockets at intervals until rescue appeared in the shape of a neutral American ship, *American Shipper*. (Young Hardie would not have known then of course, an even more interesting fact. The U-boat concerned was *U-30*, and its commander was Lieutenant Fritz Lemp, the submarine and the man who had started the battle of the oceans by sinking the liner *Athenia* on the very first day of the war.) Those stories would have been fitting for a young girl's ears, but Hardie probably would not have told her that aboard *Pikepool* he was among those who attended the sea-burial of Captain H T Phillips of *Elmbank*, who aged only thirty-five, had died in a lifeboat after losing both his legs in the torpedo attack on his ship. When Hardie and Towers said goodbye to the Institute staff as they left once more to ship out, they are reported to have said: 'Perhaps we'll see you soon again. Who knows?'

The Seamen's Church Institute at 25 South Street no longer exists. In the 1960s the SCI opened new premises at Port Newark instead. In 1913, in honour of the 1500 passengers and crew who went down with *Titanic* in the previous year, a tower which resembled a lighthouse and with a light with a range of 12 miles, was constructed on the Institute's roof. The structure can still be seen in the South Street Seaport Museum.

CHAPTER 11

The Young Navigator

The Asiatic Petroleum Company, known throughout Southeast Asia in those days as 'APC', was an organisation that matched in power and influence the famous trading houses and banks in the Far East. The company (now Shell) owned oil fields in Sarawak and the Dutch East Indies, and its refining and oil storage installations and its chain of distribution depots were spread in every direction. In addition to its fleet of deep-sea tankers, it owned many smaller craft to link this far-flung commercial empire. APC was a company that looked after its staff. When war came to the Far East on 8 December 1941 (war that is, with America and the European nations which had colonies in the area, for it must always be remembered that Japan and China had already been fighting an undeclared war for a number of years), the company began withdrawing staff and their families from vulnerable locations. It was a process that went on until the fall of Singapore and the Dutch East Indies early in 1942.

The tanker *Pinna*, run by the APC associate Anglo-Saxon Petroleum, was lying off the riverine oil port of Palembang, Sumatra, on the first day of February 1942, when she was ordered to proceed to Singapore with a cargo of aviation spirit in drums and cases. *Pinna*'s previous career had been a colourful one. Built in Germany in 1910 as Hansa Line's *Berkenfels*, she had been requisitioned by the British and handed over to Anglo-Saxon Petroleum to run. She was commanded by Captain W P 'Bill' Thomas and the Chief Engineer was Sam Bruce. Ralph Armstrong was a nineteen year-old apprentice on board.

Despite the rose-tinted news bulletins being put out by the Malayan Broadcasting Service, some of the facts about the military situation in Malaya had trickled down to Palembang, probably by word of mouth from crews of the APC craft passing between the ports. Bill Thomas and his crew may not have known that the last Commonwealth troops had, after a 55-day retreat, crossed over the Johore Strait from Malaya to Singapore Island on the previous day, but they did know the situation was serious.

Pinna sailed late that night, and on 3 February was heading north towards the southern end of the Rhio Strait when two company tankers were sighted fully laden and hurrying in the opposite direction, making south to Australia. 'Ominously,' wrote Ralph Armstrong, 'their rails were lined with civilians – mainly company families – and when they signalled us "Best of luck" we knew we were heading for trouble. Captain Thomas wondered moodily why we weren't being re-routed south as well but figured our aviation spirit was needed for our aircraft – laughable as it turned out as we had no air force to speak of anyhow.'

Shortly after 1700 hours that evening and just as the Chinese crew were settling down to an evening meal in the fo'c'sle, a formation of five Japanese aircraft was spotted at about 5000 feet. Captain Thomas immediately ordered the helm hard-a-port. Ralph Armstrong dashed up to the bridge and arrived just in time to see 'a bunch of silvery bombs screeching down towards us'. Only one of the bombs struck. 'But horribly,"says Ralph, 'it was plumb on the fo'c'sle.' Twenty-three men there died instantly. 'We dashed forward to fight the fire and rescue anyone we could, but could only get two men out both of whom died within a few hours.' Fire parties, one of them led by Apprentice Armstrong, managed to get the fires under control as darkness fell. After that, on slow ahead, *Pinna* arrived at the Rhio Strait at dawn. She was through and heading west towards Singapore by mid-morning. If Captain Thomas, in view of the aviation spirit his ship was carrying, was hoping for some friendly air cover, he was to be disappointed. A plane was sighted, but as Armstrong reported:

I thought I could see orange on the wings and thought he was Dutch and started to wave. When however I saw yellow flashes on the wings followed by tracers coming towards *me*, I knew that he was not one of ours.

I flew into the accommodation and at the same time the saloon forward bulkhead bent in towards me – the deck seemed to come up and bang me in the chest as fortunately I was horizontal by now as a red flash came in above the opened bulkhead. No.2 hold, full of aviation fuel had been hit.

On the bridge Captain Thomas and Chief Officer Watt suffered flash burns and together with the surviving officers decided to abandon ship. There was no hope of a couple of canvas hoses coping with an awesome display of pyrotechnics where forty-gallon drums and four-gallon tins of spirit were erupting to above mast height, exploding, then cascading down in red and blue stars and streamers of flames over the forward half of the ship.

My boat was the port after one and the 2nd Mate and I with a few others lowered it down after we put the Captain and Chief Officer into it first. A few others launched a raft from the after deck as being quicker and further away from No.2 hold.

Ralph added:

When we were all aboard our lifeboat the Chief Engineer Sammy Bruce, asked me could I go back to his cabin as he had forgotten his pipe tobacco – I confirmed with the Second Officer that this was just a little illogical, and we pulled away to safety.

My own most remembered personal loss was my own perfectly healthy appendix which had been removed unnecessarily in Tarakan only a few months earlier then given to me in a spirit bottle by Doctor Colign in the company hospital in Eastern Borneo.

Tom Simpkins, the ship's radio officer, found himself trapped in his cabin with Arthur Greene, the Third Engineer. They finally managed to break out and were among those who escaped on the raft. All the survivors were soon picked up by the auxiliary vessel HMS *Bulan* and landed safely at Singapore. The wounded were taken to hospital while young Ralph ended up in Connell House, the Seamen's Hostel. While he was there he visited the company offices on Collyer Quay and with, as it turned out, remarkable foresight, 'acquired', as he puts it, a sextant and a copy of *Norie's Nautical Tables*.

He was sent out to the oil refinery on Pulo Bukom, an island just off Singapore, and told to assist a demolition team in destroying as much machinery as possible. Ralph recalls that on Bukom they were never bombed and only occasionally strafed by aircraft, and puts this down to the Japanese not wanting to damage an installation they needed for their own use. He tells the following anecdote about one of those strafing incidents, a story which concerns Chief Engineer Bruce who was also on the island. Perhaps the details became etched in Ralph's mind because of the tobacco incident in the lifeboat.

> Poor Sammy Bruce while dodging machine-gun bullets jumped into a monsoon drain and slashed open his buttock on a small hip flask whiskey bottle he had in his pocket. That was the only wound I saw during that period and it was instantly bathed in antiseptic whiskey.

By the beginning of the second week of February it was obvious to any thinking person that Singapore would soon fall. The Japanese had landed on the island on the 7th, and were pushing ever nearer the city. APC set about evacuating as many of its remaining employees as possible. Two small inter-island vessels, *Ribot* and *Kulit*, were to be used to take away those left on Pulo Bukom and were commanded respectively by Captains Clayton and Moss, both in their early thirties. Other APC small craft, including one called *Mutiara* under Captain Donald Ash and which was normally used for running stores between Singapore and the off-shore island refineries, were used to evacuate personnel from the city offices.

On 12 February *Ribot* and *Kulit* sailed west in company, making for the small port of Pakanbaru on the Siak River on the east coast of Sumatra, the captains making use of their local knowledge. Ralph Armstrong and Sam Bruce sailed aboard *Ribot*. At Pakanbaru the two boats were scuttled and the crews split up, the *Ribot* contingent travelling across country by bus to the escape port of Padang on Sumatra's west coast, whilst the *Kulit* crowd, Radio Officer Tom Simpkins amongst them, made for Benkulen (sometimes spelt Bencoolen), also on the west coast but farther south, where they joined a ship and were evacuated safely to Colombo.

At Padang Ralph and other Merchant and Royal Navy escapees from Singapore were embarked on the destroyer HMS *Electra* which took them to Batavia (now Jakarta) on the island of Java. Ralph was mightily impressed there by the *Electra* captain's ship-handling, for she entered port at speed stern-first, berthed alongside, discharged the passengers in double-quick time, and then raced out to sea again.

In the harbour of Batavia lay four so-called 'Kwang boats' belonging to APC. The peacetime employment of these 800-ton shallow-draft case-oil carriers had been on the Yangtze River upstream from Shanghai. Built in Hong Kong in 1913, their only previous foray out to sea prior to the voyage in convoy to Batavia to escape capture by the Japanese had been that between Hong Kong and Shanghai in the year of their build. One of them was the *Ho Kwang* and Ralph Armstrong, with as yet no formal navigational qualifications, found himself appointed her navigation officer, for after years of sailing only on the Yangtze her British officers had forgotten most of their ocean navigation. Ralph still had with him the sextant and the copy of *Norie's* which he had filched from the APC offices in Singapore, both items being complete mysteries to the ship's regular officers.

Ralph discovered that apart from a general chart of the South China Sea, *Ho Kwang* carried no others, and none were to be had ashore. So, from the list of the latitudes and longitudes of the world's salient points in *Norie's* he took those for the Sunda Strait between the islands of Java and Sumatra, and Dondra Head, the southernmost tip of Ceylon, and drew up one of his own. He is rightly proud of the fact that after days of sailing in that old riverboat, Dondra Head was sighted dead ahead. The ship finally made it to Colombo and safety.

Ralph Armstrong arrived home in North Shields some three months later to find that his parents thought him dead. The last news they had received from the London office was to the effect that *Pinna* had been bombed and lost off Singapore and that there had been no news of any survivors. For his brave fire-fighting efforts aboard *Pinna* he was awarded both the British Empire Medal and Lloyd's Medal, of which he values the latter the most. After the war he rose to command with Shell, and after that worked for many years ashore for that company at Miri in Sarawak.

Whatever else APC might have lost when Singapore fell, it obviously had not included the company financial records. A few months after the events chronicled here, Ralph was surprised to receive a bill for 1 shilling and 4 pence from the London Office for a transaction that had earlier been carried out on his behalf in Singapore. He paid up, but reckons he got the best of the bargain for he still has the pleasure of owning the only sextant ever carried on *Ho Kwang*.

Captain Bill Thomas and Chief Officer Watts were still in hospital in Singapore when the Japanese marched in and became prisoners of war. Bill Thomas survived internment and returned to command in Shell after the war but Chief Officer Watts did not survive.

After reaching Colombo Chief Engineer Sam Bruce joined the tanker *President Sergent* belonging to Anglo-Saxon Petroleum Company. She was torpedoed in the North Atlantic on 18 November 1942 and Bruce was not among the survivors.

The *Mutiara*, of which a brief mention has been made above, sailed from Singapore on 13 February with about twenty-four people on board, all APC personnel except for two Chartered Bank officials. Two *Pinna* engineers were on board, one called Dunne, and the other Third Engineer Arthur Greene. *Mutiara* reached Rengat on the Indragiri River, Sumatra, and was there abandoned to the Dutch authorities. The party travelled overland to Padang where they boarded the Dutch *Peleleh* for Batavia on 1 March. However, after the ship had sailed she diverted to Colombo because someone on board had heard broadcasts in Japanese coming from Batavia. Arthur Greene, who died in 1995, became godfather to Radio Officer Tom Simpkins' children. Although good friends the two differed in their approach to handling their war experiences. Simpkins wrote his up, but Arthur would never even talk about his.

Ah Kwang, another of the APC case-oil carriers at Batavia, also made it to safety. She spent the rest of the war transporting aviation spirit along the North African coast for the RAF. She returned to the Far East after the war and in 1954 was sold in Singapore and converted to a dry-cargo carrier. From that port and renamed *Playaran*, she was engaged in running the Indonesian rubber-export blockade in the 1950s. As the *Sri Thai*, and by then of hoary old-age pensioner status, she was still sailing in and out of Singapore in the late 1970s.

HMS *Electra*, Commander C W May RN, was lost on the first afternoon of the Battle of the Java Sea on 27 February 1942 when she formed part of Admiral Karel Doorman's combined Dutch/British/American/Australian fleet which attempted to prevent the Japanese invasion of Java. *Electra* was leading a torpedo attack against Japanese cruisers when she was sunk. Of her complement of about 145, only 54 were picked up the following day by an American submarine. They eventually reached Australia.

CHAPTER 12

The Ordeal of Talthybius

Any sailor sighting the *Talthybius* at sea would have known from her silhouette that she was a Blue Funnel ship even when some miles off. The company's ships, almost without exception, had the unique characteristic of near-vertical funnels, which gave the impression of being too tall for them. *Talthybius*, named after the faithful servant and herald to Agamemnon, King of Mycenae and victor of Troy, was a 10,000-ton ship built at Greenock in 1912. Since March 1941 her master had been forty-nine-year-old Captain Thomas Arthur Kent, who like many another Blue Funnel man hailed from Liverpool. At Cardiff in late September of that year, the ship loaded coal in her main holds to give bottom-weight and to provide a level surface for the army vehicles to be loaded along the coast at Swansea. After that the ship received orders to proceed to the Middle East. She sailed in convoy for Freetown and then independently to Durban. It was whilst rounding the Cape of Good Hope that news came of the Japanese attacks on Pearl Harbor and Malaya. At Durban the ship's orders were changed and she was sent to Bombay. After bunkering there she joined convoy BM10 for Singapore where she arrived on 25 January 1942.

The senior of the four midshipmen on board (Blue Funnel Line used the naval term for their cadet officers) was Michael J Curtis. Mike recalls that on the date of the ship's arrival at Singapore, 'the scene on the waterfront was little changed from the way it had always been, apart from an occasional air-raid siren adding its strident note to all the other noises of the port; air-raids at that date were spasmodic.' That was soon to change.

The military cargo was discharged in three days and then work began on the coal. Air-raids had increased by then and in consequence many port labourers had disappeared. So little coal was discharged in the first twenty-four hours that the authorities decided to leave the rest on board. On the 30th the ship was moved to another berth to begin loading airfield construction equipment to save it from the oncoming Japanese. Loading was carried out by men of the Royal New Zealand Air Force, to whom the equipment belonged, and Midshipman Curtis noted that, 'the high standard of Blue Funnel cargo handling gear was never put to a tougher test' than by those amateur stevedores.

By 3 February all the equipment had been loaded and lashed in place except for a very large grader. Just as this was being lifted over the main hatch air-raid sirens sounded and Japanese planes roared in to attack the ships lying alongside the wharf. One stick of bombs fell close to *Talthybius*, and the planes then turned to come in for a second run. This time there were two direct hits on the main hatch, causing the fuel tanks of the already loaded equipment to explode. Flames soon spread to the coal underneath. One New Zealander was killed during that attack and six of the crew injured.

After five hours of fire-fighting and just as the fires were being brought under control, the supply of water from the pumps ceased. One of the original near-misses had caused hull damage in way of the engine- and boiler-rooms, and the consequent flooding of those compartments meant they had to be evacuated. The ship's portable pumps were brought into play but made such little difference that Captain Kent ordered two of the engineers to go ashore and get the fire brigade. He was taken literally, and the engineers returned 'to the ship within minutes complete with fire engine, one driving, the other ringing the bell, and hotly pursued by a carload of irate fireman who, having just extinguished a fire in one of the sheds, were having a breather before the next call'. Firemen and crew then joined forces and the fire was brought under control. Attempts to stem the influx of water met with little success. Another air-raid in the afternoon caused additional hull damage and started another fire in one of the after holds. This was all too much for the Chinese crew; Singapore was the home-port for some, and others had relatives there, and they decided it was safer ashore. That left only the British officers and gunners on board. By the time they had extinguished the new fire the weight of water in the ship caused her to list and settle on the bottom of Keppel Harbour.

On the following day it was decided to attempt to refloat the ship and get her into drydock. For that the services of a diver and a salvage pump were required. No diver was then available, but a 4-ton pump was found ashore. The ship having no power of its own, rope tackles were rigged to lift the pump aboard, using the manpower of a company of the Singapore Defence Force Volunteers. With the aid of the pump the list was reduced by a degree or two, and the water level in the ship was lowered by about a foot, but that was all. On the 5th a second pump was found and man-handled aboard, and with both working in tandem, by the next day, to everyone's joy, the water had dropped significantly. Plans were made to move the ship into drydock but they had to be shelved because no tugs were available for the purpose, the port's entire fleet then being busy assisting the burning troopship *Empress of Asia*, ashore on Sultan shoal to the south.

By that time the port and its surrounding area was not at all like the Singapore that had always been. Few ships were left alongside the once-crowded wharves, buildings were on fire everywhere, and a great pall of smoke was rolling in from the naval port at Seletar to the north, which had been put to the torch by the island's defenders as part of a scorched earth policy.

On 7 February, the day before Japanese forces landed on the island, *Talthybius* was clear of the bottom with the list down to about 5 degrees. With the aid of two tugs she was moved into Empire Dock where the water was shallower, and the pumps started again. Suddenly one of them packed up, and it was not long before the ship had settled on the bottom once more. The saga continued on the following day when, to great excitement, a diver at last turned up. All hands were set the task of carving pieces of wood into bung-like shapes for the diver to hammer into the holes in the hull. The job proceeded slowly for it had to be stopped every time there was an air-raid. At last, with most holes filled and with both pumps running, the ship came off the bottom. Not only that, the water level held. It was hoped that the diver would be able to complete the job the following day but instead he was dragged away to another job. He came back on the 9th, by which time everyone involved knew it was a race against time; there were now explosions in the harbour when there were no planes overhead, bringing the unpleasant realisation that the port was now under artillery fire. One shell set a nearby godown on fire, and the ship's officers found themselves having to deal with it as the port fire service had its work cut out elsewhere. On the 10th the diver had to give up. There was no alternative, for it was too dangerous to carry on with an artillery duel taking place overhead as the Japanese shelled the Royal Artillery positions on the island of Blakang Mati forming the southern part of Keppel Harbour.

On the 11th *Talthybius*'s ordeal came to an end. Captain Kent called everyone together and told them that nothing further could be done. After thanking them for their efforts he said it was now every man for himself. All should try to escape aboard one or other of the few ships left in the port. The first ship tried was *Empire Star*, but one look at her crowded decks and the quay alongside made them look elsewhere. They were in luck with a small ship flying the White Ensign, the requisitioned *Ping Wo*, because her commander was short of seamen and stokers as most of his Chinese crew had opted to stay in Singapore when given the choice. When HMS *Ping Wo* sailed that afternoon she had on board what was probably the best qualified deck and engine-room crew of any ship ever to have sailed from that port. Because of their youth and agility Mike Curtis and his fellow midshipmen were detailed as the shore party to cast off the mooring ropes. 'At a given signal the four lines were let go and the midshipmen as one man leapt from the quay to the ship as the current carried *Ping Wo* away.' That hardly seems an adequate way to describe what must have been some heart-stopping moments for those four young officers.

After leaving Keppel Harbour *Ping Wo* made for the Eastern Roads, and off Clifford Pier took on evacuees until there were some 200 people on board as well as the crew. There were a few women among them, and many businessmen. The largest single group were from the Malayan Broadcasting Service, the authorities having decided they must be got

The Merchant Navy Memorial, hard by the Tower of London, with Tower Bridge in the background. (Author)

(Above) Youth at war 1.
Survivors from Tatem Line's
Winkleigh, sunk by U-boat in
the North Atlantic on 8
September 1939, shown
with the captain (right), of
the Dutch *Statendam* which
took them to New York.
(South Street Seaport
Museum, New York)

Youth at war 2. Young
survivors from Bank Line's
Elmbank in New York, after
being rescued by the
Pikepool when their ship
was torpedoed on 21
September 1940.
(South Street Seaport
Museum, New York)

Memorial to 'Harry Tate's Navy', the Royal Navy Patrol Service, at Lowestoft in Suffolk. (Author)

(Below) Survivors from the *Heronspool* (sunk by U-boat on 13 October 1939), on board the rescuing ship, the American *President Harding*. Captain Sydney Bateson is in the middle of the front row, wearing a cap. (South Street Seaport Museum, New York)

Frederick Tenow, one of those who went down with the *Anglo Saxon* on 21 August 1940. (Mrs Pat Phillips)

(Below) Anglo Saxon's jolly boat, in which two of her crew survived for seventy days adrift, at the Imperial War Museum, London. (Pat Jones)

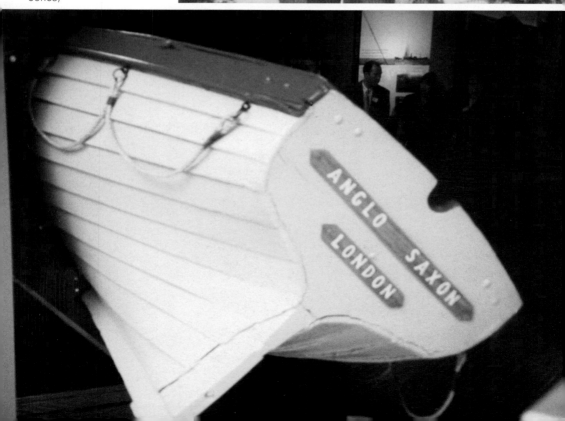

The *Automedon* before the war, in Liverpool Docks. (Donald Stewart)

Sam Harper (right) and Frank Walker of *Automedon* in 1992, holding a picture of their ship. (Sam Harper)

Second Officer (later Captain)
Donald Stewart of
Automedon. (Donald Stewart)

The German raider *Atlantis*, the ship which sank the *Automedon*. (Author)

Midshipman Michael Curtis
of *Talthybius* (taken in 1940).
(Captain M J Curtis)

(Below) In foreground, a
12-pounder gun of the type
mounted on most merchant
ships in the Second World
War. (Author)

Captain Selwyn Capon on
the bridge of the *Empire
Star*, c1939.
(Mrs Lettice Nicholls)

(Below) Empire Star shown
pre-war in a New Zealand
port. (Mrs Lettice Nicholls)

A convoy at anchor at Freetown at sunset on 14 April 1942. On the left is the cruiser HMS *Devonshire* and on the extreme right, the AMC *Alcantara*. (Imperial War Museum: A9225)

General view of a convoy under attack in September 1942. HMS *Eskimo* is in the foreground. (Imperial War Museum: A12022)

Fort Maurepas in 1946, shown with her life-rafts and gun platforms still in place. The 'Fort' class contributed greatly to the Allied victory. (Author's collection with acknowledgements to Leslie Hansen, Cardiff)

A Liberty ship, homeward-bound from Russia, rides the storm. This type of ship also played a great part in winning the war. (Imperial War Museum: A27519)

(Above) *Ah Kwang*, sister-ship of the *Ho Kwang* navigated by Apprentice Ralph Armstrong from Batavia to Colombo after the fall of Singapore, shown here at Rangoon in 1955 under her new name of *Playaran*. (Captain P J Rivers)

Poon Lim, the sole survivor from *Benlomond* (torpedoed on 23 November 1942), who endured 133 days on a life-raft. This photograph was taken after he had received his BEM at Buckingham Palace. (Imperial War Museum: HU74975)

Second Officer Gordon Rippon, senior surviving deck officer from the hospital ship *Centaur*, sunk by a Japanese submarine on 14 May 1943. (Dr Doreen Rippon)

(Below) The aftermath of the German air-raid on the Italian port of Bari on 2 December 1943. The pall of smoke over the harbour contained mustard gas. (Imperial War Museum: C5882)

Some survivors from the *Ena de Larrinaga* (Larrinaga SS Co, Captain R S Craston), sunk by a U-boat on 5 April 1941 whilst sailing independently. This photograph, taken outside the Seamen's Church Institute, New York, shows a typical mixture of races aboard British merchant ships. (South Street Seaport Museum, New York)

One of the actual models constructed by Second Officer Donald Stewart in the *Milag* POW camp for the instruction of students for Mates' Certificates. This depicts the workings of a heavy-lift derrick. (South Street Seaport Museum, New York)

Men from a torpedoed merchant ship clambering up the nets of a convoy rescue ship.
(Imperial War Museum: HU74974)

The devastation in the port of Bombay after the explosion of the *Fort Stikine* on 14 April 1944. (Imperial War Museum: IND4111)

Horror and heroism at sea. This photograph shows the *Mary Kingsley* stern-on to the *Apapa*, on fire after an attack by a German aircraft, allowing many of the *Apapa*'s passengers to leap aboard her to safety. (Imperial War Museum: HU74973)

away for fear of reprisals as MBC had been broadcasting anti-Japanese propaganda for many weeks. *Ping Wo* reached Batavia on the island of Java on the 14th, and the spirits of the *Talthybius* officers rose as they saw the distinctive funnels of at least four Blue Funnel ships in the harbour. After their marathon efforts to save one company ship, they thought the least they had earned was a lift home in another. But it did not turn out like that. There were yet more adventures in store for the Talthybians before they were finally sent home.

After the passengers had left the ship the makeshift crew was gathered together. Orders had been received that the crew was to stay aboard and take *Ping Wo* all the way to Fremantle. Not only that, the ship was to tow the disabled destroyer HMAS *Vendetta* behind her. Now, *Ping Wo* had been a Yangtze river steamer in her former life and had been designed with a minimal draught to operate in shallow waters. A deep-sea tug, any tug for that matter, needs a comparatively deep draught in order for the propeller to bite deep into the water to generate towing power. It was clear to the highly-qualified crew on board that the 2000-mile voyage ahead was not going to be an easy one.

Ping Wo took aboard some new 'passengers', including a group of Singapore Dockyard police who had earlier been evacuated from Seletar Naval Base. They were to act as stokers. A group of boy ratings, survivors from *Prince of Wales* and *Repulse*, also boarded. This meant the ship was once more crowded and that some on board would have to sleep on bare boards. After taking on the maximum amount of coal possible, including filling the cargo hold with it, *Ping Wo* sailed, and outside the harbour took aboard *Vendetta*'s towrope. The date was 15 February, the day of Singapore's surrender.

With *Vendetta* weaving along behind, *Ping Wo* headed for the Sunda Strait and twenty-four hours later Krakatoa, the volcanic island in the strait, was abeam. It was a measure of what was to come, for they had managed to cover only 100 miles in that time and that in relatively enclosed waters. Later, clear of the Strait, a southerly course was set. South of the Indonesian archipelago the prevailing sea swell is from the west. As there is nothing in that direction until one meets the African coast some 3800 miles away, that swell tends to be steady and substantial, and so it proved to be for the little Yangtze steamer and her charge. Mike Curtis says, 'both ships started to roll steadily to varying degrees, and continued to roll for the next sixteen days'. *Ping Wo*'s steering gear, un-used to the strain of sea conditions, had to have relieving tackles rigged to its quadrant. By the time the ships arrived at Fremantle on 4 March, all aboard were tired out yet as fit as fiddles, both conditions brought about by the exercise involved in transferring coal from the cargo hold to the bunkers.

At Fremantle, one by one in order of seniority, the Talthybians were placed on ships for home. At the bottom of the pecking order were the midshipmen who were left to enjoy six weeks of practically living on the beach at nearby Cotesloe, together with the hospitality of their Australian hosts. Mike says, 'One can only guess at the relief they felt when they saw us depart one by one. Feeding four healthy teenagers must have put something of a strain on Anglo-Australian relations.'

Captain T A Kent received an official commendation for trying to save his ship. The citation made in March 1943 in the usual secretive wording of those days, stated it was for 'war services'. Three months later it was upgraded to a well-deserved OBE. Kent's war adventures were far from over. His next command was *Phemius*, which was torpedoed off the West African coast on 19 December 1943 by *U-515*. Five crew members and eighteen passengers lost their lives, but Captain Kent was among the survivors. Midshipman Mike Curtis rose to many years of distinguished command with Blue Funnel Line.

It is likely that, given a few more days, the efforts of Captain Kent and his crew to salve *Talthybius* and get her away from Singapore might have succeeded. The Japanese managed to salve the ship, after which she sailed for them under the name *Taruyasu Maru*. In 1945 she struck an American mine off the coast of Honshu and sank in shallow waters. After the Japanese surrender she was raised and repaired by the Allies and became *Empire Evenlode*. She was handed back to Blue Funnel at Hong Kong in 1948. At Singapore a cargo was loaded for the United Kingdom, but the ship's poor condition necessitated a voyage around the Cape rather than risk her sinking in and blocking the Suez Canal. She arrived at Swansea in May 1949, almost eight years after her last call there. She was unloaded and then condemned to the breaker's yard. HMAS *Vendetta* went on to play a part in the Pacific War, including Operation 'Watchtower', the Allied invasion of the southern Solomon Islands in mid-1942. She survived the war and was scuttled off Sydney Heads in 1948.

CHAPTER 13

Empire Star

Captain Selwyn Capon paced the bridge of his ship. Every now and again he stopped to look down at the hustle and bustle on the deck and on the Bombay quayside, watching as his ship and cargo received the none-too-gentle attentions of the dock labourers. It was 9 January 1942, and his 10,000-ton command, Blue Star Line's *Empire Star*, had berthed three days ago after what had, for wartime, been a relatively uneventful voyage out from Liverpool. That very afternoon he had received secret orders that in ten days his ship was to join a convoy sailing for Singapore. That news, which for the time being he had to keep to himself, had given him much food for thought.

He had gone right through the last war, winning an OBE in the process, and had trained as a Lieutenant RNR. He knew how to read between the lines of official news bulletins and, on top of that experienced-based intuition, several of the army officers dealing with the ship's military cargo had dropped him snippets of information that did not feature in any bulletin. The campaign in Malaya, which had now been going on for a month, was not going well for the Commonwealth forces fighting to prevent the Japanese from taking the so-called impregnable fortress of Singapore through the back door. And now he was to take his ship there.

Captain Capon, a fifty-one year-old Norfolk man born at Acle near Norwich, but latterly living in Unthank Road in that city, was a man of middling height and portly stature, portly enough indeed for the insurance company after his last medical examination to see fit to load his personal insurance premiums. He smoked long Havana cigars and it was a rare occasion when he was seen without one in his hand, excusing this expensive habit to his family by saying that it would have looked faintly ridiculous for a man of his size to be seen clutching a tiny cigarette. He was known as an extremely able but tough shipmaster, though a fair one. Amongst *Empire Star*'s eighty-odd crew members were five between the ages of fifteen and eighteen, and one of those, Tony Higgins, who at that time was a sixteen-year-old steward's boy, says the captain was highly regarded. That sentiment is echoed by the then eighteen year-old Cadet Redmond Faulkner, one of four Australian members of the crew.

As Captain Capon gazed down on the crowded scene he took another puff at his cigar, savoured it, then sighed out the smoke. In a few days he must take his beloved ship – he had been master of her since the day she left the builder's yard in 1935 – together with its crew, into God knows what at Singapore. Then he strode from the bridge, consoling himself with the thought that there was nothing to be done about it for there was a war on. He grimaced. The fates had a way of balancing things; perhaps they had ordained the coming voyage to make up for the uneventful one out here. He decided to write a letter home.

As part of Convoy BM11, and loaded with army equipment and ammunition, *Empire Star* arrived at Singapore on 29 January 1942. The spirits of the crew, who had learned of their destination only after sailing from Bombay, had been raised during the voyage by the sight of one of the group of warships who were their escort. HMS *Exeter*, of Battle of the River Plate fame, had made a brave and comforting spectacle.

One of the other young men on board, Edward Green, an eighteen year-old assistant steward from Liverpool, wrote a memoir of the events of the next few weeks. He reported that because of its ammunition cargo, which made her a kind of floating time-bomb, the ship was at first kept at anchor in the Dangerous Goods Area from where he and the rest of the crew had a grandstand view of the ever-growing Japanese aerial bombardment of the city and dock area. At the anchorage some of her cargo was discharged into *tonkangs*, a type of local barge, but not much, for by that time many dock and barge workers had fled into the hinterland. On 5 February the crew were far-distant observers of the drama surrounding the burning and stranding of the only Singapore reinforcement troopship to be lost to enemy action, the *Empress of Asia* (see next chapter).

On the following day under cover of night, *Empire Star* berthed alongside the quay in Keppel Harbour, her cargo now being of crucial importance to the island's beleaguered defenders. No stevedores were available so 'every member of the crew went down the hatches', says Eddie Green. However, the discharging operation had barely begun when Japanese bombers came into attack. Eddie wrote, 'Panic stations, ropes cast off, and back to the anchorage. We all got the feeling our cargo was known to the Japanese'. He was probably right. There were many fifth-columnists in the city and it is more than likely that the Japanese knew that one well-aimed bomb whilst the ship was alongside could have done the work of squadrons of aircraft.

On 8 February Japanese troops poured across the Johore Strait which separates Singapore Island from mainland Malaya, and on the following day *Empire Star* was brought alongside again. 'Now it was unload at all costs', Eddie Green wrote. 'How we managed not to get hit was a miracle'. Every crew member again became a stevedore. 'Bombs were falling and shells were whistling overhead. All around us the sheds on the quayside were blazing. The ship was unloaded in record time, I can tell you,' he went on.

Eddie Green's report is confirmed by Cadet Redmond Faulkner. An Australian from East Brisbane, Queensland, he still lives in that state and is almost certainly the only *Empire Star* deck officer still with us. He says that on that day 'the crew unloaded Bofors anti-aircraft guns . . . [and these] were set up on the wharf and fired at Japanese aircraft.' He went on to say that the crew discharged about 2000 tons of ammunition.

On 11 February Captain Capon received orders that he was to evacuate women and children together with designated air force personnel, military nursing staff, and other officially authorised escapees, as part of the last large ship evacuation convoy from the island. The only thing that surprised him about the order was its belatedness. For days he had watched and listened as the city went up in flames. He had seen the ever-growing pall of black smoke rolling in from burning oil installations on the islands to the south and watched it mix with that rising from burning godowns in the port. As the acrid smell of oil and burning rubber stock-piles filled his nostrils – for some days now he had not really been able to enjoy a cigar – it had been obvious that the end was near. Sir Shenton Thomas, the Governor of Singapore, might still be quoted in the *Straits Times* as saying Singapore must and will stand and will never surrender, but any person with half an ounce of common sense knew it was nearly over. The Captain's vision went farther even than that. He guessed he might be looking, smelling and listening to the death-knell of empire, for the Commonwealth forces were facing defeat at the hands of an Asian enemy. How would the locals take that?

Alongside the wharf in Keppel Harbour the embarkation went on all day and into the night, its latter stages illuminated by the many fires burning in the docks, some deliberately lit to prevent cargo falling into enemy hands. Shells from both sides whined overhead, producing a frightening sonic backdrop to the operation.

Steward Eddie Green wrote:

> . . . we were invaded by hundreds of women and children. At noon they were flooding aboard a cargo ship with room for only twelve passengers. The captain ordered us all ashore to try to find anything edible; we had been in every shed that was left standing so we knew where to go.
>
> Later on sixty Australian nurses joined us from the military hospital – they had drawn straws with the other sixty left behind for a chance to escape. These were followed by a group of 20-25 . . . air force pilots.

Eddie reports that before the influx, a group of Scottish soldiers (probably Gordon Highlanders), who were guarding the harbour, had come aboard 'for a fag and a cuppa – nothing stronger for these lads. I borrowed writing paper and envelopes for them to write home. I finished up with forty letters and all these lads were worried about was the money for the postage. Who said the Scots are mean?'. Those letters, possibly the last post to come out of Singapore, were eventually mailed in Australia.

A number of army deserters, the majority of them Australians, forced their way aboard during the embarkation. One official RAF escapee, John Dodd (who after the war became famous as the founder of the Langley Trust involved in prison aftercare), saw a group of armed Australians surge up the gangway and push aside women and children in their way. Eddie Green recalls that the Australians were well armed, and at one point during the night Captain Capon had to persuade the Military Police not to rush his ship to get the deserters off. The Captain feared widespread bloodshed as the ship was already crammed with people, to say nothing of the quayside, which was described as 'the most God-awful melee of people you could imagine'.

At about 0200 hours on the 12th, the ship being unable to take anyone else aboard, Captain Capon ordered the gangway raised. According to Eddie Green the British soldiers on the quay, who were manning the ropes, almost caused a catastrophe. 'In the haste to help us escape they let go our mooring ropes a little too soon. Apart from the blazing buildings it was very dark, and as we floated away there was panic until the engineers got the engines going'. He went on, 'In the darkness we looked back and wondered about the fate of all we had left behind. Exhausted we flopped down where we could, our accommodation having been taken over, even if we could have managed to reach it through the crowds.'

Eddie's words provide us with a good idea of what conditions on board were like. People were everywhere, down the holds, in the 'tween decks and crew accommodation, and spread all over the deck. In his official report Captain Capon gave a figure of 2161 for those on board, but added that he was convinced this was an underestimate as no really accurate muster could be made. Another report sets the figure at nearly 3500, but the true figure is likely to have been about 2500. Whichever one of those figures was right, it was a vast number for a cargo ship of that size.

In company with the Blue Funnel liner *Gorgon* and two escorts, the cruiser HMS *Durban* and the requisitioned merchant ship HMS *Kedah*, *Empire Star*, piloted by Captain George Wright of the Singapore Pilotage Service, who was to remain on board, threaded through the port's protective minefields, keeping to a channel marked with temporary lights from small boats manned by some of the Royal Navy personnel left on the island. When clear of the minefields the ships made for the Durian Strait south of Singapore at top speed in an endeavour to be clear of its constricted waters before daybreak.

Japanese aircraft found them south of that strait at about 0900 hours the following morning, the ships still being in waters dotted with islands and shallows that restricted evasive manoeuvres. First dive-bombers screamed in, to be followed by waves of high-level bombers, in a running battle which was to last for four hours. Captain Capon produced a characteristically modest report about it all, and the following description is based on that report with additional information from other sources.

The first attack on *Empire Star* was made by six dive-bombers. The ship was hit twice, the second bomb piercing the steel deck aft and exploding in the poop space, blowing off steel beams and wooden hatch covers. Several fires broke out but were quickly extinguished by parties of crew members and volunteers led by ship's officers, including the two cadets, the youngest of whom, R Perry from Liverpool, was a lad of only fifteen. In that initial attack twelve military personnel were killed and seventeen military and crew severely wounded. The ship put up a stout defence, and a Hotchkiss gun manned by RAF personnel brought down a dive-bomber, whilst hits were scored on another one. Then high-level bombers arrived over the scene and the ship was hit again, this time a bomb striking the boat deck and exploding in the engineer's accommodation below. Another fire broke out, but that too was quickly brought under control.

Subsequent attacks were made by formations of aircraft totalling about sixty planes. With Pilot George Wright on one wing of the bridge and Third Officer James Smith on the other, both calling out the positions of the planes and angles of attack, Captain Capon skilfully conned his ship, the evasive action succeeding in reducing the salvoes of bombs to near-misses which were often not more than 10 to 20 feet away. According to V.A.D. Nurse Tommy Lucy, one of the many people down No. 2 Hold, some of the bombs were closer even than that. She says she heard 'the noise of bombs slithering down the side of the ship and exploding under the water, so the ship seemed to bounce'. On deck the Australian nurses were doing yeoman work among the wounded. One nurse was seen to throw herself protectively over one of her charges as a plane roared in low. Eddie Green saw one badly-wounded airman, who probably knew he was past all human aid, raise himself to the ship's rail and drop overboard.

The Japanese seemed to have concentrated their bombing on *Empire Star* and HMS *Durban*, for the other two ships got off virtually scot-free. Then, about one on the afternoon, the aircraft suddenly gave up. In his log entries Captain Capon paid tribute to several of those on board, specially noting the coolness and courage of the ship's company and of the RAF contingent who manned the Hotchkiss gun.

The convoy, less *Gorgon* which had fuel enough to make directly for Fremantle, arrived safely at Batavia in West Java on the 14th. On the quayside to meet *Empire Star* was a contingent of marines and sailors organised by Captain (later Vice-Admiral Sir) Peter Cazalet of HMS *Durban*, which disarmed the army deserters and took them away. The wounded were discharged into HM Hospital Ship *Karapara*, and after some patching-up *Empire Star* sailed for Fremantle herself, and later to Sydney where proper repairs were carried out. Many were the tributes poured on Captain Capon's head, and they are perhaps best summed up by just one of them. 'We had a brilliant captain who got us away', said one of the RAF men. The Captain was awarded the CBE, and sixteen other members of the crew received decorations or commendations. Amongst the latter, for the parts they played in fire-fighting, were the two young cadets.

Eight months after the events described above, *Empire Star*, still under the command of Captain Selwyn Capon but with some new crew members, sailed from Liverpool for North America. She did not sail in convoy but was routed independently because of her speed. On 23 October 1942 she had reached a point some 600 miles north of the Azores. The sky was clear but a strong wind was blowing and the sea was high. Just before 1600 hours she was struck by a torpedo fired from *U-615* (Lieutenant-Commander Kapitzky), the resulting explosion flooding the engine-room and killing four of the men working there. As the ship began to list, Captain Capon assembled the passengers and crew and ordered abandon ship, and in spite of the heavy sea, this was carried out in an orderly manner. Those aboard two of the three boats launched were picked up two days later by HMS *Black Swan*, which was searching for them after receiving the ship's SOS message. The third boat, carrying Captain Capon and some thirty sailors and gunners, was never seen again. Among those to die with his captain was Cadet Perry, then aged sixteen. Chief Officer L Vernon, one of those rescued, later wrote: 'If for any reason a boat got beam on to the sea for two or three successive heavy seas I consider that in the conditions prevailing she could easily have capsized.' That seems the most likely explanation for the loss of Captain Capon's boat.

CHAPTER 14

Empress of Asia

Lieutenant-Colonel James Dean, 125th Anti-Tank Regiment, Royal Artillery, was not a happy man when he found himself appointed Officer Commanding Troops which were due to board the *Empress of Asia* at Bombay on 22 January 1942. His unhappiness had little to do with the fact that the ship was sailing for Singapore, north of which, on mainland Malaya, British Commonwealth troops were suffering badly at the hands of the Japanese. Neither did it have much to do with the outward appearance of the troopship, once the pride of the Canada Pacific Railway Company's (CPR) fleet. Although the rusty and grimy outward aspect was dreadful enough, it was the internal condition of the ship, especially the troop decks, which concerned him. It was bad enough to be sailing into a war situation, which scuttlebutt amongst the military hierarchy ashore seemed to classify as a lost cause, but to ask men to travel there in filthy accommodation which was heaving with cockroaches was a bit too much. The author of the Official Regimental History of the 125th, says, 'what memories the mere mention of that old hulk brings back'.

Dean refused to order his men aboard until he was overruled by the Principal Sea Transport Officer ashore, who was acting under the orders of General Sir Archibald Wavell, the Allied Commander-in-Chief in the area. The 17,000-ton ship, one of the largest coal-burning ships in the world and then nearing her fortieth year, was one of the only four vessels available to load troops and equipment to form Convoy BM12, which must sail the following day.

It was no fault of the ship's master, Captain J Bisset Smith, a Scot from Banffshire, that his ship was in such a sorry state. The ship's war had already been a hard one – she had travelled nearly 47,000 miles since war began. It was not his fault either that his crew in general did not meet the company's usual high standards. It was pretty much a scratch crew. In fact the ship was not a happy one, partly due to the make-up of the crew and partly to the condition she was in. The stokehold gang, which formed nearly a third of the 400-man crew, had given considerable trouble during an earlier voyage between Capetown and Trinidad, according to Tom Pritchard, a junior engineer on board. One watch of stokers on duty had forced the door of the ship's canteen and proceeded to get drunk on the beer stored there and, says Tom, 'the ship gradually slowed down until we were nearly stopped'. On this voyage the stokers had developed a special grievance. Good-quality stoking coal was difficult to come by and the

bunkers were filled with an inferior grade which made an already strenuous job even harder. In a later interview Captain Smith had this to say:

> Well-trained Chinese firemen got the best out of the two coal burners from
> the Pacific fleet, but by the time World War Two broke out there was a real
> dearth of firemen accustomed to coal and after our Chinese firemen re-
> turned home we had to rely on what the Merchant Seaman's Pool could
> scrape up.

This voyage had begun in Liverpool, and trouble started there when seven
men deserted. On the way out, at Freetown, one man had been arrested
and imprisoned. Five men deserted at Durban and when Captain Bisset
Smith sought to land some other troublemakers there, the South African
authorities refused permission for him to do so. Another seaman had
deserted in Bombay itself. No, the *Asia* was not a happy ship at all.

The troops boarded at last and the ship sailed on the 23rd in company
with *Felix Roussel, Devonshire, City of Canterbury* and *Plancius*, their naval
escorts including the cruisers HMS *Exeter* and *Danae*. Only when the ship
was at sea did troops and crew alike learn of their destination and that
knowledge did not make the ship any happier. The stokehold crew
especially, many of whom were Liverpool Irish and, being citizens of
Ireland, officially neutral, did not much fancy being taken into the
Singapore war zone.

The first part of the voyage was uneventful. The convoy sailed south,
entering the South China Sea by way of the Sunda and Banka Straits. It was
on 4 February, the day before the scheduled arrival at Singapore, that the
convoy came under attack by Japanese planes. *Empress of Asia* suffered only
slight damage during that first attack but it was enough for the 'black gang'
(as stokers are called), to down shovels and crowd up on deck. Fifth Engineer Tom Pritchard reports, 'Before the explosion all the firemen had been
shovelling coal but now there was nobody there, only me'. Despite any
extenuating circumstances that existed, this amounted to a mutinous incident, and it is one that became indelibly etched on the minds of some of the
troops on board. Tom Brown, for instance, recalls that the stokers 'were
ordered back down at the point of a revolver'. Another, E Pearlman, wrote,
'When the stokers refused to work the captain asked for volunteers from
amongst us. We had quite a few ex-miners with us and they manned the
fires until the stokers were persuaded to go back to work'.

It must be mentioned here that the situation with the *Empress of Asia*
stokehold crew, the Liverpool Irish amongst them, was unusual. The
majority of Irish nationals who served in British merchant ships during
the war, and there were many of them and they did not have to be there,
displayed exemplary conduct.

The combination of the initial cessation of stoking and the subsequent
amateur efforts of the soldiers caused steam-pressure to drop, and the
ship fell behind the rest of the convoy. Captain Smith was not telling the
whole story when he later reported, 'We had been allotted this position on

account of our steaming difficulties, the ship almost invariably dropping astern of station when fires were being cleaned.'

On the morning of the 5th a black smudge was seen ahead, 'which everyone thought was a cloud – we later found out it was Singapore with a pall of black smoke hanging over it'. Suddenly, Japanese planes again roared into attack. *Felix Rousell* was hit twice and there was some loss of life aboard. However, the planes singled out the laggard for special attention. Soldiers aboard *Empress of Asia* put up a curtain of fire with the ship's guns and with their own small arms, but this did not prevent the ship being hit. One bomb passed through the officers' saloon and exploded somewhere below. That was followed by more hits, and fire took hold in many places. The author of the History of the 125th says that a fire-party made up of off-duty members of the black gang tried to put out one of the fires but due to the low steam pressure only a trickle of water came out of the fire-hoses. 'Had the circumstances not been so serious.' he added, 'we could have appreciated the humour of the situation'. Tom Pritchard says that after this second attack, 'all the firemen had gone again'.

In a great feat of seamanship Captain Smith sailed his blazing ship as close to Singapore as he could, and then ran her ashore on Sultan Shoal. Boats from other ships in the convoy, and tugs, water-boats, and other craft from Singapore itself, rescued many men. The Australian sloop *Yarra* gallantly went alongside the burning vessel and took off over a thousand soldiers and crew members. Due to the efforts of the rescue craft, only 15 soldiers and one crew member – First Radio Officer P L Harkins – of the 3000 souls aboard, lost their lives, although a number of others were wounded or suffered burns.

Three young soldiers were particularly lucky to be saved. A Singapore Police launch under Inspector Frank Pestana, which had rescued many men during the evacuation of the ship, went back during the night after receiving reports that some survivors were still adrift. He found the three clinging to some wreckage. In 1946 Inspector Pestana, who later rose to be a Superintendent of Police in Singapore, was awarded the King's Police Medal for Gallantry for his efforts during the *Empress of Asia* incident. He eventually retired to Western Australia and died there in 1992.

None of the military equipment on board was saved. A few days later the ship was nothing but a burnt-out hulk. The *Empress of Asia* was the only ship carrying troop reinforcements to Singapore to be lost.

By the time Singapore surrendered ten days after the grounding, most of *Empress of Asia*'s officers and many of the deck and engine-room crew, including the stokers, had been posted to other ships and so escaped from the port-city. Before they left most of the crew had been housed in the famous Tanglin Club. The stokers gave trouble even there. 'Having no respect for property', reports Tom Pritchard, 'they were throwing chairs in the beautiful swimming pool and generally making a nuisance of themselves . . . they were shipped out on one of the other [convoy] ships and I can't say I was sorry to see them go.'

Senior Second Engineer Bert Stainton and Tom Pritchard were appointed engineers aboard the small steamer *Ampang*, commanded by a naval officer. They were soon joined by about a dozen of their former shipmates, including Chief Officer Donald Smith. *Ampang* was an oil burner and, as neither engineer had any previous experience with oil engines, the ship had only two speeds during the coming voyage, 'flat out and stop'. *Ampang* managed to reach the river port of Palembang, where she was abandoned. The crew then commandeered a bus and in it, and later on foot, managed to reach a railhead. They were lucky to be able to board, albeit in a goods van, the last train out of the place, and reached the port of Oosthaven in southern Sumatra the following day. They caught a small Dutch vessel for Batavia, and there were taken aboard the Dutch vessel *Marella* and made it safely to Fremantle.

The *Asia* catering staff, almost to a man, were used for orderly and kitchen duties in Singapore hospitals in the last few days before the city fell. They ended up as prisoners of the Japanese. Altogether 143 of the *Asia*'s crew became prisoners of war. One Liverpool-Irish crew member used his status as a neutral to avoid internment and under the alias 'Stephen Early' wrote several anti-British pieces for *Shonan Shimbun*, the Japanese successor to the *Straits Times*. The ship's Purser, Brian Moran from Stratford in London, was appointed Commissariat Officer at Changi, where his conduct, efficiency and integrity under the most difficult conditions made him highly respected. He survived internment and rejoined CPR after the war. He retired in 1966 and died in 1992, aged 86. Captain Bisset Smith was awarded the OBE, and First Officer L H Johnston the MBE, for their efforts to save the ship.

CHAPTER 15

Small Ship, Big Heart

Captain Thomas Wilkinson, who was always called 'Tam', came from Widnes in Lancashire. He was fifty-one years old when his ship *Li Wo* was requisitioned by the Royal Navy as an auxiliary patrol vessel in June 1940. Wilkinson, who never had a day's formal naval training in his life, was retained in command and given the temporary rank of Lieutenant RNR.

The 700 ton, 160 foot long *Li Wo* was built in Hong Kong in 1938 for the Indo China Steam Navigation Company. Designed to operate on the upper reaches of the Yangtze River, she was flat-bottomed and a coal-burner. After requisition she may for a time have been used as a river patrol vessel out of Shanghai, taking the place of one of the British gunboats which had been withdrawn from the area, but by late 1941 she had sailed south and, fitted with an ancient 4-inch gun, two machine-guns, a depth-charge thrower, and with some regular Royal Navy ratings added to her crew, she then operated as a patrol vessel out of Singapore. Although life became more hectic for Tam Wilkinson and his crew after Japan attacked northern Malaya on 8 December 1941, the ship took no part in any aggressive action but instead, carried on patrolling the waters around Singapore Island.

On Friday 13 February 1942, only two days before Singapore surrendered, *Li Wo* received orders to proceed to Batavia in Java. Before sailing she took on extra people which brought her complement up to eighty-four, including some survivors from HMS *Prince of Wales* and *Repulse*, which had been sunk by the Japanese in December. One of those from the latter ship was Chief Petty Officer Charles Rogers, always called 'Lofty'. Lofty was a specialist gunner and was placed in charge of *Li Wo*'s 4-inch gun. He was a professional and not too happy with his lot when he discovered that the ship carried only thirteen rounds for the weapon and that even those were only practice shot.

Having survived four air attacks, one by no less than fifty-two aircraft and during which she had suffered considerable damage, *Li Wo* reached the Java Sea by the 14th. That afternoon two Japanese troop convoys were sighted, escorted by warships including a cruiser and several destroyers. The convoys were, in fact, the spearhead of the Japanese invasion fleet heading for Sumatra.

Tam Wilkinson may not have had any naval training but he had had time to imbibe some naval tradition. On top of that, he was a natural born leader. He called his scratch crew together and told them that rather than try to escape he intended to attack and fight to the last, hoping at the very least to inflict some damage on the enemy. In the words of the writer of the later official citation, 'Lieutenant Wilkinson drew resolute support from the whole ship's company.'

With battle ensigns flying and with thick black smoke belching from her funnel, *Li Wo* closed on the nearest Japanese transport. This action by the lone, small, dirty-looking ship apparently confused the Japanese, for she was able to get in close before opening fire. Under the firm hand of Lofty Rogers, the gun-crew's aim was excellent and by the time all thirteen rounds had been expended, the trooper's superstructure had been wrecked and the ship was on fire.

Rogers afterwards recalled, 'The damaged ship was now approaching *Li Wo* still firing, so the CO decided to ram her. We hit her at top speed amidships and became interlocked, our bows being buckled back.' A machine-gun duel now began, one of *Li Wo*'s which was manned by an RAF flight sergeant being particularly effective.

Wilkinson rang for full astern, and as his ship pulled away from the transport, it came under heavy fire from Japanese warships, including the cruiser. Tam knew his ship well, and using her twin rudders to good effect and despite the bow damage, he handled her superbly as he dodged this way and that for over an hour to avoid the shells. The end was inevitable, however, and after *Li Wo* had received several hits Wilkinson ordered abandon ship. That amateur naval officer, but far from amateur merchant seaman, had led his ship's company into battle and fought it in the highest traditions of the service he knew so precious little about.

Many years later Chief Petty Officer Rogers said, 'The last sight I had of the *Li Wo* as she started on her last voyage to the bottom was something I shall never forget – her ensigns were still flying and the Captain was standing on the bridge; although listing to port, she was still under way. Then, suddenly, she disappeared.'

The Japanese fired on the *Li Wo* survivors in the water, and only one officer, Sub-Lieutenant R G Stanton, and nine men, Lofty Rogers amongst them, were eventually plucked from the water. Tam Wilkinson disappeared with his ship. The ten survivors became prisoners of war and not all survived the Japanese camps. Those that did told the story after the war, and Tam Wilkinson was posthumously mentioned in despatches. A year later, however, he was awarded a posthumous Victoria Cross. Lieutenant Stanton received the DSO. Lofty Rogers was mentioned in despatches. It was the second time for him, for he had received the same for operations on the Malayan coast after *Repulse* had been sunk. He left the Navy in 1950 and died in 1997.

The Japanese admire courage and it is surprising they saw fit to machine-gun the *Li Wo* survivors in the water. That conduct should be compared with the honourable treatment meted out to the survivors from HMS *Peterel* when she was sunk by the Japanese in the Shanghai River on 8 December 1941, the first day of the war with Japan.

Peterel, a small gunboat being used as a communications ship at Shanghai, was lying close to the Japanese cruiser *Izumo* when war began; *Izumo* signalled *Peterel* to surrender, but instead, Lieutenant Stephen Polkinghorn RNR, another merchant seaman, opened fire on the cruiser with his armament, which bore no comparison with the 8-inch and 6-inch guns of her adversary. *Izumo* fired back, blowing the gunboat out of the water. The survivors, including Polkinghorn who was later awarded the DSO, were picked up and treated as heroes by the Japanese, the gunboat's action even being featured in Japanese news bulletins of the time. HMS *Peterel* was the first Royal Navy victim of the Japanese war, HMS *Prince of Wales* and *Repulse* meeting their fates off the coast of Malaya two days later.

CHAPTER 16

Sunk – by a Gentleman

The *City of Cairo* (Ellerman Lines) sailed from Bombay for the United Kingdom in October 1942. It was a voyage the elderly ship had made many times before, but now in wartime she was making the passage via Durban and Cape Town instead of via the Suez Canal. Despite being old the ship was comfortably appointed, especially so for the ninety-odd European passengers on board. Her exterior surfaces might now be painted warship grey, but inside the ship looked much the same as she had when she left the shipyard twenty-seven years earlier. Her mahogany-lined public rooms served to remind everyone of earlier and more peaceful times. If one criticism was voiced by some of the more elderly passengers, it was that the public rooms were on the small side, especially as on this voyage there were twenty rumbustious children on board. In its holds the ship carried cotton, manganese ore, and 100 tons of bullion in the form of 2000 boxes of silver rupees.

In command of the ship, its 155-strong crew, and all else he surveyed, was a forty-six year-old Ellerman Lines veteran, Captain William Rogerson from Liverpool. In a profession in which its leaders, the shipowners, were ever rather sparing in the bestowal of kudos (and consequently a profession in which the giving and receiving of compliments by those further down the chain was never undertaken lightly nor without a great deal of embarrassment), Bill Rogerson was highly regarded. He was now one of Sir John Reeves Ellerman II's senior masters, and if the war permitted, could look forward to one day becoming the Line's senior master.

Even in wartime good masters tend to attract good officers and men, and so it was with Rogerson. His chief officer was Sidney Britt MBE, a rather dapper, self-confident, extroverted man. Britt was an excellent seaman, had a fine singing voice, and possessed all those diplomatic skills necessary for dealing with passengers. The ship's chief engineer was another good man. In fact, there was almost a plethora of good officers on board for, in addition to the ship's own set, there were several more sailing as passengers on their way home to join new ships. Among the comparatively few European crew members who were not officers, were Quartermasters Angus MacDonald and Bob Ironside, both about thirty and both with excellent records. Amongst the catering staff was the able and experienced Jack Edmead, and two stewardesses. One of these was sixty-four year-old Annie Crouch, a Liverpool lady who had retired from the sea some years before and then gone back to get away from the bombing at home. The other stewardess was fifty year-old Ada Taggart, who suffered badly from arthritis. Most of the deck crew, and all of the engine- and boiler-room staff, were Lascars, and there were an additional forty or more Indian seamen on board who were travelling to England to join ships there, bringing the total number of people on board to 313.

Among the passengers was bespectacled, but slim, attractive, and vivacious, Diana Jarman. This girl was to play a brave part in some of the events to come and as her courage is even more remarkable because of the facts that lay behind her presence on the ship, it is necessary to say something of her background. Before her marriage in India two years earlier at the age of nineteen, her surname had been Tyrrell. Her father, Major H C Tyrrell, was second in command of the 2/16th Punjab Regiment, Indian Army, and her husband to be, John Jarman, was a subaltern in the same regiment. Within weeks of the marriage which took place in October 1940, the regiment sailed for Malaya leaving Diana behind in India. Contrary to what the author of a book about the *City of Cairo* has written, when Diana boarded the ship in October 1942, eight months after the fall of Singapore, she was unaware of the fate of either her husband or her father during the Malayan Campaign, for the first lists of prisoners of war in Japanese hands were not forthcoming until well into 1943. In fact, Captain John Jarman had been killed on Singapore Island three days before its surrender to the Japanese, and her father, who had earlier been promoted to Lieutenant-Colonel to take command of the 1st Bahawalpurs, was a prisoner of war. But Diana knew nothing of this and it was this awful lack of information which drove her to take passage to England in order to join her mother there. One imagines that not knowing the fate of her husband and father must have been worse for Diana than if she had known, but she gave little indication to her fellow travellers of the inner torment she must have been suffering. It was not long before she became the darling of the ship. (The name of Captain J D Jarman is engraved on Column 263 in the Kranji War Cemetery, Singapore. Immediately above it is the name Captain P S V Heenan of the same regiment. Captain Patrick Heenan was the 'Singapore traitor', the man who spied for the Japanese and who was largely responsible for the destruction of many British aircraft in the north of Malaya during the first two days of the campaign. He was arrested and sentenced to death. Two days before Singapore surrendered he was taken down to the harbour by military policemen and there shot in the back of the head. The body was then pushed into the sea.)

Another lady passenger with more than a degree of sadness in her past was Mrs Dulcie Kendall. She was travelling home with her three year-old son. Her husband, a railway engineer in Burma, had taken part in a trek of refugees from northern Burma to Assam in India to escape from the advancing Japanese. The trek was made through the disease-ridden and almost impenetrable Chaukkan Pass. Cyril Kendall was one of the many who did not reach safety, and was buried along the way. Dulcie was aware of the fate of her husband.

The ship was in mid-Atlantic, about 480 miles south of the island of St Helena, when at 2030 hours on 6 November, a torpedo from the German submarine *U-68* struck, and the vessel began to settle by the stern. Captain Rogerson rang 'stop engines' and ordered abandon ship. The ship had been plunged into darkness immediately after the torpedo hit, but in the light of fires burning at the seat of the explosion, the evacuation was conducted in a reasonably orderly manner thanks to the many boat-drills that had been held. Seven of the eight ship's boats were safely launched, but one had been damaged and was lying alongside water-logged. Captain Rogerson, Chief Officer Britt, the Chief Radio Officer and about ten others were still aboard the ship when a second torpedo struck home. With his ship now rapidly going down by the stern, Rogerson ordered the group down into the last boat, but it was too late. The ship sank, taking the boat with her, leaving its would-be occupants in the sea and struggling against the enormous suction generated by the sinking vessel. Rogerson, Britt and two others managed to fight back to the surface but the others had disappeared. They were not the only ones in the water, for the blast from the second torpedo had destroyed another boat, tossing its occupants into the sea, amongst them Quartermaster MacDonald and Diana Jarman. Two of the remaining boats moved in to pick the swimming people up.

U-68 came to the surface close by, and the nearest boat was ordered alongside. The submarine captain, Commander Karl Merten, called out for the ship's name and was given it. Merten then asked for the captain and received the stock reply that he had gone down with the ship, which seemed to satisfy him. (Captured masters were often taken aboard submarines for interrogation.) Merten then gave the ship's position and advised that a course of 005 degrees be set for St Helena. 'Goodnight, sorry for sinking you', were his final words before the submarine submerged. Those last words may not have been very helpful but they were gentlemanly and certainly memorable.

At first light Captain Rogerson, who had been picked up by Boat No.5, ordered the others to close on him, and he then took stock of the situation. The survivors, some of whom were injured, numbered 292, which meant that 21 must have gone down with the ship. Each boat was well provisioned, but as in all such situations, it was the water supply that was critical. There was a sextant in one of the boats, but no adequate timepiece, a necessity to correctly work out the longitude. After discussing the available alternatives with his officers, including staying in the vicinity in the hope of rescue arriving in answer to the distress message which had been sent from the ship, Rogerson decided to take the German captain's advice and make north for St Helena. He made an estimate of the number of days needed to reach the island and ordered water to be rationed accordingly. The weight of responsibility lying on Rogerson's shoulders in making the decision to sail north towards a small island that could easily be sailed past without being sighted, was made no lighter by the fact that scattered throughout four of the boats were the twenty children.

In the light of information that came out only after the war, it was as well he did not decide to stay where the ship went down. The ship's radioed distress message had been answered by a station purporting to be the one at Walvis Bay, but it had not been that station at all. The distress message had been intercepted and answered by *U-68*'s radio men using the code letters of the South African station. As far as the British authorities were concerned, the *City of Cairo* was still on her way home.

At first the six boats tried staying together but some were faster sailers than others, Boat No.1 under Chief Officer Britt proving to be the fastest of all. During the first two days his boat was sometimes so far ahead as to be almost out of sight of the others and he had to wait for the others to catch up. This gave Britt the idea that it might be better for him to forge on ahead, reach the island, and send back help for the others, but Captain Rogerson refused permission, partly on the grounds that Britt's boat had no navigation instruments on board apart from a compass. However, on the fourth day, after repeated requests from Britt, Rogerson let him go, a decision that was against his better judgement. Perhaps the Captain was influenced by the first death amongst his charges; a man had fallen overboard during the night in bad weather.

Boat No.1 left the flotilla to a chorus of rather envious farewells from the others. In the boat with Britt were fifty-three people including Angus MacDonald, Bob Ironside who was injured, Jack Edmead, Diana Jarman, and the two stewardesses, Annie Crouch who was also injured and Ada Taggart who was ill. There were no children on board. For the remainder of that day those left behind watched Britt's sail grow smaller and smaller, and by the following morning it was out of sight.

Many tribulations were in store for those in the remaining five boats which, after a few more days, tended to drift away from each other. Suffice it to say that on all of them men and women died and that the children were soon in a piteous state. Dulcie Kendall aboard Boat No.6 with her three year-old son Colin, says she amused him by planning what 'we would do and eat when we reached land, and all the toys I would buy him'. She added, 'he slept a lot'. There were quarrels and some men came to blows. Some of the Lascars and at least one European drank sea-water and became demented. But that was just one side of the coin. Several of the women did splendid work in treating the wounded with the few facilities available, and one Indian seaman was seen giving up his water ration to a child. Just occasionally a rain shower brought some relief from thirst and from the heat.

On the thirteenth day after the sinking, first one boat and then two others, including Captain Rogerson's, were sighted by the British *Clan Alpine* and the survivors taken aboard. They totalled 150 out of the original 166 carried by the three boats, but two more men were to die before the ship reached St Helena. On that same day, and about 150 miles farther south, a fourth boat with 47 from its original complement of 55 still alive, was sighted by Ben Line's *Bendoran*. They were taken to Cape Town, the ship's next port of call. Thankfully, with the rescue of that boat, all twenty children from the *City of Cairo* were safe.

When Sydney Britt took his boat away from the others he estimated he would reach St Helena in five or six days. The boat was overloaded with 54 people and needed continuous bailing, but nevertheless she was a very fast sailer. Britt and Captain Tom McCall, an elderly master mariner with Cable & Wireless who had been on his way home as a passenger, looked after the navigation, and they together with Diana Jarman who proved to be something of a boat-handler, took most of the turns at the tiller. Angus MacDonald was placed in charge of the sails and was stationed in the bows. His fellow quartermaster, Bob Ironside, had seriously injured his back in the sinking, and he and the other sick and injured were looked after the best she could by the ubiquitous Diana. Jack Edmead was in charge of issuing rations. An elderly engine-room serang (petty officer) called Bedruddin Baba proved very reliable in dealing with and encouraging his fellow Lascars.

Within a day or two an elderly Briton died, and to the horror of those on the boat, his body had no sooner been committed to the deep when it was attacked by sharks. By the time the sixth day had passed with no sight of the island, tempers began to fray, especially in the heat of the day. By that time everyone was suffering from thirst and sunstroke. Britt, who was perhaps beginning to rue his decision to sail on ahead, had become more autocratic in his behaviour. (He had no way of knowing, of course, that by that time the flotilla he had left behind had begun to separate anyway.) That night three Lascars died.

They now experienced a period of flat calms during which the sails were lowered and oars shipped. 'We didn't make much headway', Angus MacDonald reported later, 'but the work helped to keep our minds and bodies occupied.' He noted that there were a few Europeans who never gave a helping hand, and that they were the first to fail mentally. The sick Ada Taggart spent most of the time lying down and in consequence her back became a mass of festering sores; the only available treatment was to bathe them in salt water, a task undertaken by Diana Jarman. Ada died on the same day as another elderly European and that night there were three more deaths among the Lascars. MacDonald noted that by that time many people chose to do nothing else but sit all day with their heads on their chests, in complete contrast to Diana who went about helping others as much as she could and 'was always cheerful and bright'. He noted also that at night the Lascars tended to huddle together for warmth and comfort and in doing so sometimes upset the stability of the boat. By the tenth day it was obvious to all that the previously self-confident Britt was suffering grievously from exactly the opposite characteristic, self-doubt, something he had probably never before experienced. He began to disintegrate before their very eyes.

Water was down to only a few day's supply. Annie Crouch who had suffered her injuries bravely, died on the thirteenth day, leaving Diana the only woman on board. The day after that, after laying down in the boat, Second Officer Britt died along with Bob Ironside. Angus Mac-Donald now took charge of the boat, for Captain McCall was already failing and was to die the following day. Having no idea where the boat was in relation to St Helena, MacDonald decided to maintain the present course in the hope of meeting up with a ship.

People were now dying regularly. On the seventeenth night MacDonald awoke from a fitful sleep to find the boat filled with water, for a young European passenger had pulled out the plug. 'He was not in his right mind', reported MacDonald. 'He said, "I'm going to die so we might as well go together."' The young man died along with eight others two days later. At the end of the third week only seven men, MacDonald, Jack Edmead and the tough old serang Bedruddin Baba, amongst them, and Diana Jarman, were left alive. There were only a few drops of water left, for not once during the previous days had they met with any rain. A few days later a dog-fish landed on board, and during his efforts to kill it with an axe, MacDonald gashed his hand. The fish was chopped up and its blood and flesh distributed, but it tasted so foul no one could swallow it. Angus MacDonald's hand festered, and it was Diana who tended the wound.

They were now drifting aimlessly on the ocean, and when three of the men died it took the others almost a whole day to push the bodies over the side. Sometime after that, for all sense of time had been lost, Bedruddin was found unconscious in the bottom of the boat, and on top of all the other afflictions, Diana was suffering from an extremely sore throat. Soon, Bedruddin, described by MacDonald as a grand old man, and a European died, leaving only three survivors. Sick as she was, MacDonald says Diana always managed to force a smile and say that everything would be all right if only it would rain. Then one night it did rain, not for long but long enough for a few pints to be collected in the sail. Three days after that, their thirty-sixth in the boat, the three were picked up by the *Rhakotis*, a German freighter running the Allied blockade. The lifeboat had sailed past St Helena and was 500 miles north-west of it and had been lucky to be spotted, for the *Rhakotis* was in that part of the ocean precisely because it was largely unfrequented.

The ship carried a doctor and the three survivors were well looked after, but it was found that Diana could not swallow food and so had to be fed by injections. After five days the ship's captain told the recuperating men that Diana would die unless the doctor operated on her throat, and asked permission for the operation to be carried out, which they gave. MacDonald and Edmead visited the girl before the operation and found her still smiling though very weak. During the operation that evening Diana Jarman died, her heart being too weak to cope with the anaesthetic. It was then and only then, that Angus MacDonald, a Scotsman of small stature but with a heart that Robert the Bruce might have been proud of, broke down and cried. He was not alone, for Jack Edmead did the same. Diana Jarman was given a military funeral by the Germans in a coffin covered by the Union flag. 'A gallant end to a brave and noble girl', wrote MacDonald.

The adventures of MacDonald and Edmead were not over yet. *Rhakotis* was making for Bordeaux, having sailed from Yokohama ten weeks earlier with a cargo that included 4000 tons of rubber much needed by Germany. On New Year's Day 1943, and not far short of her destination, she fell in with the cruiser HMS *Scylla* and was sunk. Jack Edmead, in one of the ship's lifeboats, ended up on Spanish soil, whilst Angus Mac-Donald aboard another boat was rescued by a U-boat and taken to St Nazaire. (Of 257,770 tons of cargo shipped on blockade-runners to Germany from Japan, only 111,490 tons got through. In the reverse direction, 57,000 tons out of 69,300 tons despatched reached Japanese ports. Some of this traffic was carried by submarines. The German blockade-runners also doubled as supply ships for submarines and Armed Merchant Raiders. During this voyage home *Rhakotis* had met up with the raider *Michel* (also known as No.28) somewhere in the South Atlantic.)

With that rescue by *Rhakotis*, only one of the *City of Cairo* boats remained to be accounted for. This was Boat No.4 under the charge of Third Officer James 'Knocker' Whyte. The smallest of the boats, it had only seventeen persons on board, sixteen men and one woman, an Australian called Margaret Gordon. This boat had early lost touch with the others, and like Boat No 1 sailed past St Helena. On 23 November, the seventeenth day, by which time all ten Asians aboard had died, Whyte decided to head west for the coast of South America, 1500 miles away. It was a big decision for a twenty-five year-old, especially as one or two of the older men on board were inclined to argue against it. But head west they did. One by one the others perished until only Margaret Gordon and Whyte himself were left alive. On the fifty-first day, having sailed to within 80 miles of the American coast, they were rescued by the Brazilian corvette *Caravellas*.

Jack Edmead was repatriated home to England from Spain. He was awarded the BEM and spent several months on a tour of factories organised by the Ministry of Information. He spoke to workers, inspiring them with his story of endurance. He died in 1981. Angus MacDonald became the sole member of *City of Cairo*'s crew to end up at *Milag*. He too was awarded the BEM. He returned to sea after the war before 'beaching' himself and becoming a National Union of Seaman official in Manchester. He died in 1975. Captain Rogerson was awarded the OBE, and after the war did rise to become Ellerman Line's senior master. He died in 1972 and at his own request his ashes were scattered at sea. Margaret Gordon was awarded the BEM and saw the war out as a Wren attached to a Royal Navy group serving in the United States. She returned to Australia after the war. Her sole survivor companion, 'Knocker' Whyte, was awarded the MBE. After convalescence he joined the *City of Pretoria* at New York at the end of February 1943. The ship had a part cargo of munitions. On 4 March she was torpedoed in mid-Atlantic by *U-172*, and blew up. There were no survivors. Dulcie Kendall remarried, becoming Mrs Kup. She says that for several years after the events depicted here, her son Colin used to wake screaming in the night, perhaps a legacy of those dreadful days in the boat. The *City of Cairo* was the last ship sunk by Commander Karl Merten. On returning to base he was promoted and appointed to command a submarine training establishment. After the war he became an executive in the German ship-building industry.

At least two feasibility studies have been made in recent years regarding the possibility of raising the silver coin in *City of Cairo*'s cargo. However, the treasure lies in nearly 3000 fathoms of water, and anyway, perhaps the ship should be left undisturbed as it is in a sense a war grave.

The *City of Cairo* incident was far from being the worst wartime tragedy for the Ellerman Line, for that had happened two years previously, and it also involved children. The *City of Benares*, carrying 191 passengers and 215 crew, sailed from England in September 1940. She was making for Canada and of her passengers about ninety were children being evacuated under a scheme known as 'seavac', with another ten who were travelling privately. Seamen are superstitious lot, at least where their ships are concerned, and it was said that *Benares* had been built from the thirteenth plan at Barclay Curle's yard in 1936, something which did not augur well for the future. On top of that she sailed on what turned out to be her final voyage on Friday 13th, a date no sailor likes to set sail on.

Four days later, at night and in rough weather, the ship was torpedoed by a submarine. Herded by their escorting adults, the children, just as they had been trained to do during many boat drills, went to their lifeboat stations singing, a sound that some survivors have never forgotten. The ship sank in little over half an hour with some boats capsizing as they were launched. In the bitter cold of the North Atlantic, in water-logged boats, many died from exposure during the night. Two hundred and forty-eight people, including seventy-seven children, lost their lives before help in the form of the destroyer HMS *Hurricane* arrived on the scene. At first it was thought that the death roll was far higher, but ten days after the sinking, the destroyer HMS *Anthony*, called to the scene by a Sunderland Flying Boat, rescued forty-five survivors from a lifeboat in charge of a very young Fourth Officer. Six of them were children, and it had been one of them who had spotted the plane.

CHAPTER 17

A Tanker Fights Back

The saga of the tanker *San Demetrio* (Eagle Oil Shipping Company) is well known, for a book and film was made of it. That tanker was part of Convoy HX84, in which the gallant armed merchant cruiser *Jervis Bay* met her end whilst trying to save the convoy from the German pocket battleship *Admiral Scheer*. *San Demetrio* was badly damaged by shellfire and abandoned, but then reboarded by survivors from her crew and sailed back to England. The similar saga of the tanker *Ondina* is not so well known even though it includes an epic sea battle against considerable odds.

Under International Law the armament carried by merchantmen is for self-protection only. Merchant ships are not supposed to instigate warlike action or even use their guns in support of another ship under attack. Such rules, of course, were bent during the Second World War, but possibly never to such good an effect as during the action fought by *Ondina* in the Indian Ocean on 11 November 1942.

Ondina was a Dutch ship carrying twelve Dutch officers and thirty-five Chinese ratings. Her story is included here because she was operated by the British Ministry of War Transport and because at the time of the action she was under orders of the Royal Navy. Furthermore, the Chinese crew members were from Hong Kong and eight of her nine DEMS gunners were either Australian or British. The DEMS men were led by Australian Bert Hammond and they were all highly trained professionals who took pride in keeping the ship's one 4-inch gun, which was sited aft on the poop-deck, in immaculate working condition.

The Japanese 10,000-ton AMC *Hokoku Maru* first came to the attention of the Allies when, operating in tandem with a sister-ship *Aikoku Maru*, she sank the American freighter *Malama* on 2 January 1942 near the Tuamotu Islands in the South Pacific. The two ships, each fitted with six 6-inch guns, two torpedo tubes, and two aircraft, then moved into the Indian Ocean where they doubled as submarine supply ships. On 9 May they captured the Dutch tanker *Genota*, and a month later sank the British *Elysia* (Anchor Line). On 14 July, whilst the Japanese ships were on their way home, the British cargo vessel *Hauraki* became their fourth victim.

On 5 November, about the same time that *Hokoko Maru*, under Commander Imatsato Hirishi, moved once more into the Indian Ocean, this time in consort with the seaplane tender *Kunikawa Maru*, the *Ondina* under Captain Willem Horsman sailed from Fremantle, Western Australia. She was making for the Middle Eastern oil port of Abadan via

Diego Garcia, an island in the Chagos Archipelago. In one of her tanks she carried 250 tons of bagged grain for the island. *Ondina*'s escort as far as Diego Garcia was to be the Indian Navy's 730-ton minesweeper HMIS *Bengal*. A new ship recently built in Australia's Cockatoo Dockyard, she was armed with one 12-pounder and three smaller guns. She was under the command of acting Lieutenant-Commander W J Wilson, RINR; his crew of about seventy were predominately Indians.

At 1145 hours on 11 November, the weather being fine and the sea calm, the lookout aboard *Bengal* sighted a ship on the port bow proceeding their way at high speed. Commander Wilson altered course towards the unknown vessel and as he did so sighted a second one. Wilson directed his tiny ship towards the approaching vessels as his yeoman signalled a challenge. At a range of about 3500 yards, the lead ship, which turned out to be the *Hokoku Maru*, opened fire. Wilson rang for full revolutions and made for the enemy ships, at the same time signalling *Ondina* to escape north-eastward with all speed. At first Captain Horsman complied with the order.

Horsman and his officers watched as *Hokoku* poured shells in *Bengal*'s direction, the minesweeper sometimes disappearing from view amid shell-splashes. Captain Horsman was faced with a quandary. At his ship's maximum 11 knots or thereabouts, there was little chance of escaping the Japanese ships if and when they put paid to the escort, and if he joined in with his gun the Japanese might not give his crew the chance to abandon *Ondina* before sinking her. The sight of *Bengal* bravely firing at the enemy, which was still out of range of her 12-pounder, made up his mind for him, for the leading enemy ship was within range of his own, larger 4-inch gun. Much to the satisfaction of Bert Hammond and his men who were crouched ready and waiting over their gun, Horsman ordered open fire.

Ondina's first two shells bracketed *Hokoku Maru*, the third one striking high up in the bridge superstructure. Aboard *Hokoku*, Commander Imatsato altered course to present a broadside to the interloper, but was too late. A shell from *Ondina* hit the ship aft where her two spotter aircraft were housed. Perhaps the planes had bombs aboard or perhaps ammunition, bombs or torpedoes were stored in the area, but, for whatever reason, the raider's stern suddenly disappeared in a mass of flames. *Ondina*'s crew burst out cheering. Unaware that *Ondina* had joined in, the *Bengal* gunners began to cheer too, but then a shell from *Kunikawa Maru* struck the minesweeper's bow. Wilson now turned his fire on the second raider.

Aboard the burning *Hokoku*, which had come to a stop and was settling by the stern, Commander Imatsato turned all the guns that would bear on the tanker. A shell hit *Ondina*'s mast bringing down the radio aerials, and others struck the bridge and destroyed a lifeboat. Fires broke out. By then the action had become spread over a wide area, and *Bengal* and *Ondina* were out of communication with each other. Aboard the minesweeper, which had been repeatedly hit and was belching smoke, some of it made deliberately as a screen, Wilson decided to draw the *Kunikawa Maru* away from the still-fleeing tanker. His gambit worked, for the Japanese ship gave chase, but several more of its shells found their mark on the minesweeper. From *Ondina*'s bridge it seemed as if the distant *Bengal* was doomed, whilst aboard the minesweeper Wilson thought he had bought the tanker time to escape. *Ondina* continued to fire at *Hokoku Maru* but no more hits were scored, and as it turned out, no more were necessary, for at about 1230 hours, about an hour after the engagement began, a violent explosion rocked the Japanese ship.

The commander of *Kunikawa Maru*, assuming the *Bengal* was finished, now turned his guns on the tanker at a range of about 4000 yards, hitting her with a salvo. *Ondina* fired back until all her ammunition had been expended. With the Japanese ship approaching fast, Captain Horsman now had only one option, one made slightly more palatable in that, remarkably up to that point, no one aboard had been killed or even injured. He stopped engines and ordered two white sheets to be flown from the yardarms. Then he ordered abandon ship.

The white 'flags' had no effect, for the Japanese ship continued to fire. A shell hit the bridge and Horsman fell mortally wounded. As the Chief Officer and Chief Radio Officer between them dragged the Captain towards one of the boats, he died. In under five minutes, and still being fired upon, the remainder of the crew got away from the ship in three lifeboats and two rafts. As the survivors pulled away they had the satisfaction of seeing and hearing another explosion on the *Hokoku Maru*, after which the raider sank. The *Kunikawa* now fired two torpedoes at short range into *Ondina*, and the ship took an ominous 30-degree list to starboard. The Japanese then turned guns on to the lifeboats, raking them with machine-gun fire. Fortunately most of the men in them had guessed what was about to happen and had thrown themselves over the side. The machine-gunning stopped after ten minutes as *Kunikawa* made for the area where the *Hokuko* had disappeared.

Despite the intensity of the hail of machine-gun bullets only two men had been killed and four wounded, although an hour later one of the latter, the Chief Engineer, died from a head wound. Barely had the dead been committed to the deep when *Kunikawa* raced back to fire another torpedo in the direction of *Ondina*. It missed, and this time the Japanese took no notice of the boats and raced off northwards and was soon out of sight.

Chief Officer Maarten Rehwinkel assessed the situation. All three lifeboats had been holed and needed constant bailing and the nearest land, the Cocos Islands, was over 500 miles away. He decided that their best hope would be to reboard the still-floating tanker, which was showing no sign of sinking. After getting back aboard, he and other officers took a quick survey. Despite the list and a few small fires burning here and there, and considering the hammering she had suffered, the ship was in remarkably good condition and the engines were working perfectly. Rehwinkel set about making the vessel as seaworthy as possible. The list was corrected at the expense of making the ship very low in the water. The steering gear had been damaged, so the emergency gear was rigged. The deck fires were extinguished, but just as everyone thought the main work was done, a fire was discovered in the bagged grain cargo and it took several hours to put it out.

At last the ship was ready to make the 1400-mile voyage back to Fremantle, and on the bridge Rehwinkel rang full ahead and set the course. Navigation was going to be difficult as the chronometer had been destroyed, and with shell holes in the hull and a low freeboard he knew that any bad weather could bring disaster.

On the second day Captain Horsman's body was reverently committed to the deep. On the fifth day the ship was spotted by a Catalina aircraft of the Royal Australian Air Force, and a rendezvous was made with a hospital ship which took off the wounded. On the 18th *Ondina*, with her flag at half-mast in honour of the dead, entered Fremantle harbour. On the day before *Ondina*'s safe arrival, HMIS *Bengal* limped into the harbour of Diego Garcia. Although badly damaged she had suffered no casualties.

This unique sea action was an outstanding victory; a small minesweeper and a tanker had taken on two fast and heavily-armed raiders equipped with all modern devices, and had sunk one of them. Despite that, the battle became the subject of an inquiry and some controversy, the Dutch authorities in London wanting to know why *Bengal* had apparently run off leaving her charge to its fate. Perhaps the best way to sum up the course of the battle is to say that *Bengal* thought the *Ondina* had got away, whilst those aboard *Ondina* thought the minesweeper had been lost; the Japanese for their part thought that both Allied ships had succumbed.

Lieutenant-Commander Wilson was awarded the DSO and eight of his Indian crew also received decorations. Captain Willem Horsman received a posthumous mention in despatches, and other awards went to members of his crew and to the DEMS gunners, including a DSM to Ah Kong, a Chinese quartermaster who had stayed at the wheel throughout the action. Captain Horsman's honour seems a rather niggardly one. It is likely that the British Admiralty took some exception to the fact that he had seen fit to disobey Commander Wilson's orders, though it is clear that had he not done so, the battle would almost certainly have ended in a Japanese victory.

Kunikawa Maru picked up all but seventy-six of the *Hokoko*'s 350-man crew, but not her commander, who went down with his ship. The commander of the *Kunikawa* was not amongst those Japanese naval officers brought to trial after the war for war crimes, though he should have been for firing on life-boats.

That sea battle was not the end of *Ondina*'s direct involvement in warlike activities. After repairs she again voyaged to Abadan, and this time got there and back safely. Then, in September 1943 she became the refuelling ship off the north coast of Australia for the small boat involved in Operation 'Jaywick', the attack by a Special Operations Executive group on Japanese shipping in Singapore Harbour. The boat involved was the *Krait*, a captured Japanese fishing vessel (now on view at Sydney's Maritime Museum). After hiding *Krait* among the Rhio Islands to the south of Singapore, the Anglo-Australian group led by Captain (later Lieutenant-Colonel) Ivor Lyon of the Gordon Highlanders used folboats to reach Singapore and blew up 50,000 tons of enemy shipping with limpet mines. The attackers then escaped, and back aboard *Krait* safely reached Australia.

Ondina's battle was an epic for a merchant ship but there was another engagement during the Second World War that was even more so. The ship involved was American, and the story is included here as a tribute to the men of the American Merchant Marine who operated side by side with their British colleagues from December 1941 onwards, and because the engagement directly avenged the sinking of two British ships.

The Liberty ship *Stephen Hopkins*, Captain Paul Buck, was in mid-South Atlantic bound for Bahia from Cape Town when, on 27 September 1942, she fell in with the German raider *Stier* in consort with the blockade runner *Tannenfels*. The weather was misty and *Stephen Hopkins* was within two miles of the German ships, which were lying stopped for maintenance purposes, before there was a mutual sighting. *Stier*, with a trained naval crew, six 5.9-inch guns, six smaller ones, two torpedo tubes, not to mention two Arado seaplanes, cleared for action. For want of a better expression, so did *Stephen Hopkins* with her single 4-inch gun manned by US naval reservists. The American had only one thing going for her; the *Stier* was at very close range and it might be possible for the 4-inch to score some hits. That is exactly what happened.

The Liberty ship's first salvo wrecked the raider's steering gear, cut off the oil supply to the engines, and put the torpedo tubes out of action. The ferocious action, in which both ships scored repeated hits, lasted for twenty-two minutes and when the firing ceased both ships were lying close together and heavily damaged, just like a sea battle of old. Inside the hour *Stephen Hopkins* sank, taking 42 members of the crew with her. A boat carrying 15 survivors reached the Brazilian coast thirty-one days later. Aboard *Stier*, fire was blazing out of control and endangering the torpedo store, so Captain Gerlach gave orders to abandon ship. Just as he and his men were boarding *Tannenfels*, which being unarmed had taken no part in the engagement, *Stier* blew up and sank.

Stier was the last German commerce raider sent to sea, and the least successful. In a four-month career she sank only three ships prior to the engagement with *Stephen Hopkins*, the Panamanian tanker *Stanvac Calcutta*, and two British freighters *Gemstone* and *Dalhousie*. Now, she herself had been sunk by a merchantman armed with but a single gun. The embarrassment and stigma attached to that must have been too much to bear. Captain Gerlach saw fit to lie to the authorities when he reached Germany, for his Official War Diary stated that the American freighter carried 'six 4.7-inch guns and smaller weapons'. Or perhaps he was not lying. Maybe it had seemed like that.

CHAPTER 18

Poon Lim's Marathon

The seventy-day open-boat ordeal of Tapscott and Widdicombe, the two seamen from *Anglo Saxon* in late 1940 (see Chapter 3), was far from being the record for such acts of endurance during the Second World War.

Ben Line's *Benlomond*, Captain J Maul, was on an unescorted voyage in ballast from Cape Town to Paramaribo in Dutch Guiana in November 1942. By the 23rd the ship had reached a position some 30 miles north of the equator and less than 250 miles from the nearest point on the Brazilian coast when, at 1145 hours, she was hit by a torpedo in the engine-room and water flooded in so fast that the ship sank within a few minutes; so quickly did she go under that there was no time for any boats to be lowered.

A Chinese steward called Poon Lim leapt overboard as the ship sank and, clutching a lifejacket, managed to swim clear. He spotted one of the ship's life-rafts which had broken adrift as the ship sank – as they are designed to do – and, in fear of sharks, hastily swam over to it and clambered aboard. By standing on its deck he was able to see another raft and was close enough to recognise the five men on it as the ship's gunners, but as neither raft had any means of propulsion, not even a paddle, no contact could be made. Poon Lim watched helplessly as the other raft drifted away eastward. It was never seen again. It was not long after that when he sighted a surfaced submarine in the distance and assumed it to be the one which had sunk his ship. From his description of the colours painted on her side, the submarine was later identified as Italian. No one aboard the submarine took any notice of him and soon it was out of sight. Poon Lim was now on his own and completely at the mercy of wind and current.

On the raft he found some provisions, a small first-aid kit, some distress flares, and a quantity of water, all in containers let into the deck. From the very beginning he rationed himself strictly. As it turned out, there was no need to eke out his fresh water supply as the raft was in an area of frequent torrential rainstorms and he was able to refill the water tank regularly by funnelling rain into it with the aid of his life-jacket. On the second or third night Poon sighted the silhouette of a ship and fired off distress flares. They worked perfectly and Poon was convinced they must have been seen by the lookout aboard the blacked-out ship which, however, proceeded on its way. Maybe the flares were seen, but war is war and perhaps those aboard the ship thought the flares to be an enemy ruse.

Over the following days he was to sight several more ships, but nothing he did succeeded in attracting their attention.

Poon augmented the provisions on the raft by occasionally catching fish and seagulls. The raft had a life-line around it and he managed to detach part of it and fashion a fishing line from its strands. The hook was more difficult to manufacture, it taking him days to gouge out one of the galvanised nails which held the raft together, and then bending it into a hook shape with his teeth. For bait he made a paste from ship's biscuit, allowing it to dry hard in the sun before using it. The first fish he caught was small and he cut it up to use as bait for larger ones. The monotony of a raw fish diet was relieved on the rare occasions he managed to catch gulls when they alighted on the raft, and sometimes even on his shoulders.

The days turned into weeks. For most of the daylight hours he was exposed to the direct rays of the equatorial sun from which his clothing, which soon rotted into shreds, afforded him little protection. The raft had no bulwark for him to shelter behind and the combined effect of sun, wind and salt caused his skin to become a mass of blisters. But Poon continued to hope, and fight to stay alive. Around the 100th day, and for about a week, no rain came, and he ran desperately short of water. But he fought through until at last it rained again. On the 120th day, or there-abouts, a plane flew low over the raft. It rocked its wings and Poon's spirits soared for he knew he had been sighted and thought he was safe at last. But it was not over for him yet. Although a search for the raft was made by Brazilian aircraft in the general area reported by the first plane, no further sighting was made.

Poon was so weak by this time he could not sit up, let alone fish. When on the 133rd day he was finally found by Brazilian fishermen, he was nothing but a scarcely breathing bundle of bones in the last stages of starvation. He was landed at Belem and was cared for at the Beneficiencia Portuguese Hospital there. The British Consul visited him and Poon reported the loss of *Benlomond*, which up to then had been listed as missing. To the amazement of the doctors and nurses, in a little over a fortnight Poon Lim's body had regained its former condition. From the crew of forty-seven, Poon was the only survivor. During the 133 days of his ordeal the raft had drifted to within 10 miles of the Brazilian coast, covering an average of 1.8 nautical miles a day. He was later awarded the MBE.

The experience of that brave Chinese sailor is amongst the most remarkable stories of survival at sea. However, neither in length of time adrift nor in distance travelled was Poon's marathon a record for the Second World War. That record is held by two other Asian seamen.

Fort Longueuil (Chamber's Castle Line) commanded by Captain C G Edwards, sailed from Barry to the Middle East with a cargo of ammunition at the end of August 1943. After discharging her cargo at Kossier and bunkering at Aden, she sailed from the latter port on 10 September for

Newcastle, New South Wales. Nine days later, when south of the Chagos Archipelago, she was torpedoed by a Japanese submarine. The ship sank in minutes and only seven survivors managed to scramble aboard a life-raft. The submarine surfaced and came alongside, only for the captain to call out he could do nothing for them. He then left the survivors to their fate.

The raft carried rations for only two days and one by one the men died until by the twenty-fifth day only two remained alive. Both were Indians and their names were Mohamed Aftab and Thakur Miah. The pair drifted with the ocean currents for 3400 miles, subsisting on fish and any rain-water they managed to catch. On 1 February 1944, after no less than 135 days on the raft, they drifted ashore on the island of Sumatra. Natives found the sailors, who were in a dreadful condition, and handed them over to the Japanese Occupation Forces. They nearly met their deaths at the hands of the Japanese military. Since their conquest of Malaya, the Dutch East Indies and Burma, the Japanese had sent Indians trained in subversion, and who were antagonistic to British rule in their homeland, back into India as spies. It was probably this that at first caused the Japanese to treat the two men as spies coming in the opposite direction; they just did not believe that men could have stayed alive on a raft for that length of time. The Japanese had second thoughts later and the two Indians ended up in a prisoner of war camp. Eighteen months later, at the end of the war, they were freed by British troops, flown to Rangoon and from thence repatriated home.

CHAPTER 19

The Merchant Navy George Cross

Far from all Merchant Navy deck officers in the 1930s began their careers as cadets, midshipmen or apprentices, for many came up through the ranks. The organisation of the Merchant Navy was diverse, and officers were free to move around from company to company – providing there was a job available – with the result that an officer's background was sometimes unknown to his fellows, but even when it was known that an officer had once been a deckhand, the fact was not held against him. This attitude was in contrast to that of the Royal Navy of those days. Such officers were much less common in that service and the process of rising to officer status from the ranks was rather disparagingly described as 'coming up through the hawse-hole'. (It had not always been like that in the Royal Navy. In the seventeenth century more than a few captains and admirals rose from the ranks. Admiral Sir Christopher Myngs, the first of two County of Norfolk-bred admirals to fall mortally wounded on the deck of a ship called the *Victory*, was one of them, and so was his distant relative, Admiral Sir Cloudesley Shovell. Such officers whose rise was due to merit and experience were known as 'tarpaulin captains' to distinguish them from others who had gained rank through patronage, and it was not a disparaging term.)

George Preston Stronach was a merchant officer who rose from the ranks. Born in the seaside hamlet of Portgordon near Lossiemouth on the Moray Firth, he first went to sea as a Deck Boy in 1932. He rose through Ordinary Seaman to Able Seaman before taking the examination for Second Mate at Glasgow in 1937. Passing with flying colours, he then joined Clan Line as a junior officer. By March 1940 he had the necessary sea-time in to sit the Mate's examination and, having passed, joined the trampship firm of H Hogarth & Sons. This company was known as 'Hungry' Hogarths. (This was not at all a unique epithet, for several other lines whose names began with 'H' were also so honoured; sailors have always been given to the bestowal of alliterative adjectives on shipping lines, adjectives which appropriately summed up their experiences with them, especially in the gastronomic field.) Hogarths was one of the larger tramp organisations, and most of their ships were named *Baron* something-or-other. George Stronach's first company ship was *Baron Stranraer* which he joined as Second Officer, being promoted to Chief Officer a year later. In March 1942 he came ashore to sit for, and pass, his Master's examination. Up to that time his wartime experiences had been largely uneventful.

In August that year Stronach joined *Ocean Voyager* at Liverpool in the rank of Chief Officer. The ship had been built by a yard in Richmond, California for Britain's Ministry of War Transport, and was only three months old. She was managed by Hogarths and commanded by Captain D Mackellar. Loaded with military cargo, she sailed for the Middle East, proceeding via Takoradi, Cape Town, Suez and Port Said to the Palestinian port of Haifa. The British Eighth Army was then fighting its way westward in North Africa, and Tripoli was one of its major supply ports. *Ocean Voyager* became one of the ships servicing the route to that port from Alexandria, and her cargo on the voyage which began during the second week of March 1943 included a highly dangerous mix of 3000 tons of aviation spirit in drums and almost the same tonnage of ammunition. *Ocean Voyager* arrived at Tripoli on the 16th and anchored in the Roads close to the breakwater. Discharging into barges and other miscellaneous craft began almost immediately; for the Eighth Army were preparing to attack the Afrika Korp's Mareth Line less than 200 miles to the west, and the cargo was required urgently.

On the 19th, with about half the cargo unloaded, three flights of German bombers and torpedo aircraft attacked the port. So low did some of the aircraft fly in that the blast from one of several bombs which struck *Ocean Voyager* caused one of the planes to hit the ship's foremast and crash alongside in flames. Other aircraft came in with cannon fire and very soon most parts of the ship were enveloped in flames. The bridge superstructure collapsed into No.2 hold, and it was probably then that Captain Mackellar lost his life.

At the time of the attack George Stronach was in his cabin. He made a run for the lower bridge but the blast from a bomb blew him unconscious under one of the lifeboats. Coming to a few minutes later, he found the air filled with exploding tracer bullets from the cargo. Some of the crew had already got away in boats, but fifteen men were trapped in the fore part of the ship. Braving fire and exploding ammunition, Stronach made his way forward, found the men and after leading them back along the deck, saw them safely down into a boat which was lying alongside.

In the knowledge that Captain Mackellar was almost certainly dead and that therefore he himself was now in command, Stronach was not about to leave the ship until he was sure no one else was left alive. Before beginning a search he lowered a boat, making it fast alongside. He coupled a fire-hose to the mains and used the trickle of water coming from it to wet himself down. The fact that there was any water at all in the mains was due to the valiant efforts of Second Engineer Hezekiah Hotham who, down in the engine-room and working without lights, was struggling to keep the pumps going.

Dragging the hose after him, George Stronach made for the ruins of the officer's accommodation. He found the wounded and badly burned Second Officer, dragged him clear and lowered him into the boat alongside. By then some of the accommodation bulkheads were glowing red-hot, but

Stronach went back anyway. He found the injured Chief Engineer jammed in a porthole from an effort to escape, and pulled him clear. Hotham
had now come up on deck, and with his help and that of a DEMS gunner
who until then had been busy firing an Oerlikon gun at the attacking
planes, the injured man was lowered into the boat, the gunner following
him down. Stronach had still not finished, and neither had Hotham who
returned to the engine-room to attempt to get more pressure on the
pumps. Stronach found one of the radio officers with a broken leg and
other injuries, and carried him to the ship's rail, from which he hailed a
nearby raft and lowered him down on to it.

The ship was now a blazing inferno and the air was filled with shrapnel,
but that did not put Stronach off from attempting to make a final tour of
the ship. After calling Hotham back up on deck, he managed to reach
No.3 hold in which bombs were stowed, but was driven back by fierce
flames. As he made his way back amidships he stumbled across the unconscious body of an engine-room greaser and dragged him over to the
ship's rail and towards the waiting Hotham. As Hotham clambered down
a ladder which was hanging over the side, Stronach strapped a life-jacket
on the greaser and lowered him to water level. Only then, after having
spent well over an hour on the ship since the time of the first attack, did
Stronach jump overboard. He swam to an empty raft and paddled it back
to pick the other two men up. Pulling clear, they were rescued shortly by a
naval pinnace. It was not long after that when *Ocean Voyager* blew up.
Captain Mackellar and five of his crew had been lost, a death toll that
would have been far higher had it not been for the extraordinary bravery
of two men.

Eight months later the *London Gazette* carried the news that George
Stronach had been awarded the George Cross and Hezekiah Hotham, the
George Medal. Stronach had suffered a serious back injury during the
rescue operation, and was hospitalised for some months before being sent
home. He never went back to sea and in late 1943 became a Clyde Pilot.
For a number of years before his retirement in 1979 he was the Pilot
Master on that river.

In mid-1942, well before the *Ocean Voyager* incident, a high-powered
committee headed by Sir Horace Wilson, Permanent Secretary to His
Majesty's Treasury, had looked into the subject of awarding the George
Cross to deserving merchant ships, much as earlier in that year, on 16th
April, the award had been made to the island of Malta. Though well
disposed towards the idea, the Committee recorded there were certain
snags, the biggest one being that the most deserving ships, 'the noblest' as
the report called them, 'are often lost'. It was decided that the cons
outweighed the pros and that it was better to carry on the present system
of giving a series of awards to representative individuals who had shown
special gallantry on a ship. Had the 'corporate' George Cross proposal
been agreed, it is likely that crew members' Discharge Books would have
been endorsed with the award against the ship's name.

CHAPTER 20

The Horror of the Centaur

Centaur, requisitioned in January 1943 and commissioned two months later as an Australian hospital ship, was, at only 3222 tons, a little on the small side for such a role. She had been built in Greenock nineteen years earlier to join two other vessels on Blue Funnel's feeder service between Western Australian ports and Singapore, linking up at the latter place with the Line's main service to and from Far Eastern ports. Like all the Company's ships she was registered in Liverpool, a port she visited only once in her long life, and that before her maiden voyage took her out east never to return. She was designed to carry general cargo and, in upper and lower 'tween decks, fitted with removable stalls, livestock, which walked aboard through side-ports. These livestock decks, easily convertible into wards, together with the ship's shallow draft which made her ideal for use in the bays of New Guinea where Australian troops were fighting, were probably the main reasons for her selection as a hospital ship. Another reason might have been her thicker than usual hull plating, which had permitted her to take the ground safely in such West Australian ports as Broome and Derby which dry out at low water, and might prove useful in picking up wounded men from beaches.

Until she was requisitioned the ship had seen little of the war apart from one incident late in 1941 when she was involved in the search for survivors from the German raider *Kormoran*. On 19th November that year off the west coast of Australia, the raider had been sunk in a battle with the cruiser HMAS *Sydney*, but not before damaging the cruiser so badly that it had later disappeared with all hands. (No news of the actual fate of *Sydney* has ever come to light though rumours persist that a Japanese submarine assisted *Kormoran* in the battle nearly three weeks before Japan entered the war. There is, however, no firm evidence of this.) A few days later some *Kormoran* survivors were picked up by the troopship *Aquitania* and others by the Shell tanker *Trocas*. Another boatload reached the Australian coast to the north of Carnarvon on the same day. The search for more survivors – and for the *Sydney* – then went into high gear as every available aircraft took to the skies and all ships in the vicinity were put on the alert. On the 26th November a lifeboat was sighted from *Centaur* crammed with sixty survivors from the German ship, including its captain, Commander Theodor Detmers. Fearing that such a large contingent of the enemy might attempt to take over the ship, the survivors were not permitted to board but instead the lifeboat was taken in tow. On the next day the German boat was swamped and the survivors were transferred into two of *Centaur*'s own boats and late that afternoon the ship and its tows safely reached the port of Carnarvon.

In its new occupation as a hospital ship *Centaur* was still officered by Blue Funnel men under the command of Captain George Murray. The forty-four year-old Murray had been born in Buckie, Banffshire, and he and his wife had recently made their home in Australia. A stocky, shy sort of man, he walked with a distinct roll. When he laughed, which tended to be rather infrequently, he did so in a way that was recognisable as his very own even from a cable or two away. As ever, Blue Funnel only employed the best, and Murray had the reputation of being an exceptional seaman and navigator. The Chief Engineer was also a Scot. Ernie Smith had been *Centaur*'s very first Third Engineer, and since then had served on other company ships before rejoining *Centaur* in charge of the engine-room. Chief Officer Harry Lamble was a Devonian from Kingsbridge. A bachelor of thirty-one, he had recently been stepping out with a WAAF officer. Also unmarried at that time was Second Officer Richard Gordon Rippon, a twenty-nine year-old Yorkshireman from Whitby. He came from a family with a tradition of seafaring, for his father had been a master mariner. Rippon had served on the ship for a couple of years, originally as Third Officer, and now he was looking forward to being appointed Chief Officer as Lamble was due to be posted to another ship. The ship's present Third Officer was Ernie 'Monty' Banks, of about the same age as Rippon. He had been born in South Africa although his mother now resided in Bristol. Having already survived being torpedoed three times, Monty must have been pleased when *Centaur* was converted into an hospital ship, which supposedly made her immune from attack. Apart from the officers the ship's original crew had been Asians. Their places had now been taken mainly by Australians and Britons, although there were also a Swede, a Finn, an Icelander, a Norwegian, and a Maltese amongst them. The crew was now seventy-four strong.

The neutral Swiss had earlier in the year, and in accordance with that part of the Hague Convention applicable to hospital ships, been requested to inform all enemy countries (Germany, Italy, Hungary, Finland, Romania and Bulgaria in the west, and Japan and Thailand in the east) of the ship's new role. She made her initial mercy voyage in April, bringing back to Australia 200 wounded Australian and American soldiers from Port Moresby.

On 12 May 1943 *Centaur* sailed from Sydney on its second mission to Port Moresby. In addition to the crew she carried 52 men and 12 nursing sisters, who together comprised the ship's medical staff, and 193 members of the 2/12th Field Ambulance. Also aboard for this voyage, which was routed inside the Great Barrier Reef, was Captain Richard 'Jock' Salt, one of that select band of experienced seamen who made up the Torres Strait Pilotage Service and who knew the waters of northeastern Australia as they knew the lines on the palms of their hands. At sixty-seven, Salt was already past retirement age but had been persuaded to stay on because of the increased burdens of war. Altogether there were 332 souls on board when the ship sailed.

For the ship's crew the first, and as always very busy, day of a voyage had already slipped into the dull peace of familiar routine by late on the 13th. The shakedown part of the voyage over, and secure behind the protection afforded the ship by international convention, everyone from captain down to deck boy had quickly settled into that dreamlike state of sameness that all seamen know so well. By the early hours of the 14th the ship was steaming north about 30 miles off the Stradbroke Islands on the west coast of Australia, islands that together with another called Moreton a few miles to the north guard the entrance to the river on which the city of Brisbane lies. That night the citizens of the Queensland capital lay soundly in their beds in the comforting knowledge that the nearest war front lay in New Guinea 1300 miles to the north. Though the city was one of the main bases in the Allied South-west Pacific Area, and though it provided the headquarters for about two dozen Allied intelligence agencies, it was a long way from any fighting. No one could have guessed that one of the war's most horrific acts of aggression was about to take place on their maritime doorstep.

Centaur presented an unusual sight for wartime at sea, for she was ablaze with light. Arc lights lit up her white hull with its wide green band interspersed with large red crosses – three on each side – together with its assigned identification number, 47, on either side of the bows, all strictly in accordance with the international conventions for such ships of mercy. An enemy vessel sighting her could have been in no doubt of her status; she was a non-combatant merchant ship and therefore sailed with immunity.

The night was clear and the sea slight as towards the end of his midnight to 0400 watch Second Officer Gordon Rippon used a running fix to find the ship's position and prick it off on the chart (a method used by navigators to find the ship's position when only one position line is available. In this case Rippon used a bearing of a shore light he had taken earlier.) At 0400 hours he would be relieved by Chief Officer Lamble and he was looking forward to handing over the bridge, for so well lit was the ship it caused eye-strain to rake the night horizon above the reflected glare of the lights.

Cruising on the surface and inshore of *Centaur*'s track at that fateful hour was the Japanese submarine *I-177* under forty-one year-old Lieutenant-Commander Nakagawa Hajime. Nakagawa must have been an unhappy man. Since sailing from the Japanese Naval Base at Truk in the Caroline Islands he had sunk only one ship, the 8724-ton *Limerick*, not exactly a large haul for five weeks at sea. Soon it would be necessary to return to base and he would have to face the shame of returning with most of his torpedoes unfired. On top of that, he had much to make up for. In 1939 the submarine he then commanded had rammed and sunk another

Japanese submarine in the Bungo Strait, drowning eighty-one of its crew. For nearly two years he had been in the dog-house and made to do hated shore duties. Now back with a sea command he ached to make a name for himself.

At 0410 hours one of two torpedoes fired from *I-177* slammed into *Centaur*. (A soldier who happened to be on deck saw the other pass astern.) It struck the ship on the port side just forward of the bridge, the blast tearing through the engine-room and the oil tanks. Within seconds the oil vapourised and exploded with devastating effect. A fireball roared fore and aft through the 'tween decks which, acting like wind tunnels, sucked fire into every compartment. A gigantic flame accompanied by a noise like thunder also hit upwards in the direction of the bridge and the accommodation which lay under it. Everyone on duty in the engine-room must have died instantly, and as the engines disintegrated the ship began to slow. The sea pouring through the huge hole in the side must have finished off anyone in the vicinity who had survived the initial fireball. On deck it was raining burning oil and in less than a minute there were fires burning everywhere. The bows of the ship began to dip and only three minutes after the torpedo struck she heeled to starboard before diving down into the depths. It is perhaps surprising that anyone survived those three minutes of hell, but many did.

Pilot Jock Salt came awake to the explosion and managed to fight through fire to the deck by throwing a wet blanket over himself. Even so, his face and hands were badly burned by the time he was suddenly confronted by a torrent of water which lifted him bodily over the side. The explosion also wakened Chief Engineer Ernie Smith, who tore out of his cabin to bang frantically on the door of his next door neighbour, Fourth Engineer Maurice Cairnie. The pair managed to reach the deck only by putting their shoulders to a jammed door. They parted there, Smith making for the emergency dynamo room situated near the engine-room casing, and Cairnie making for his lifeboat station. A sea swept Smith overboard before he had gone a few yards.

Second Officer Gordon Rippon had just that minute undressed and settled in his bunk when the explosion came. In a letter he wrote afterwards to his father he said:

> . . . there was a most almighty crash and I was picking myself up from the floor. I got up and looked out of the door of my room which was near the bridge on the boat deck and saw a sight I will never forget, and which has since been flashing through my mind hundreds of times. The ship was way down by the head. All the forepart was one vast sheet of flames, and it was raining drops of burning oil. At first I thought I was cut off but I grabbed my life jacket and dashed outside.

He found the boats on the port side smashed beyond recognition, and so ran round to the starboard side where he found Captain Murray, Chief Officer Lamble and some stewards fighting to free the two boats on that side. The group were joined there by Fourth Engineer Cairnie and others. Lamble was in agony; he had been out on the wing of the bridge at the time of the explosion and had taken the upward blast of fire full in the face. As a wall of water rushed towards the group, Rippon and Cairnie threw themselves clear of the ship after calling for the others to follow them. Rippon wrote:

> I learned later that Captain Murray, Chief Officer Lamble and two doctors had been clinging to a raft which had sunk under them because the drums had been pierced. [The raft in question was one of the type supported by drums. The drums were supposed to be packed with kapok and then sealed, but this work had not been carried out in the dockyard.]

It is known for certain that three of the twelve nursing sisters managed to reach the deck where they fell in with the CO Troops, Lieutenant-Colonel Clem Manson, who directed them to jump with him from the rail. Only one of group survived. Sister Ellen Savage found herself sucked down by the sinking ship, but after sustaining serious injuries from striking a part of the ship underwater, she then shot to the surface 'very breathless from the ordeal', as she later put it. She had been saved by her life jacket. A fourth nursing sister, Mary McFarlane, may also have made it into the sea. It may have been she who was heard screaming in the water during the night, but by the morning there was no sign of her. Right aft in the ship, Swedish bosun Gustav Brandin tried to organise the release of some life-rafts. Seconds before the end he yelled out 'Every man for himself!', before diving over the side himself. He was another one who was not around in the morning

No-one knows how many of those on board made it safely into the water and clear of the ship before it sank. Gordon Rippon later estimated it to be about 200. Whatever the number was, most were either naked or half-naked, and suffering from burns and other injuries. They were struggling to stay afloat in a sea covered with oil, which mercifully was not on fire. As eyes grew accustomed to the dark most swam over to nearby pieces of debris, hatchboards, an upturned and damaged lifeboat, or to the wheelhouse roof which had somehow survived the conflagration. A large raft had floated clear and was soon filled with survivors, with others clinging to its grab-lines. One of those aboard the raft was Third Officer Monty Banks, having now survived his fourth torpedoing. Some smaller rafts, mostly damaged, also bobbed to the surface, and were soon filled. The injured Sister Savage was found and assisted aboard a piece of wreckage by Private Tom Malcolm.

The awful silence which hung over the scene was punctured every now and then by screams and agonised cries as some survivors were taken by sharks. Others, perhaps badly injured or without lifebelts, were just unable to keep afloat. By first light those that were left were scattered about an oil-slick spread over an area of about two square miles. The largest concentration of about forty were either on or clinging to the large raft, or lying on the nearby wheelhouse roof, or clinging to the upturned boat. Another thirty or so were more widely spread in smaller groups. Dotted here and there were solitary men, each clinging to his own piece of debris. There may have been more survivors at that time but if so they were out of sight of the main bunch.

Rippon, one of those astride the wheelhouse roof, as the most senior surviving deck officer began to take charge. He yelled out for the separated groups to paddle towards each other, to use whatever lay at hand to give motive power. Soon the raft, the upturned boat and the wheelhouse roof were lashed together. One of the ship's stewards, twenty year-old Jim Watterston from Bassendean, Western Australia, volunteered to swim across with a rope to the improvised raft on which lay Sister Savage and her soldier saviour, and that done it was hauled over to the large raft on to which Sister Savage was transferred. She was more than pleased to see that Dr Leslie Outridge of the 2/12th Field Ambulance was aboard complete with a medical kit, although she made no mention of her own internal injuries. It was soon after Watterston's brave swim that the first shark of the morning was seen.

Few of the survivors were in anything but a bad way. Most had swallowed oil which brought on fits of vomiting; the oil had also got into their eyes. Many had burns, others had suffered abrasions and bad bruising. Everyone, even those aboard the raft, which was so overloaded as to be half-submerged, was suffering from hypothermia and various degrees of shock. Dr Outridge, badly burned himself, together with Sister Savage, set about doing what they could for those in their immediate vicinity, for it was impossible to move around much on the crowded raft.

Some emergency rations and about two gallons of water were saved from the wrecked lifeboat and placed in charge of Sister Savage. The lifeboat lockers also gave up some signal flares. Rippon ordered that the available rations be issued to last for four days, for he guessed that there had been no time for any distress message to be sent from the ship, although there was no way to know for sure as none of the ship's three radio officers appeared to be among the survivors. It was therefore a matter of waiting until they were either found accidentally or the authorities ashore realised the ship was missing and instituted a proper search. The waiting game was made worse by the knowledge that land lay only a few miles over the western horizon.

The weather that day was typical for the season and though the warmth of the early morning sun was at first welcomed by the cold and wet survivors, as it rose higher in the sky it brought severe discomfort to those with burns. Occasional showers brought some relief but also brought back the chills. It was in mid-morning when spirits were raised as a plane, which Rippon identified as a Catalina flying boat, was seen, but despite the firing of flares it flew unheeding on its way. To add to the general dejection, more and more sharks were circling the area and seemed to be growing bolder as they nudged against the rafts. At midday a tanker was sighted only five miles to seaward, but she too did not sight the flares.

Throughout the day more survivors on makeshift rafts paddled over to join the main group. In an endeavour to keep everyone's spirits up, Sister Savage organised sing-songs in between doing what she could for the injured. Another ship was sighted towards the end of the afternoon, by which time several more planes had flown over. As dusk fell it brought with it the realisation that now no rescue would be possible until the morrow, and perhaps not even then.

That night Rippon and Banks oversaw a position-swapping roster so that all who could do so had a turn at occupying the safest places. It was during the night and as she was accidentally jostled when someone moved, that the true extent of Sister Savage's injuries became known; she had kept them to herself until then. Also during that long, cold night, Army Ambulance Driver Jack Walder, the most badly burned of the survivors, died. There was a discussion about what to do with the body and Sister Savage's view that it must be kept until the morning and then given a proper sea burial prevailed. At dawn Walder was committed to the deep.

After the brief ceremony, the morning was much like the previous one as the ship's officers and Sister Savage strove to keep up morale. Time seemed to crawl by. Midday passed and then early in the afternoon an aircraft was spotted flying much lower than those of the previous day. A flare was lit and suddenly the prayers of those on the rafts were answered, for the aircraft altered course to fly directly overhead. It was an RAAF Avro Anson from Lowood Air Base out on an anti-submarine reconnaissance mission, and the last thing the pilot had expected to come across was an area of ocean seemingly littered with makeshift rafts from which people were waving madly up at him. The plane came in low, the pilot signalling by lamp that he would bring help, before flying off north-westward in the direction of an American destroyer only a few miles away and engaged in escorting a single merchant vessel. In fact, a vigilant lookout aboard the USS *Mugford* had already sighted the flare, and, ordering his charge to proceed north on its own, the destroyer's captain, Lieutenant-Commander Howard Corey, brought his crew to action stations, turned his ship and raced at full speed in the direction of the flare. Inside two hours *Mugford* had rescued sixty-four survivors, the oldest amongst them being Captain Salt, and the youngest, sixteen year-old Ordinary Seaman Robert Westwood. After that Corey quartered the area but although much debris was sighted, no other survivors were found. Subsequent searches of the area by other ships hastily sent out from Brisbane also failed to find anyone else. A total of 268 people from the ship, including 11 women and another sixteen year-old lad, Deck Boy David Abbot, had met their deaths either at the time of the sinking or in its aftermath.

It was Commander Corey's radio message to the Naval Officer in Charge, Brisbane, that he was engaged in picking up survivors from the Hospital Ship *Centaur* which provided officialdom ashore with the first indication of the tragedy. By the time *Mugford* reached its berth at Brisbane a little before midnight, preparations for receiving the survivors were well in hand.

As soon as the news was released, newspapers all over the world headlined the sinking of the hospital ship with such words and phrases as 'barbarism', 'murder at sea', and 'a crime to repay'. The *Melbourne Herald* called it 'A Foul Atrocity At Sea', while the *Liverpool Echo*, in the home port of Blue Funnel, borrowed the phrase used by the Allied Supreme Commander South-west Pacific, General MacArthur, and described the incident as 'Limitless Savagery'. A leader in London's *Daily Telegraph* said it was one of the many foul outrages that were a disgrace to Japanese arms. As it was, the incident would probably have had even greater publicity had it not been vying for headlines with the contemporary RAF Dambuster raids on the Ruhr.

On 15 May, the day after the sinking of *Centaur*, and either by a remarkable coincidence of timing or in what could have been an attempt to head off international outrage over the incident, Radio Berlin, quoting Japanese sources, broadcast a protest against an American air attack on a Japanese hospital ship which had taken place at Rabaul three weeks earlier.

At the end of May, Australian Prime Minister Curtin issued a strongly-worded note of protest about the sinking of the *Centaur*, which was relayed to the Japanese through Swiss channels. He called it a wanton act which disregarded international law and the principles of common humanity, and demanded punishment for those involved. The protest did not exactly fall on deaf ears, for after a delay of several months Tokyo rejected it, stating that after investigation there were no facts that justified the Australian allegations that a Japanese submarine had been involved. In the meantime the Japanese had made their own official counter-protest about Allied attacks on no less than six of their hospital ships. To be fair, after General MacArthur ordered an investigation into the six allegations, two were found to have some justification. MacArthur himself put forward the theory that *Centaur* may have been sunk in retaliation for the attack on, and damage to, the hospital ship *Ural Maru* at Rabaul on 3 April 1943 though his aircrews had reported that the ship was not carrying any of the required markings. (When the *Ural Maru* finally met her end off the Philippines on 27 September 1944 by a torpedo from the US submarine *Flasher*, she was being used as a troop transport and not a hospital ship.)

The actual circumstances surrounding the decision to sink *Centaur* will probably never be known. A discovery by the Allied Translation and Intelligence Service after the war of a secret order No. 442 by the Japanese Imperial General Headquarters, sent out on 10 January 1942, may be relevant. The translation reads:

> Naturally the rules of international law dealing with hospital ships will be respected. However, it has become known that the enemy (especially Britain and the Netherlands) had resorted in desperation to utilising the immunity of these ships for the escape of important personages. Upon sighting an enemy hospital ship, therefore, an inspection will be made and, if any suspicious persons are aboard, they will be detained. Every effort will be made to uncover and put a stop to illegal actions of this kind.

Maybe that signal was all the justification Lieutenant-Commander Nakagawa had needed for his actions.

Another possible reason for the attack has been mooted. It revolves around the question of whether under international law the carriage of the men and equipment of the 2/12th Field Ambulance to New Guinea effectively changed the ship's status to that of a troop carrier. There were more than a few Japanese agents operating in Sydney, and maybe information about the boarding of the unit was relayed to Tokyo. Gordon Rippon once wrote: 'Probably the kindest reason for the sinking is that the Japanese submarine had honestly thought that the Field Ambulance Unit were ordinary combat troops and had acted accordingly.' It should be noted however, that at no time did the Japanese use this excuse for sinking the vessel, preferring to maintain the fiction that they had not been responsible.

The Japanese submarine *I-177* which sank the hospital ship was herself sunk by the US destroyer escort *Samuel B Miles* on 3 October 1944 north of Palau. She was then under the command of Lieutenant-Commander Watanabe Katsuji, and was lost with all hands. Her previous captain, Nakagawa, will feature again later in this book.

Gordon Rippon, whose efforts in keeping the survivors together received considerable praise in the Australian Press, was repatriated to England and spent some months training seamen at the Outward Bound School before returning to sea with Blue Funnel. He went on to become a master with the company, serving over twenty years in that capacity. In 1963 he married the lady who was serving as ship's surgeon on his ship. He retired in 1974 and died at Whitby, Yorkshire in September 1996 at the age of 82. Monty Banks, the born survivor, who was also praised by the Press, became a pilot in the port of Durban and died there in 1987. Chief Engineer Ernie Smith retired from the sea in 1967; having long since taken up permanent residence in Australia, he died there twenty years later. Pilot 'Jock' Salt eventually recovered from his burns although an ankle injury also sustained in the incident was to worry him for the remainder of his life. The voyage on the *Centaur* was in fact his last. For her courage and fortitude in the *Centaur* incident, Sister Ellen Savage was awarded the George Medal in 1944. The citation stated that although suffering from severe injuries herself, she displayed great heroism during thirty-four hours on the raft. She died in 1985 on Anzac Day.

A stained-glass memorial window to those who died on the ship was unveiled at the Repatriation General Hospital, Concord, New South

Wales in May 1990, and in December 1992 the Australian Returned Services League opened the Centaur Memorial Home at Caloundra, north of Brisbane. On 14 May 1993, the 50th anniversary of the sinking, the Centaur Memorial Stone was unveiled at Point Danger on the Queensland coast near Coolangatta. Robert Westwood, who at sixteen had been the youngest survivor from the ship, was amongst nine survivors to attend the ceremony. Australia Post issued a special stamp to coincide with the event.

Centaur was not the only hospital ship sunk by the enemy during the war. Three were lost during operations off Dieppe and Dunkirk in May/June 1940, and *Ramb IV* was bombed and sunk in the Mediterranean off Tobruk on 10th May 1942. She was carrying 269 sick and wounded when German aircraft roared in. The ship's Chief Engineer reported:

> The ship had her big awnings up bearing the Red Cross in addition to the usual markings. One bomb struck B ward and caused a great fire. By the time it was extinguished nothing was left but white ashes; even the iron bedsteads had been consumed. Just one tin hat lay there. We kept the ship's head to the wind to prevent the flames spreading . . . We estimated that about 180 of the wounded were burned to death.

Others Allied hospital ships to be lost were *Talamba, Newfoundland* and *St David* during the Italian campaign, and the *Amsterdam* off Normandy in August 1944.

CHAPTER 21

The Bari Poison Gas Disaster

One of the best-kept secrets of the Second World War, at least until December 1943, was the fact that the Allies kept stocks of poison gas close to most front lines so that they were available for use if required. They were there for retaliatory purposes, for it was feared that Germany might emulate its First World War use of chemical weapons. In the Far East it was known that Japan had used such methods on many occasions during its war with China, one such incident having resulted in the deaths, or maiming, of 1600 Chinese soldiers in 1937.

In Germany's case, Allied concern over this matter grew as the German Army was pressed back on the various European fronts; it was thought the enemy might use gas as a weapon of last resort. Earlier in the war there had been no need for the Germans even to consider its use, for gas is more suited to conditions of static trench warfare than to rapid *blitzkrieg* tactics in which its use would have slowed down advances. It certainly was not required, for example, when German tanks struck through the Low Countries and into France in 1940. On the other hand it might have made military sense for the Germans to use it at Dunkirk, but they did not do so. By that time Hitler was hoping for a peace treaty with Britain and the best way not to get one would have been to have gassed British soldiers on the beaches, not to mention the effect any such action would have had on world, and especially American, public opinion.

In fact, after Dunkirk when Britain stood alone in that desperate summer of 1940, it was the British who mooted the use of gas. General Sir John Dill, Chief of the Imperial General Staff, put forward a proposal that if German troops invaded Britain, mustard gas should be used against them. Though Dill's memorandum had a very restricted circulation, it nevertheless met with considerable opposition. The main point made by opponents of the scheme was that Britain would lose the moral high ground by doing so. Dill withdrew his memorandum, only to find that the views he had expressed had the support of Winston Churchill who in his own words was 'prepared to go to all lengths' to beat off an invasion, and it is therefore likely that gas would have been used by the British had the Germans implemented their invasion plans in 1940. Although morally reprehensible, its use would have been understandable by a country with its back to the wall. Later in the war the Allies attributed the same kind of thinking to the Germans.

Even in far-off Malaya, Britain held stocks of gas for use in the event the Japanese used it first. During the Malayan Campaign, December 1941 to February 1942, there were several reports of Japanese use of chemical weapons, but the incidents were of a minor nature and no retaliatory action was considered. At the time of the Japanese invasion of Malaya the stock of 25-pounder mustard gas shells held by the British Army there amounted to 11,800 rounds. On top of that, the RAF held a stock of 500 × 250lb and 4000 × 30lb mustard gas bombs, in addition to 300 × 500lb 'refill tanks' for the Smoke Curtain Installations, or SCI, which were normally used for laying smoke-screens from the air (a simple change of nozzle converted the tanks into gas-laying contraptions). All this deadly stuff had been shipped east in British merchant ships, the first consignment arriving in Singapore aboard *Medon* on 4 September 1941, the second on *Silver Beech* two days later. So secret was the movement of these cargoes that only the ships' captains and chief officers and the army specialists who sailed with them knew what it was they were carrying; this ignorance no doubt allowed crew members to sleep more soundly in their bunks. The ships' cargo manifests listed the gas as 'Chem Y', the 'Y' standing for 'Yperite' from Ypres where the Germans first used this type of gas in 1915. In the last few days before Singapore fell to the enemy, the task of getting rid of the gas stocks took on major proportions. Cables from London urged that it be shipped out because other theatres of war were short of such supplies, but there was no available ship on which to load it. It could not just be left where it was, for if the Japanese found it, the propaganda value of the discovery would have been enormous. There was only one other alternative. With Japanese shells flying overhead making the operation extremely hazardous for those involved, men from the British and Indian Armies laboured frantically to load it aboard lighters from which it was dumped in the deepest part of Keppel Harbour.

Churchill was never to lose his willingness to authorise the use of gas under certain circumstances, although by 1941 it 'had been accepted that we [Britain] should not initiate the use of gas unless it suited our book to do so during the invasion [of Europe]'. As late as 27 March 1943, in a signed minute to his military advisor, General Ismay, to pass on to the Chiefs-of-Staff Committee, Churchill wrote:

> In the event of the Germans using gas on the Russians, my declaration of last year of course stands. We shall retaliate by drenching the German cities with gas on the largest possible scale. We must expect their counter-measures. Is everything in readiness for this contingency both ways?
>
> It is possible that another warning like I gave last year might check them off at the last minute, but we must be ready to strike and make good any threat we utter with the utmost promptitude and severity.

The secrecy surrounding the global movement of this type of cargo did not end with keeping it from the notice of most ships' crew members, as had happened in Malaya. Few people on shore in any theatre of war were let in on the secret, for had the stockpiling become known to the enemy it might have been used by them as an excuse to initiate gas warfare, and furthermore there was the danger of the stocks being deliberately attacked by the enemy. The degree of secrecy surrounding chemical weaponry, under which only the senior commander in an area and a few members of his staff were in the know, was to have horrific consequences at the Italian port of Bari in early December 1943.

Unlike Churchill, President Roosevelt found the very idea of chemical warfare particularly repellent. Nevertheless, having the Chinese experience in mind, and out of fear that the Japanese might one day unleash gas warfare against the United States, the President was prevailed upon to set in motion a gas production programme, even before America was in the war. Not only that, from the winter of 1940, twelve months before Pearl Harbor, America began supplying Britain with about 200 tons of phosgene gas every month, all shipped in foreign bottoms to preserve the image of American neutrality.

The United States also formed an elite group of chemical warfare specialists. One of them was Lieutenant Howard Beckstrom, a member of Army 701 Chemical Maintenance Company based at Baltimore, Maryland. His particular expertise was in the transportation of the end product, and in November 1943 Beckstrom and his five-man team received orders to board the American 7100-ton Liberty ship *John Harvey* at Baltimore to supervise the loading and subsequent ocean transportation of 2000 M47AI 100lb mustard gas bombs. The shipment was carried in the ship's 'tween decks, as a small part of the ship's total cargo destined for Italy.

The United States has always tended to improve on industrial processes imported from abroad, but that was not so with poison gas, perhaps because no one concerned had any heart for the job. Instead the Americans used a cheap and speedy method to manufacture mustard gas which produced a rather inferior end product, so inferior that amongst the comparatively few in the know, it was notorious for its instability. Beckstrom and his men must have been exceedingly brave, for throughout the month-long voyage to Bari via Sicily the 'tween decks in which the bombs were stowed had to be kept well ventilated, and each bomb casing regularly checked for signs of leakage and corrosion. Whether any leaky ones were found and if so what happened to them, is not known, but as the Singapore experience shows, the sea provides a handy repository.

It is likely that Captain Elvin Knowles, a veteran of Arctic convoys to Murmansk and now in command of *John Harvey*, knew at least something about the special nature of part of his cargo. He would hardly have allowed six soldiers to mooch around the 'tween decks of his ship without demanding some sort of explanation. However, when on 28 November his ship arrived at Bari, a port on the eastern side of Italy just north of that country's 'heel', only to find it crowded with Allied shipping, he made no use of the knowledge he probably possessed to demand priority unloading and neither, it seems, did Lieutenant Beckstrom. The entire matter had to be kept hush-hush and any sign of queue-jumping might have set tongues wagging. So it came about that Captain Knowles' ship was ordered alongside Pier 29, there to wait its turn in the queue. It was still waiting on 2 December.

That day there were over thirty Allied ships in Bari harbour, twenty-five of them being cargo ships. Seven of those flew the Red Ensign. *Testbank* (Bank Line), under the command of Captain Herbert Jones of Leigh-on-Sea, was carrying ammunition and for safety reasons was berthed alongside the outer mole astern of the American *John L Motley*, which had a similar cargo. *Testbank* had a crew of seventy-five, about two-thirds of them from India. The three youngest members of the crew were the apprentices, seventeen year-old David Carr, and Peter Green and Joseph Wheatley who were both a year younger. *Fort Athabaska* (J & C Harrison Ltd) was a new ship not long off the stocks and under the command of Captain Walter Cook of Cardiff. Of her forty-odd crew, three were under eighteen, Cadets Geoffrey Lewis from Monmouth and Anthony Williams from Blantyre, Nyasaland, and Ordinary Seaman Henry Shead from London. Other British merchant ships lying alongside the wharves were *Devon Coast*, *Crista*, *Fort Lajoie*, and *Brittany Coast*, whilst lying at moorings was *Lars Kruse*, a requisitioned ship under the management of Lambert Brothers of London. (*Lars Kruse* has previously been mentioned in this book as having taken part in a Murmansk convoy.) She had arrived that very day from Barletta, a small port farther along the Italian coast, loaded with a cargo of aviation spirit in drums.

The ubiquity of the Liberty ship at that time in the war is indicated by the fact that of the seven American merchant ships at Bari, no less than six were of that type. In addition to *John Harvey*, the others with exactly the same silhouettes were *John L Motley*, *John Bascombe*, *Joseph Wheeler*, *Samuel J Tilden* and the *Lyman Abbott*. The seventh American ship was the tanker *Aroostook*, loaded with 19,000 barrels of high octane gasoline. The other merchant ships in port were four Norwegian, two Polish, one Dutch, and four Italians. (By that time Italy had converted to the Allied side.) A number of Allied warships were also in the harbour.

By 2 December the Allied front line in Italy was well north of the port, so far north in fact that on that very day Air Marshal Sir Arthur Coningham, Commander Allied Tactical Air Forces in Italy, saw fit to announce at a press conference that the Allies had total air supremacy over southern Italy. 'Maori' Coningham – although Australian-born he had served at Gallipoli with the New Zealand Canterbury Mounted Rifles, hence the nickname – then went further. He would consider it a personal affront and insult, he said, if the *Luftwaffe* attempted any significant action in his area. Late that evening he must have wished he had eaten those words for by then he had been affronted by the worst Allied port disaster from enemy air action since Pearl Harbor.

At 1930 hours a hundred German bombers came roaring in from seaward. So crowded was Bari harbour that there was little need for the air crews to waste much time taking aim. When the aircraft flew off twenty minutes later they had sunk no less than seventeen ships and badly damaged another eight. The American ammunition ship *John L Motley* received a direct hit and exploded, taking the nearby *Testbank* with her. *Fort Athabaska* also got a direct hit and blew up. Alongside another berth, *Devon Coast* was ablaze and sinking. The American Liberty ship *John Bascombe* was a blazing wreck. All round the port there were fires and explosions. The tanker *Aroostook* blew up, the blast from it causing windows in houses many miles inland to shatter. Gasoline from the tanker mixed with aviation spirit from *Lars Kruse*, which had sunk after a direct hit, forming a highly dangerous mixture on the surface of the water, a mixture that was soon to become even more lethal. It has been estimated that around the harbour and in the adjacent town about a thousand people were killed during the air-raid itself. As it turned out, they were the lucky ones, for later some of the living must have come to envy the dead.

The *John Harvey* had also taken a direct hit and was well on fire though still afloat as the German planes left the scene. At the later Official Inquiry it was suggested that Captain Knowles, perhaps on the advice of Lieutenant Beckstrom, had made an effort to scuttle his ship, but no one could be sure because Knowles, Lieutenant Beckstrom and all five men of his gas team, the only ones around who knew what the ship was carrying, had lost their lives along with every other member of the crew. What is known is that very soon the ship was blown apart by an explosion which ejected her deadly cargo over the harbour and town. Some of the mustard gas was burning, whilst some evaporated to rise into the night sky, there to mix with the smoke from many fires. The contents of other bombs leaked into the sea to form a deadly cocktail with the gasoline and aviation spirit already floating there. Mustard gas smells much like garlic and an onion-like stench hung everywhere, but there was no one left alive to recognise it for what it was.

All over the harbour survivors from stricken and burning ships had taken to lifeboats, whilst many others were in the water clinging to the life-lines of rafts or hanging on to pieces of floating debris. Over their heads hung a deadly cloud and not only were they breathing in mustard gas fumes, but much, much worse, many were swimming in a solution of the stuff. Rescue teams hauled men from the harbour and rushed them to hospital where doctors and nurses had their work cut out to cope with hundreds of casualties. During the rescue process, many rescuers became contaminated themselves. The medics, having no knowledge of *John Harvey*'s cargo, assumed they were dealing with cases of exposure, aggravated by 'ordinary' burns and by the effects of immersion in oil, and acted accordingly. Survivors were wrapped in warm blankets to await their turn to be examined, cleaned up and treated, and all the while beneath the blankets the solution was taking its deadly course.

Over the next day or two 75 of the 600 or so gas victims died, and others had lost their sight. Yet others, suffering from what had been taken for first-degree burns, were shedding vast stretches of skin. Some had lost all their body hair. In many victims the worst effect was around the genital area, with penis and scrotum swollen to several times their normal size. All were in terrible pain. In Bari town similar cases had developed among the civilian population. It was later estimated that over a thousand civilians died, while many others had fled inland. The few ships that had not been badly damaged in the raid hurriedly left the burning port, some of them plucking survivors from the water as they went. The destroyer USS *Bistera* plucked thirty men from the sea before making south for the port of Taranto. By the time the ship arrived there she was in the gravest peril for, from both direct and indirect contamination, many of her crew, including every deck officer, had gone blind and were suffering from other effects of poison gas.

On 7 December, Lieutenant-Colonel Stewart Alexander, the Consultant in Chemical Warfare Medicine attached to General Eisenhower's HQ in North Africa, flew in and confirmed that the victims were suffering from mustard gas poisoning. As victim after victim died from the symptoms, scientists from Porton Down, England's chemical and biological warfare establishment, and from Edgewood Arsenal, Maryland, the American equivalent, began arriving at Bari. According to Colonel Alexander's report, pathological specimens of forty 'representative cases' were despatched to those centres for microscopic examination and study. Whether this meant, as one author has suggested, that forty bodies were sent back, is not known. What can be inferred is that the disaster had presented scientists with a never-to-be-repeated opportunity for research. As the proverb goes, 'it's an ill wind that blows nobody any good.'

When news of the disaster had first reached General Eisenhower's headquarters, panic had reigned for it was not known whether or not the Germans had initiated a gas attack. When the truth came out, the panic remained but took off at a tangent. If the Germans discovered what had happened, might not they use it as an excuse for initiating gas warfare anyway? An attempt was made to localise the matter and keep it under wraps. The order went out that all deaths must be attributed 'to burns due to enemy action'. The attempt at secrecy failed, for too many people were involved including civilians the military had little control over; and had not a ship from Bari arrived at another port with its crew in a dreadful state? None of that stopped Winston Churchill saying, in answer to a question asked in the House of Commons, that he 'did not believe there were any mustard gas casualties at Bari on the night of 2nd December 1943'.

It was soon clear that there was no chance of covering the matter up from anyone, the Germans included. In February 1944, within two months of the disaster, and in order to take the heat out of the situation, the Allied Combined Chiefs of Staff issued a communiqué stating it was not Allied policy to use gas unless the Axis did so first.

Of *Testbank*'s crew, seventy lost their lives. The names of the forty-four Indian crew members from that ship who died are inscribed on War Memorials in Bombay and Chittagong. The body of Captain Jones lies buried in the War Cemetery at Bari. The ship's three young apprentices were not among the bare handful of survivors. Their bodies were never found and their names are inscribed on the Merchant Navy and Fishing Fleet Memorial at Tower Hill, London. The names of the naval gunners who died can be found on either the Portsmouth or Plymouth Naval Memorials. It was a similar story with *Fort Athabaska*, for thirty-nine of the crew lost their lives. Captain Cook's body lies in the cemetery at Bari not far away from that of Captain Jones, and the names of the three youngest members of the crew are inscribed at Tower Hill.

Casualties were not nearly so high aboard the other two British ships sunk in the harbour, *Lars Kruse* and *Devon Coast*. However, others who died aboard the damaged *Crista, Fort Lajoie*, and *Brittany Coast* brought the total of British seamen to die in the disaster up to 118. The number of American casualties was higher, and there were casualties on other Allied ships, the Norwegian *Lom*, for example, losing seven members of its crew.

Not all those who lost their lives at Bari died from the effects of gas, of course. But those that did have left a sort of legacy, over and above the fact that their names are engraved on memorials and gravestones in scattered parts of the world. An important lesson was learned from the disaster for very soon after it, Allied High Command issued a directive that the presence of chemical warfare weapons in his area must be notified to the Chief Military Medical Officer concerned, in order that his staff could be immediately informed in the event of another such occurrence.

On 2 January 1944, Allied HQ in Algiers issued this confirmation of an earlier instruction regarding the documentation of the Bari gas deaths.

Following nomenclature will be used for record purposes.
(A) Skin infections and burns – enemy action.
(B) Lung and other complications, bronchitis etc. – enemy action.
(C) Death, shock, haemorrhages etc. – enemy action.
(D) Injuries to eyes – enemy action.
Considered these terms will adequately support future claims by those injured for disability pensions, etc.

Most of the gas shells which had been dumped in Singapore Harbour in February 1942 were recovered by British Army salvage teams after the war, but not all. Over succeeding years several of the weapons were found washed up on nearby beaches. One senior British Army officer who made his home in Singapore after the war, recently wrote: 'I would never go swimming from any of the beaches in that part of Singapore.' The Singapore salvage operation begs a question. What happened to the shells that were recovered which by that time must have been in an extremely unstable state? It seems likely they were transported out to sea and dumped again. There is an area marked on charts as an 'Ammunition

Dumping Ground' about fifty nautical miles east of Horsburgh Light-house at the South China Sea end of the Singapore Strait. This author knows from personal experience that at least up to 1957, British LSTs (Landing Ships Tank), based at Singapore, were being used to convey unwanted ammunition to that dumping ground. On one occasion, a metal container dumped there went off like a small depth charge. The crew of LST *Frederick Clover* had plenty of freshly-killed fish to eat that day.

A ship built in 1917 as the *Glennevis* (Furness Withy & Company) was requisitioned by the Ministry of War Transport during the war. She was renamed *Botlea* and placed under the management of Reardon Smith & Sons. In December 1945, it being deemed that the old ship was worth only her scrap value, she was loaded with gas shells and taken out into the Atlantic and scuttled. As has been said previously, the sea makes a handy repository.

CHAPTER 22

Japanese Atrocities against Merchant Seamen

The horrors of the 'unlimited warfare' campaign waged by submarines during the First World War caused the Big Five naval powers (the United States, Great Britain, France, Italy and Japan), to include the famous Article 22 in the Naval Treaty signed in London in 1930. It provided that:

(1) In action against merchant ships submarines must conform to the rules of International Law to which surface vessels are subject.
(2) In particular, except in the case of persistent refusal to stop on being duly summoned, or of active resistance to visit and search, warships, whether surface vessel or submarine may not sink or render incapable of navigation a merchant vessel without having first placed passengers, crew and ship's papers in a place of safety. For this purpose the ship's boats are not regarded as a place of safety, unless the safety of the passengers and crew is assured in the existing sea and weather conditions, by proximity of land, or the presence of another vessel which is in position to take them aboard.

Another clause in the Treaty ensured that Article 22 remained binding without time limit even after the Treaty itself was allowed to expire on the last day of 1936. It should be noted that Germany was not a signatory to the Treaty. However, as one of the signatories, Article 22 was still binding upon Japan when that country entered the Second World War in December 1941. Furthermore, Japan had confirmed that obligation when in November 1936 she signed a protocol in London acknowledging that the provisions of the London Treaty relating to submarines still applied. No country, Axis or Allied, kept strictly to the Article 22 provisions during the war. However, it pays to be on the winning side, and it was only the Axis nations who were called to account for transgressions against it in 1945.

The only known case of a German *submarine* atrocity against survivors occurred on 13 March 1944 when the Greek steamer *Peleus* (Nereus Steam Navigation Company), three days out of Freetown bound for Buenos Aires, was torpedoed and sunk by *U-852*. The U-boat subsequently surfaced and rammed and machine-gunned the ship's boats. One of the boats with three survivors and two dead men on board was picked up thirty-eight days later by the Portuguese *Alexandre Silva*, and so the story was

out. After the war *U-852*'s commander, Heinz Eck, and two of his
officers, were sentenced to death and other members of the crew received long terms of imprisonment. (The case of Captain von
Rucktenschell of the German surface raider *Widder* has already been
mentioned in Chapter 3.)

Eck's behaviour should be compared with that of Commander
Wilhelm Kleinschmidt of *U-111* when he sank *Cingalese Prince* (Furness
Withy) in the Central Atlantic on 20 September 1941. Kleinschmidt
surfaced and provided the seventeen survivors on four linked rafts with
provisions and sailing directions. Twelve days later the survivors, led by
Chief Engineer P H Wilson, were picked up by a Spanish ship. On 4
October, only three days after that rescue, *U-111* was sunk in an engagement with the British Armed Trawler *Lady Shirley*. There were forty-five
survivors from the submarine but sadly, Commander Kleinschmidt was
not amongst them.

Throughout 1940/1941 German U-boats did their utmost to cut British
supply routes, whilst the British fought with might and main to keep
them open. At times it was a close run thing for Britain. Then Japan's
attack on Pearl Harbor in December 1941 brought America into the war,
and Hitler was not slow to realise that this provided the Allies with an
almost inexhaustible ship-building capacity. One way to tackle this shipping preponderance, he decided, was to ensure a lack of suitable crews,
and he issued instructions that crews should no longer be rescued, but
instead should be exterminated. It is fortunate indeed that many of Admiral Dönitz's U-boat commanders chose to ignore the latter part of the
order, and sometimes the former part too. The captains of most German
armed raiders also disregarded the instruction.

Early in 1942, about a month after Japan entered the war, Hitler held
talks with Japanese Ambassador Oshima Hiroshi in Berlin, and the fate
of captured merchant sailors was among the many matters discussed.
General Oshima, who had previously been Japan's military attaché in
Germany, heartily agreed with the extermination policy and passed the
Fuhrer's observations to Tokyo, adding his own endorsement of them. As
throughout the war Oshima's messages from Berlin to Tokyo, which were
sent in diplomatic code, were systematically being intercepted *and
deciphered and read concurrently*, by Allied code-breakers, the Allies were
aware of this change in policy.

There is little doubt that Admiral Dönitz was personally opposed to the
policy of extermination. Before September 1942 he did nothing much to
dissuade his U-boat commanders from aiding survivors in spite of the
Fuhrer's orders. However, on the 12th of that month an incident occurred
which caused him to issue his Standing Order No.154, which read:

> Rescue no one and take no one on board. Do not concern yourselves with
> the ship's boats. Weather conditions and the proximity of land are of no
> account. We must be hard in this war.

The incident which provided the *fons et origo* for Dönitz's order concerned the Cunard liner *Laconia*; in fact, Order No.154 came to be called the '*Laconia* Order'.

Laconia, of 19,965 tons and under the command of Captain R Sharpe, was requisitioned as a troopship during the war. On 12 September 1942 the ship was about 500 miles south of Cape Palmas on the West African coast, homeward bound from Suez via the Cape. In addition to her large crew of 692, she carried 766 passengers including families of British colonial civil servants, together with 1793 Italian prisoners of war. That day she was sighted by Commander Werner Hartenstein of *U-156*, and torpedoed.

Hartenstein surfaced as the ship sank and began plucking survivors from the shark-infested waters. From some of the first taken aboard his craft Hartenstein learned about the Italians and without hesitation began broadcasting in English, asking all ships in the vicinity to proceed at once to the rescue, and assuring them they would not be attacked. Those transmissions augmented *Laconia*'s own SOS messages. Hartenstein had thus initiated what could have become one of the great humanitarian stories of the war had it been allowed to run its course.

Commander Hartenstein radioed Admiral Dönitz about the action he had taken and Donitz answered by instructing two other U-boats in the area, *U-506* (Lieutenant-Commander Wurdemann) and *U-507* (Commander Schacht) to join in the rescue. Also soon on the scene was the Italian submarine *Cappellini* (Lieutenant-Commander Revedin). Through diplomatic channels Dönitz requested the help of the Vichy-French navy based at Dakar and Casablanca, and the cruiser *Gloire*, the sloop *Dumont D'Urville*, and the minesweeper *Annamite* were ordered to sea from those ports. When *Laconia*'s SOS was received at Freetown, the British merchant ship *Empire Haven* was immediately despatched to the scene, as was the AMC *Corinthian* from Takoradi. Up to that point everything was happening in the very best traditions of the sea.

The United States 1st Composite Air Squadron on Ascension Island, about 500 miles south-west of the incident, apparently received *U-156*'s message in garbled form, and was not informed of the rescue operation being led by U-boats. The squadron was asked to supply air escort for the British ships, and a Liberator bomber belonging to the USAAF 343rd Bombardment Squadron, which had landed on Ascension on its way to Africa, was flown off for the purpose. It was piloted by Lieutenant Harden, USAAF.

The Axis submarines, crowded on deck and below with survivors and each with several packed lifeboats in tow, were making for an agreed rendezvous with the Vichy-French ships when one of them, Hartenstein's *U-156*, was spotted from the American Liberator. The aircraft circled over the submarine and its charges before flying off. Lieutenant Harden must have been overhead long enough to fathom out something of the nature of the unusual scene going on beneath him. He referred the matter by radio to Captain Richardson, Commander of the 1st Composite on Ascension, who ordered him to attack. Half an hour later Harden was back overhead and, despite flashed signals, radio messages, and the display of a Red Cross flag, roared in to attack the submarine and dropped five bombs before flying off again. (At the subsequent American inquiry into the incident, Harden proffered the explanation that the two British ships he was there to escort were endangered by the presence of the U-boat.)

U-156 had been damaged by near-misses, and Commander Hartenstein had no recourse but to return his survivors to the water, although Dönitz ordered the other submarines to carry on with their part of the rescue operation. On 17 September they made rendezvous with the three French ships and 1041 survivors were taken off the German submarines and another 42 from the *Cappellini*. However, a further 2100 souls had perished in the incident, amongst them the *Laconia*'s master, Captain Sharpe.

Among the charges brought against Admiral Dönitz after the war was one of murder for issuing the *Laconia* Order. He was acquitted on that charge (but not of others) after American Admiral Chester Nimitz testified that in the war in the Pacific the US Navy had followed the same general policy. The Germans have a knack of inventing single words, albeit rather long ones, to describe complex concepts. This seems to be the place to mention one of them. *Schrecklichkeit* means that war is a brutal business and not one to be conducted as a game between gentlemanly sportsmen. Here, too, might be the best place to mention that several American authors have stated that the *Laconia* rescue mission was broken up by British actions. The latest writer to do so was Edwin P Hoyt who in 1988 wrote, 'the rescue mission was upset by British bombings'. Perhaps the Germans have a word to cover that too.

The Japanese proved to be by far the worst of the Axis partners in perpetrating atrocities against merchant seamen. The worst spate of atrocities by their submarine commanders was triggered by an operational order dated 20 March 1943 issued by Rear-Admiral Mito Hisashi, commanding the 1st Japanese Submarine Force at Truk in the Marshall Islands. It read:

> All submarines will act together in order to concentrate their attacks against enemy convoys and totally destroy them. Do not stop with the sinking of enemy ships and cargoes; at the same time carry out the complete destruction of the crews of the enemy ships; if possible seize part of the crew and endeavour to secure information about the enemy.

The straightforward, calculated evil of this order was matched only by the eagerness and apparent pleasure with which some Japanese submarine commanders, especially those of the 8th Submarine Flotilla based at Penang, carried it out.

It is almost certain that the doctrine behind Admiral Mito's order, perhaps even the order itself, began higher up the Imperial Japanese Naval Command chain than himself, although the exact origin of it did not come out at the War Crimes Tribunals after the war. An input by Higher Command is indicated by an operational order of March 1944, a year after Mito's, issued by Admiral Takasu Shiro, C-in-C South-west Area Fleet, when a Japanese raiding force of three cruisers, *Aoba* (Vice Admiral Sakonju Naomasa), *Tone*, and *Chikuma*, was ordered into the Indian Ocean. Known to the Japanese as Operation Z, the main object of the raid was to disrupt Allied communications in that ocean, and as by that time Japan had lost nearly half its merchant shipping tonnage, it had the secondary object of capturing and bringing in Allied merchant ships, the cruisers carrying specially trained boarding parties for that purpose. Admiral Takasu's order to Vice-Admiral Sakonju included the instruction that all merchant ship crews were to be killed except for certain specified categories, such as Radio Officers, who were to be retained for interrogation.

This mission was undertaken because the Japanese merchant marine suffered heavily during the war, losing a total of 2345 ships amounting to 8.6 million tons, together with 108,000 officers and men killed or missing. Unlike the Allies, the Japanese shipyards could not keep up with the attrition rate. In an attempt to fill the gap, all over the Far East Japanese salvage and repair teams were busy raising sunken vessels and repairing damaged ones, whilst the Allies were equally busy trying to prevent them doing so. Two such ships, the Italians *Sumatra* and *Volpi*, both under repair in Phuket harbour, Thailand, were attacked and sunk by two human torpedo 'chariots' launched from the submarine HMS *Trenchant* on the night of 27/28 October 1944. The four seamen manning the chariots were awarded DSMs. One of the four, Wilfred 'Bill' Smith, was commissioned after the war and retired in 1987 with the rank of Lieutenant-Commander. He died in 1998.

A copy of Admiral Mito's 1943 order to his submarine captains was captured by the Americans in the Marshall Islands early in 1944, but they kept it quiet, not even informing the British of it until March 1945. However, even had the British been told earlier it is doubtful whether much would have been done about it. Although Allied merchant seamen sailing the Indian Ocean soon learned via the nautical grapevine of the incidence of atrocities, strenuous efforts were made by both Britain and America to throw a blanket over such news. It was feared that if the media got hold of it, an irresistible demand for convoys might be created in the relevant areas which would have the effect of diverting naval ships away from the battle zones. The main British protagonist for keeping the atrocities under wraps was Lord Halifax, the Ambassador in Washington, though there can be little doubt that Winston Churchill was of the same mind.

Between 14 December 1943 and 29 October 1944, Admiral Mito's order was faithfully carried out by some, though not all, Japanese submarine commanders. As we shall see, Admiral Takasu's order to his cruiser commanders was also carried out, but not without some delay and opposition.

The British steamer *Daisy Moller* (Moller & Company, Shanghai) would probably have been a contender for first prize had there been a competition for the slowest ship on the Indian Ocean when she sailed from Colombo for Chittagong on 8 December 1943 with a cargo of military stores. A little over 4000 tons and built in 1911, she was capable of only 8.5 knots flat out. According to the diary of Admiral Sir James Somerville, C-in-C Eastern Fleet, in the entry for 3 January 1944, the ship might have been in line for another prize too. The Admiral wrote:

> While I was at Bombay, the *Daisy Moller* was torpedoed N of Madras. This ship had made more false sighting reports than any other ship out here, and at first we concluded it was probably just another scare; unfortunately the wolf was there this time . . .

Most of *Daisy Moller*'s crew of seventy-one were Indians and Chinese, although the officers were Europeans. Forty year-old Captain Reg Weeks was from Devon, and the other officers came from either Britain, Norway, or Denmark, except for one who was an émigré from Tsarist Russia. To man its single 4-inch gun the ship carried six DEMS gunners, three from the Royal Navy and three from the RA Maritime Regiment.

Because his ship was sailing unescorted, Captain Weeks had been ordered to keep well inshore along the east coast of India before making a dash, if for such a slow ship it can be called that, across the neck of the Bay of Bengal to its destination. No doubt the Naval Control Officer at Colombo thought the shallow waters along the coast would prove a deterrent to submarines. It proved not to be so for *RO-110* under Commander Ebato Kazuro. At 0420 hours on 14 December a torpedo from the submarine struck *Daisy Moller* on the starboard side between holds 1 and 2. Almost immediately the ship took a heavy list to starboard and began to sink. Radio Officer Patrick Healy, on duty in the wireless room, was flung from his chair by the explosion but although stunned, managed to send the signal SSS, 'I am under submarine attack', together with the ship's position. The message was received by the radio station at Vizagapatam to the north.

Thankful that the Indian coast was only three miles away, Captain Weeks ordered abandon ship. Every member of the crew got off in three lifeboats except for the gunners, who used the two rafts situated aft. Weeks and his men were engaged in watching their ship sink when, with the loud sound of water blowing from its tanks, *RO-110* surfaced not more than a hundred yards away.

Without warning, Commander Ebato commenced carrying out his admiral's orders. At full speed it rammed Captain Weeks' boat, spilling its occupants into the sea and then began machine-gunning those in the water. He then did the same with the other boats before concentrating his fire on the two life-rafts on which were the gunners.

In his affidavit to the International Military Tribunal after the war, Captain Weeks reported:

> The sub approached my boat after firing tracer bullet at us . . . approximately three minutes later the sub rammed my boat at an approximate speed of 16 knots, opening fire with machine guns directly after. I swam to a raft about one and a half miles away. The submarine then rammed the other two boats and machined gunned the water over a large area.

No less than fifty-five of the seventy-one men who had abandoned *Daisy Moller* lay dead in the water by the time Ebato left the scene. The bodies of the dead were discovered later that day by Lieutenant Maxwell-Clarkson RINVR aboard the tug *Zerang*, sent out in answer to the ship's distress signal. When the bodies were pulled from the water it was found they were riddled with bullet holes. The tug searched the area but no survivors were found. However, Captain Weeks and twelve others had managed to board the rafts, and by using oars as masts and awnings as sails were able to reach the shore three days later after having been swept south by the current. On that same day three exhausted Indian members of the crew were found clinging to an upturned lifeboat by fishermen.

In view of the fate of most of her crew, was ever a ship more ironically named than *British Chivalry*? On 22 February 1944, this British Tanker Company vessel, commanded by Captain Walter Hill, was sailing unescorted and in ballast to the south-west of the Maldives when she was torpedoed by the Japanese submarine *I-37*. In command of the submarine was Commander Nakagawa Hajime, the man who in May of the previous year had sunk the Australian Hospital Ship *Centaur* in his previous command, *I-177*. Nakagawa was a man who knew nothing of chivalry. It is more than possible that the tanker was lured into breaking radio silence, and therefore into giving away its position, by bogus transmissions from the submarine purporting to be from the radio station at Colombo. If so, no blame is attributable to Nakagawa for that, as deception is a much-used practice in warfare. But what followed the torpedoing is not recognised practice.

Of the fifty-nine people on board, which included fourteen DEMS gunners, all but six got away from the stricken ship in two lifeboats after the torpedo hit in the engine-room area. Four rafts had also been released, but they were floating empty. Chief Officer Pierre Payne's boat was the only one with a motor, and from the other boat Captain Hill called over for Payne to collect the rafts together as the stores they carried would be required for the boat voyage ahead. As Payne began this task, the submarine surfaced about a mile off and opened up with her deck gun. The first shells fell close to the boats, which lay between the submarine and the tanker, but then Nakagawa concentrated his fire on the ship. The gunnery was not good, and it took another torpedo to finally sink the ship.

That accomplished, Nakagawa turned tracer fire on the boats, but stopped as his submarine drew closer. He signalled Chief Officer Payne's boat alongside, and a Japanese asked in bad English whether the captain was in the boat. When Payne answered in the negative he was ordered to tow the other lifeboat alongside. Having done that Payne went astern putting about a hundred yards between the submarine and his boat. As he watched he saw Captain Hill climb aboard the submarine after which the other lifeboat, now under Second Mate Mountain, also backed water away from the sub.

The submarine then moved off east and Payne, taking the other boat in tow and using his engine, began to move in the opposite direction. Suddenly someone facing aft yelled out a warning. The submarine had turned and was heading back towards them. Guessing the submarine commander's intent, Payne warned his boat's crew to be ready to go over the side on his order. When less than a hundred feet away the submarine opened fire on Mountain's boat with machine guns. Payne's crew went over the side, but some of those in the other boat were too late in following suit. Bullets thudded into and through its hull as in a frenzy the Japanese gunners poured round after round into it.

As he crouched low behind the hull of his own boat, Payne just had time to note that a man on the submarine's conning tower was filming the attack, before his own boat came in for similar attention. For over an hour Nakagawa switched his gunners' attentions, first to one boat and then to the other, seemingly set on leaving no one alive. Payne yelled for his men to swim away from the boat and to feign death by floating face down, a ruse that did not save some of them as Nakagawa cut a way through the group with his craft's stem. After what seemed a lifetime to the men still alive in the water, Nakagawa called a halt to the firing and the submarine once again made off eastwards. Despite the ferocity of the attacks, thirty-nine men were still alive although five were badly injured. Mountain's boat had sunk and Payne set about the task of making the other one seaworthy, for it was now peppered with bullet holes. The engine was no longer serviceable and so was jettisoned, and that made room for everyone to board. Pierre Payne decided to sail west and so began a fight for survival that lasted for thirty-seven days until they were picked up by the British motorship *Dulane* on 29 March. Only one man was lost during that time, one of the wounded.

On the evening of 26 February, only four days after the sinking of *British Chivalry*, the 5189-ton *Sutlej* (J Nourse & Company, a subsidiary of P & O) on a voyage from the Red Sea to Fremantle, and under the command of Captain Dennis Jones, fell in with Nakagawa's command. A torpedo struck the ship between Nos 1 and 2 holds, the explosion sending smoke and debris mast-high together with an enveloping dust-cloud from the ship's cargo of phosphate fertiliser. In under four minutes the ship went down by the head. (Fortunately, a steel box carried on deck and containing diplomatic mail, went down with the ship. An Admiralty report on the sinking noted, 'all went down with the ship and there is no chance of compromise.')

Chief Engineer Richard Rees was one of three men to clamber aboard a small raft which had somehow floated clear. Standing on the raft Rees looked around and estimated from the number of lifebelt lights among the floating debris, that a large number of the 73-man crew had managed to get off the ship before she took the final plunge. As Rees and his companions were busy pulling aboard as many men as could safely fit on the raft, they were lit up by a searchlight from *I-37* which had come to the surface. As the submarine neared, a line was thrown and the raft hauled alongside. From the conning tower someone demanded the whereabouts of the ship's captain. Rees called back that he believed the master had gone down with the ship. At that Nakagawa ordered the raft away before making an unsuccessful attempt to ram it, the raft being saved only by being pushed aside by the submarine's bow wave. Then the submarine's gunners opened fire but somehow missed those on the raft before concentrating on the men still floating in the water. For an hour Nakagawa moved around the area with guns blazing before moving off. The men aboard Rees' raft sighted two larger rafts that must have broken away from *Sutlej*, and twenty-two survivors were soon spread between the two. Some distance away, Third Officer Frank Newell, together with one of the DEMS gunners and five Indian sailors, managed to reach an overturned lifeboat, which they righted and boarded.

Forty-two days later and within sight of the coast of Madagascar, and having had one man die on him, Frank Newall and the five remaining men in the lifeboat were rescued by HMS *Solvra*. Without compass or charts, the twenty-five year-old third mate had navigated 1300 miles and reached a point only ninety miles south of Diego Suarez, the port for which he had been aiming. A week after that the two rafts containing Richard Rees and his men were sighted by a Catalina aircraft out of Diego Garcia, some 700 miles north-east of the place where *Sutlej* had gone down. They were subsequently rescued by HMS *Flamingo*.

The last week of February 1944, at the end of which he was due to return to base at Penang, was turning out to be a busy one for Commander Nakagawa, and it was not over for him yet. The British steamer *Ascot* (Watts, Watts & Company) had sailed from Colombo on the 19th, making for Fremantle via Diego Suarez. She was under the command of Captain Jack Travis. A little past noon on the 29th she steamed into the periscope sights of *I-37*. A torpedo struck *Ascot* on the starboard side in the vicinity of the engine-room, and the ship leant heavily to port only to come upright as the engines stopped. But then she began to settle. Both starboard lifeboats had been smashed to smithereens by the torpedo blast and one of those on the port side carried away as it was being lowered. Most survivors got away on the fourth boat whilst others leapt into the water to make for the only raft to be released. The second lifeboat was rapidly recovered and Captain Travis distributed the survivors among the three floating craft.

I-37 surfaced about a mile away, and from his place on the raft Apprentice Harry Fortune, an eighteen year-old lad from Hartlepool, watched as the submarine began shelling the still floating *Ascot*. Suddenly the shelling ceased and the submarine began to head for the boats, only to stop when it drew close. A burst of machine-gun fire was followed by a shouted demand for the captain to make himself known. Captain Travis stood up and was ordered to bring his boat alongside. After questioning Travis on the deck of the submarine, a man taken to be the commander of it appeared to lose his temper and slashed at Travis's hands with a sword before having him thrown overboard. On seeing this, Harry Fortune and the men on the raft began paddling quietly away. They saw Captain Travis being hauled aboard the nearest lifeboat.

Nakagawa and his men now went about their usual routine. The lifeboats were rammed, one of them sinking immediately, and then a machine-gun opened up on the men in the water. Seeing the machine-gun being turned in the direction of the raft, Fortune yelled for its occupants to get into the water. Some were too late and died, but young Fortune and six others managed to find safety by keeping the raft between themselves and the submarine.

Nakagawa then turned his attention back to the still floating *Ascot*, and as he did so the men in the water who were still alive, Captain Travis amongst them, began climbing back either into the remaining boat or on to the raft. To the background noise of some two dozen shells being pumped into the ship, Travis, who was aboard the boat, had a tow rope passed to the raft and then made to clear the area. With *Ascot* now on fire from stem to stern, Nakagawa again turned his attention, and his machine-guns, on the survivors. Once more Fortune flung himself into the sea as bullets tore into the raft and the surrounding water, with those in the lifeboat following his example. For two hours Nakagawa cruised the area, shooting at anything that moved before leaving the area with the lifeboat in tow.

As *I-37* disappeared, seven exhausted men swam to the raft and dragged themselves aboard; two apprentices, two Able Seaman, two gunners, one of whom was wounded, and a cook. On the following morning after a mostly sleepless night, the lifeboat was seen some way off. It had been cast adrift by the submarine and, unbeknownst to the Japanese, one of the gunners, Sergeant Hughson, had lain alive in the bottom of it, although wounded. It took a day for the two craft to draw together. As the senior of the two apprentices, Harry Fortune took charge, and after examining the boat decided it was too damaged to use. Hughson and the boat's stores were transferred to the raft, after which Fortune shaped up to make for Madagascar, 900 miles to the south-west. On the following day, however, they were sighted by the Dutch *Straat Soenda*, which conveyed the only eight men to survive Nakagawa's latest horror to Aden.

We turn now to Japanese surface craft. The three-cruiser task force under Vice-Admiral Sakonju which entered the Indian Ocean on the first day of March 1944 was by the 9th of that month engaged in sweeping a sixty-mile corridor south of the Cocos Islands for possible victims. A low-lying mist covered the sea that morning, although the cruisers' masthead lookouts were above it. At about 0900 hours, smoke was seen by the lookout on *Tone*, which proved to be coming from Hain Line's *Behar* on route from Melbourne to Bombay. *Behar* was almost brand-new, having been completed on the Clyde only ten months earlier. Under the command of Captain Maurice Symonds, it had a crew of 102, including a larger than normal contingent of DEMS gunners; there were 17 on board to man the ship's two guns and its rocket launchers. On this passage she was also carrying nine passengers, including two ladies.

It was about 1000 hours when *Behar*'s officer of the watch, Third Mate James Anderson, had the heart-stopping experience of seeing *Tone* emerging from the mist to starboard. Captain Symonds rushed to the bridge just as the Japanese cruiser made a signal to heave-to. As his ship's gunners ran to action stations, Symonds ordered Radio Officer Cumming to send out an RRR distress signal, 'I am being attacked by a surface raider'. It was a gallant gesture, but the transmission was picked up by *Tone*, which immediately opened fire with her 8-inch guns.

Firing at almost point-blank range *Tone*, commanded by Captain Mayuzumi Haruo, poured shell after shell into the cargo ship and within minutes she was ablaze and sinking; the gunners had no chance to get off even a single shot before the order came to abandon ship. Under continuous bombardment, four lifeboats were launched, loaded with people, and were pulled away from the ship. As some crew and passengers were missing, Captain Symonds and Chief Officer William Phillips remained on board to search for them Three were found dead but five more, including the two lady passengers, were found alive. As by that time the ship was settling fast, the group went over the side, Captain Symonds being the last to leave. They were soon picked up by the lifeboats.

As the lifeboats clustered together, *Tone* stopped a cable or two away. The boats were ordered alongside and the survivors taken aboard. On deck they received some rough treatment from their captors and their hands were tied behind their backs, including those of the two ladies, and when William Phillips remonstrated about that he was beaten with a baseball bat. Subsequently a Japanese officer had the ladies' arms released. Captain P J Green, one of *Behar*'s passengers and who was a master with the Indo-China Steam Navigation Company, wrote of boarding the *Tone*:

> Arriving on deck I found myself facing six to eight men armed with rifles ready to shoot. Other Japanese sailors removed most of our clothes, leaving us only in shirts and trousers. My hands were then tied tightly behind my back with marline. My arms were forced up behind my back and the rope put round my throat.

Admiral Sakonju aboard his flagship *Aoba* was not at all pleased over the sinking of *Behar*. Not only had the chance been lost of adding a splendid ship to the Japanese merchant navy, but because the victim had managed to get off a distress message he considered it advisable to leave the Indian Ocean and return to Batavia on the island of Java, for he guessed the Allies would soon be out looking him. His displeasure deepened when he learned that *Tone* had 108 prisoners on board in direct contravention of Admiral Takasu's extermination order. He instructed Captain Mayazumi to keep the required few for interrogation and to dispose of the others forthwith.

Mayazumi may not have been above allowing his men to maltreat prisoners but he was no cold-blooded killer, and all his prisoners were still alive when his ship arrived at Batavia six days later. Mayazumi confronted Sakonju there and pleaded for his prisoners' lives, but was told in no uncertain terms that the order must be carried out. Captain Symonds, Chief Officer Phillips, and thirty-four other survivors, including the two women, were taken ashore to become prisoners of war, but the other seventy-two were taken to sea on *Tone*. A group of Japanese led by a certain Lieutenant Ishihara formed a killing squad, lined the prisoners up on deck, felled them with a kick, and then beheaded them.

Yet another atrocity took place in what for merchant seaman in the Indian Ocean was the terrible month of March 1944. On the 18th, at about 0830 hours and when about 600 miles south of Colombo, the *Nancy Moller* (Moller & Company, Shanghai) was torpedoed by *I-165* commanded by Lieutenant-Commander Shimuzu Tsuruzo. Struck by two torpedoes the ship sank in under a minute and there was no time to launch lifeboats or release life-rafts, although one of the former rose upturned to the surface after the ship sank, together with some of the latter. In spite of the suddenness of it all, it seems that many of its complement of fifty-three survived the sinking, but Captain James Hansen and Chief Officer Neil Morris were not amongst them. The senior deck officer striving to survive was Second Mate Chu Shih Kao from Hong Kong. From a position astride the keel of the upturned boat, Chu saw the *I-165* come to the surface less than a hundred feet away. The submarine manoeuvred close to one of the rafts on which were crouched DEMS Gunner Dennis Fryers, two Chinese and three Lascars. A Japanese in the conning tower called for the ship's captain and received the standard answer, which in this case was true, that he had gone down with the ship. Fryers and the others on that raft were then taken aboard and the gunner was forcibly dragged below. The two Chinese were shot in the back and kicked overboard, whilst the Lascars were merely thrown over the side. Shimuzo then circled the area as his gunners shot at everyone in sight. When the submarine left there were only thirty-two men alive in the sea, one of them seriously wounded. Second Officer Chu distributed the survivors among the four life-rafts and under oars made northwards. Four days later they were rescued by the cruiser HMS *Emerald* and taken to Mauritius.

It was not only crews of British ships who were on the receiving end of Japanese atrocities. A submarine commander even more sadistic and evil than Nakagawa, Commander Ariizumi Tatsunosuke, was responsible for two others, one involving a Dutch ship, another an American one. So evil was Commander Ariizumi, that he earned the nickname 'the Butcher'.

Tjisalak of Royal Interocean Lines was heading for Colombo, and was some 600 miles short of her destination by 26 March 1944. Most of the officers under Captain Hen were Dutch, although there were three Britons amongst them. The crew were mainly Hong Kong Chinese and all ten DEMS gunners were British. Inclusive of the passengers, there were 103 people on board. At about 0600 hours on that day, Commander Ariizumi's submarine *I-8* fired two torpedoes which struck *Tjisalak* abaft the bridge, the resulting explosion almost lifting the ship out of the water. Even as the ship was sinking, her gunners turned their 4-inch gun on the now surfaced submarine, three shells landing so close to it that Ariizumi hastily submerged. Perhaps it was that which raised his especial ire. (As with *Sutlej*, this ship carried sensitive mail that went down with the ship. It was naval mail from the Royal Netherlands Navy, Melbourne, to its counterpart in Colombo.) As the ship sank, all but three of those on board got away in boats or on rafts. *I-8* then surfaced, its commander ordering the lifeboats alongside and the men in them to board the submarine. There, forced to squat on the casing, the survivors saw the boats cut adrift as the submarine got under way. Then the killing began. In ones and twos the prisoners were taken abaft the conning tower after which those left behind heard sounds of shooting. When it came to the turn of Second Officer Jan Dekker someone swung at his head with a heavy hammer. The blow was a glancing one, though hard enough to knock him down. Dekker looked up to find a gun pointing at him, but somehow managed to twist and throw himself over the side and swim away. Chief Officer Frits de Jong, Radio Officer James Blears, and Third Engineer Spuybroek all had similar experiences to Dekker's. The story of a fifth survivor, an Indian called Dhange, was somewhat different. By the time there were only about twenty crew members left to kill, all of them Asians, the Japanese had apparently grown tired of the original method of slaughter. The remaining seaman were each tied to a long rope attached to the submarine which then dived. Only Dhange, the last one on the rope, managed to free himself. All five men eventually managed to reach one of *Tjisalak*'s lifeboats, and two days later they were rescued by the American Liberty ship *James A Wilder*, but only after that ship, mistaking the lifeboat for a submarine's conning tower, had fired on it.

On being told of the *Tjisalak* affair, Admiral Somerville wrote in his diary: 'I hear with grave concern that shocking atrocities were committed by the Japanese submarine', and the following day he wrote:

I sent a signal to the Admiralty giving a list of the atrocities which had been committed in this Theatre by the Japanese on the crews of torpedoed ships; in every case these were independently sailed ships and I expressed the view that when the news of these atrocities leaked out there might be a reluctance on the part of crews to sail in unescorted ships. A review of the

additional escorts required to put all the ships into convoy showed that
would require the following additional long range escorts:–
Australia to India and Ceylon   18
Colombo to Aden   10
South Africa to India   8

The second ship to have the misfortune to fall in with Commander
Ariizumi in one of his fouler moods was the American *Jean Nicolet*. This
Liberty ship had loaded a military cargo at the Californian port of San
Pedro and was bound for Calcutta, having last called at Fremantle for
bunkers. In addition to its seventy-man crew the ship carried about thirty
US Army personnel. On 22 July 1944, in a position about 150 miles west
of Diego Garcia, she was struck by three torpedoes from Ariizumi's *I-8*.
Everyone aboard *Jean Nicolet* got away on boats and rafts. *I-8* surfaced,
and as with the *Tjisalak*, ordered the survivors on board where their hands
were bound behind their backs. Many were then forced to run the gauntlet, and after a succession of blows from iron bars and the like, were
pushed into the sea. There were about thirty survivors still awaiting a
similar fate when the submarine's klaxons blared and she began to sub-
merge. One survivor had managed to loosen his bonds and he was able to
release six others before they were dragged beneath the surface. Two days
later, twenty-three men, all that remained alive of *Jean Nicolet's* crew,
were plucked from the sea by HMIS *Hoxa*. They were found clinging to
pieces of debris, several of them without lifebelts.
    I-8 was sunk with all hands bar one off Okinawa at the end of March
1945, but by that time Ariizumi had moved on to command Submarine
Squadron 1 in the Inland Sea of Japan, flying his flag aboard the giant
new submarine *I-401*. After the Japanese surrender and whilst his squadron was being escorted by American warships round to the port of
Yokosuka near Tokyo, Captain Ariizumi shot himself. Commander Ebato
Kazuro, the man who sank the *Daisy Moller*, died when his submarine was
sunk with all hands on 11 February 1944, in an action in the Bay of
Bengal involving a gunboat of the Royal Indian Navy and two Australian
minesweepers.
    Commander Nakagawa, who was responsible for sinking the hospital
ship *Centaur* and who afterwards in *I-37* committed atrocities against the
crews of *British Chivalry*, *Sutlej*, and *Ascot*, lived to face the music after the
war. *I-37* itself, under another commander, had been sunk with all hands
by American destroyers in November 1944. Allied war crimes investiga-
tors were not able to prove conclusively for the benefit of the War Crimes
Tribunals held during 1946-48 that it was Nakagawa's command which
sank the *Centaur*. This was partly because the relevant Japanese submarine operational documents had disappeared, and partly because
Nakagawa lied through his teeth. During the investigation he attempted
to place the blame on the commander of another Japanese submarine who
had been off the Australian coast at the time and who had rather conven-
iently been lost when later his boat was sunk. In July 1948 Nakagawa was

sentenced to eight years' hard labour for his actions against the crews of some of his other victims. This seems a very light sentence in view of the gravity of his offences, especially as he served only six years of it. He was released in 1954 and died in May 1986, aged eighty-four. The same tribunal sentenced Rear-Admiral Mito to eight years as the man who issued the order to his submarine commanders to take no prisoners.

Vice-Admiral Sajonju, who had ordered Captain Mayuzumi of the cruiser *Tone* to execute his prisoners, was sentenced to death. The court had some sympathy for Captain Mayuzumi himself for at least trying to save the victims. He was sentenced to seven years imprisonment. Lieutenant-Commander Shimizu Tsuruzo, who was responsible for machine-gunning survivors from *Nancy Moller*, was for some reason never brought to trial. Not only that, he subsequently rose to the rank of Rear-Admiral in the Japanese Maritime Self-Defence Force.

Captain Walter Hill of *British Chivalry* survived internment by the Japanese, as did *Behar*'s chief officer, William Phillips. Gunner Dennis Fryers of *Nancy Moller* survived several months of internment in Singapore's infamous Changi gaol.

The Allies were not above committing what almost certainly would have been classified as atrocities at sea had the war turned out to be an Axis victory. In the interest of fairness it is necessary to comment on one of these. On 5 March 1943 in the Bismarck Sea after eight Japanese troop transports were sunk, American PT boats, under Lieutenant-Commander Barry Atkins and acting under higher orders, machine-gunned many hundreds of Japanese soldiers in the water or aboard life-rafts. It should be noted that 'acting under orders' was not considered an acceptable defence at the War Crimes trials the Allies held after the war.

It is worth noting too, that in the Mediterranean war, after two Italian destroyers had been sunk off Pantellaria, Admiral Cunningham signalled the Italian naval authorities the position of life-rafts on which were survivors from the ships. For his pains Cunningham received a severe rebuke from Churchill, who complained that such chivalry was bad for morale at home. One would have thought that, on the contrary, propaganda based on that act of maritime chivalry would have had completely the opposite effect on public opinion back home.

CHAPTER 23

Khedive Ismail, Troopship

The troopships and escorts comprising Convoy KR8 were in the middle of the Indian Ocean about 60 miles north of the equator. It was a fine afternoon to be at sea, even if there was a war on. The light airs were just enough to ruffle the water, and the sun shone brightly overhead. The date was 12 February 1944. As commodore ship *Khedive Ismail* was leading the middle row of the convoy, with *Ekma* astern of her. Leading the port row was the main escort vessel, the old cruiser HMS *Hawkins*, with *City of Paris* steaming astern of her. To starboard was *Varsova*, with *Ellenga* keeping station behind. Over on the flanks and slightly ahead of the convoy, the modern 'P' Class destroyers *Petard* and *Paladin* were fussing around like mother hens.

The destroyers had only joined the convoy on the previous day, having arrived via Suez from the Mediterranean. Their appearance on the northern horizon had been greeted with much relief, not least by Captain J W Josselyn DSC RN in command of the *Hawkins*. There had been no warnings of enemy submarines in the area, but as his elderly ship was not fitted with Asdic and with about 9000 troops in the convoy to protect, Captain Josselyn had been a worried man until the two sleek greyhounds of the sea had arrived. The convoy had sailed from Mombasa for Colombo on the 5th with at that time five smaller naval craft also in attendance, but, having reached the edge of their fuel range by the 9th, they had detached and gone back.

Khedive Ismail was only a few years younger than HMS *Hawkins*, but was well appointed. She belonged to Khedivial Mail Line of Egypt, but had been requisitioned as one of His Majesty's Troop Transports earlier in the war, and was placed under the management of the British India Steam Navigation Company. She was under the command of Captain R W M Whiteman and had a crew of 183, of which 144 were Indians and Chinese. The European contingent consisted of twenty-two European officers and petty officers, five medical staff, and twelve DEMS gunners, six each from the Army and Navy. Captain Whiteman had been in command of the ship for over a year and was the most senior and experienced of the five merchant navy captains in the convoy – he had earlier been awarded the DSC – which was why his vessel was commodore ship.

This convoy was rather unusual in that the Senior Officer, Escort (SO,E), in this case Captain Josselyn, was of the same rank as the captain of the commodore ship, although of course, Josselyn was Royal Navy and

Whiteman was Merchant Navy. In most convoys the SO,E, was junior in rank to the Commodore, and the Admiralty had never laid down that one command should be under the other and was unwilling to place a senior officer under a junior. So, in its wisdom, it always left the two officers, whose duties were interdependent, to achieve smoothness of operation by tact and goodwill. Both those attributes, in fact, played important parts in the pre-sailing conferences of ship commanders held before any convoy set sail. In this case, the fact that Josselyn was as senior as the Commodore, and was therefore held to be ultimately responsible for any decisions made, was to go hard with him at a later Official Inquiry.

In addition to its crew *Khedive Ismail* was carrying over 1300 military and naval personnel. They included about 1000 men of an East African Division and the 301st Field Regiment RA, and 200 from the Royal Navy. Also on board were eighty-five women; ten from the ATS, twenty-two Wrens, fifty-two nursing sisters of 150th General Hospital, and a Mrs Merrill, a civilian who was accompanied by her young son.

It was mid-afternoon and the convoy was steaming at 13 knots on a course of N85E. It kept on a straight course, for Captain Josselyn had decided before sailing that the delay to the convoy caused by zig-zagging would have meant an unacceptable additional night at sea in potentially dangerous waters. Down in the spacious saloon of *Khedive Ismail*, with the whirling giant overhead fans providing extra background noise, a crowd of 300 or so were enjoying a concert put on by some of the nursing sisters. One of the sisters was playing the grand piano. Seconds before two torpedoes struck the starboard side of *Khedive Ismail* almost simultaneously, Cadet Norman Smith on the bridge of *City of Paris* saw something through his binoculars and exclaimed to the officer-of-watch, 'that's a funny fish'. What he had probably seen, though much too late, was the periscope of the Japanese submarine *I-27*, which under Commander Fukumura Toshiaki, had manoeuvred into a position just astern of *Varsova* to fire a fan of torpedoes from a range of less than 800 yards.

On watch on the bridge of *Khedive Ismail*, Second Officer C H R Munday was talking to a signalman when he saw the track of a torpedo pass the ship's stern heading in the general direction of the Hawkins. He reported later:

> Immediately afterwards we were struck by a torpedo in No. 4 hold . . . followed 5 seconds later by a second torpedo which struck in the boiler-room. There was a loud explosion with the first torpedo which caused the vessel to list 12 degrees to starboard; the second explosion which was more violent than the first, may have caused one of the boilers to explode. . . . the second explosion caused the main stairway and troop deck to collapse, thereby trapping a great number of people. The vessel continued to heel over to starboard until she was on her beam ends . . .

As the ship rapidly heeled to starboard, the furniture in the saloon including the grand piano slid to the low side, along with most of the people there. Only two of those in the saloon managed to escape by hauling themselves out of portholes on the port side, which was now on top. No one else in there had a chance, for one minute and forty seconds after the torpedoes struck, the ship went down.

Second Officer Munday recognised the seriousness of the situation and yelling 'every man for himself', ran down the bridge ladder. He met up with Chief Officer J Duncan, who, along with Troop Officer R I Leleu, was urging everybody over the side. One of the ship's radio officers, John Ainslee, afterwards reported that he thought he was the last person to see Captain Whiteman alive. 'He was standing holding on to the rail outside his accommodation; he was not making any attempt to leave his ship'. The ship went down leaving survivors floundering in the water. Some of those who got off were killed when they were struck by lifeboats and life-rafts sliding off the ship as it rolled over and sank.

The remaining troopships and HMS *Hawkins*, following standing orders, began to take evasive action. The two destroyers raced in to attack the submarine with depth charges, and this went on for an hour and a half. Both destroyers then lowered motor launches, and while *Petard* went on with the hunt for the submarine, survivors from *Khedive Ismail* were picked up and taken aboard *Paladin*.

Suddenly the submarine broke surface between the destroyers and both turned to ram with all guns firing, but on seeing the submarine was badly damaged Commander R C Egan of *Petard* hauled off, and signalled *Paladin* to do the same. *Paladin*, commanded by Lieutenant E A S Bailey, also turned away, but too late, and the submarine's hydroplane guard, acting like a can-opener, caught *Paladin*'s side below the water line and sliced open her hull from amidships to abaft her after guns. Second Officer Munday who had been picked up by *Paladin*, reported that 'water poured into the ship and everybody was ordered on deck'. Now on her own, *Petard* carried on the fight against the submarine, which refused to surrender. In his report Commander Egan said, 'A running action now ensued for nearly an hour during which time the enemy circled blindly, having lost her periscope.' He went on to praise the enemy's 'amazing tenacity in battle'.

Sub-Lieutenant Peter Wood RNVR, the torpedo officer on *Petard*, later reported, after stating that both destroyers had left the Middle East without any armour-piercing shells on board and that they were carrying only high-explosive shells which were not effective against metal hulls:

> . . . our guns large and small were firing at the sub; it was a gruesome sight to see the stream of little yellow men scrambling out of the conning tower to try to man their gun only to be shot to bits before they reached the deck.
>
> In a few minutes the sub's gun and conning tower had disappeared over the side but still it kept underway as we fired salvo after salvo of our H/E shells into the hull. The noise to the wretched Japs inside the hull must have been unbelievably terrifying, but the H/E shells couldn't penetrate the pressure hull, and after a time we ran out of shells. The sub was still a lethal war machine capable of firing torpedoes from both ends. As it continued

circling we had to be careful not to cross either its bow or stern. The only weapon we had left capable of finishing it off were torpedoes. [These] were normally fired in a spread of 4 or 8 in the hope that one or more would straddle the target. On this occasion the captain decided that as I was completely inexperienced, I had better fire only one at a time. Well, I did just that. 1, 2, 3, 4, 5, 6, 7, watching the stopwatch with bated breath as the minute and a half elapsed before the torpedo should have reached its target. Just as I was about to tell the captain for the 7th time, 'Torpedo missed, sir', there was a mighty explosion and the sub disintegrated. Not a trace was left except for an oil slick.

Sub-Lieutenant Wood says:

> I had some explaining to do about why I had expended 7 torpedoes. The navy would have been quite happy if I had fired four or eight, but 7 required a detailed report. However, I was booked in to the first available Torpedo Control Officers' training course as a matter of priority.

A South African by birth, Peter Wood now lives at Hawkes Bay in New Zealand.

Of the nearly 1500 people on board *Khedive Ismail*, only 214 were saved, including 113 Africans and 22 members of the ship's crew. Of the eighty-five women on board, only six were rescued, three nursing sisters, two Wrens, and one ATS girl. Mrs Merrill and her son were not among the survivors. There were no survivors from the Japanese submarine.

HMS *Paladin* was so badly damaged it was at first thought she might not be able to reach port. After all survivors had been transferred to *Petard* from *Paladin*, everything capable of being jettisoned was thrown over the side and the remaining torpedoes were fired in order to lighten her. She was taken in tow by *Petard* and the two ships reached Addu Atoll in the Maldives the following day. *Petard* then took all the survivors on to Colombo. Commander Egan DSO, DSC, was awarded a bar to his DSC for sinking the submarine. *Paladin* was subsequently repaired and continued to serve in the Royal Navy until broken up in 1962. When Admiral Somerville left his Eastern Fleet appointment to head the British Admiralty Delegation in Washington, DC, he voyaged part of the way aboard HMS *Petard*. That ship continued in service until 1967.

So many lives had been lost in the incident there was bound to be a call for an inquiry, and Admiral Sir James Somerville, Commander-in-Chief, Eastern Fleet, ordered one to be held at Colombo under Rear Admiral R S G Nicholson. In his diary for 13 February 1944, Somerville wrote:

> In view of the *Khedive Ismail* sinking I informed the Admiralty I felt we were no longer justified in accepting, as we have had to hitherto, such light escorts for troop convoys, and that until troop movements at present envisaged were completed I must take destroyers from the Fleet for the purpose.

The Board of Inquiry was held on 16/17 February 1944, and evidence was given by some of the survivors, by the captains and some officers of the other five troopships, and by naval officers. The Board concluded that the number of escort vessels for the convoy had been inadequate. Its report also stated that Captain J W Josselyn of HMS *Hawkins* had made an error of judgement in deciding not to zig-zag, a view endorsed by Admiral Somerville. On 2 September 1944, the Lords Commissioners of the Admiralty sent Captain Josselyn a letter to the effect that he had made errors of judgement in accepting 'the 13 knot advance schedule for the convoy which left no time in hand for zig-zagging' and in dispensing 'with the elementary A/S [anti-submarine] precaution of zig-zagging to avoid extra time at sea.'

The *Khedive Ismail* incident was far from being the worst Allied troopship disaster of the war. That occurred to the Cunard liner *Lancastria* during the evacuation of troops from St Nazaire on 17 June 1940, a fortnight after Dunkirk. The ship, under Captain J Sharp, and crammed with about 6000 personnel including 300 members of the crew and some civilian women and children, was preparing to sail when it was attacked by German bombers. One bomb went down the funnel, exploded, and blew a huge hole in the hull, and the ship capsized and sank in about thirty minutes. Many men were trapped inside the hull as the ship went down. Those that did get off, and the many small craft which hastened to the rescue, found themselves being machine-gunned from the air.

One soldier survivor, J F Sweeney, has reported:

> Within a short space of time, hundreds of heads were bobbing up and down in the water, amidst a mass of flotsam. Some of those heads were struck by fresh objects hurtling from the decks. Some of those heads sank and never rose again.

Official records show that only 2477 of the estimated number of people on board were saved and taken aboard other evacuation ships. It is reckoned that a few more managed to reach the shore to eventually become prisoners of the Germans. Captain Sharp was amongst the crew survivors. The sinking of *Lancastria* resulted in the single biggest loss of British lives in the Second World War. A blanket of secrecy was thrown over the event, and despite many rumours, news of the disaster was not made public until after the war.

CHAPTER 24

The Great Bombay Dock Disaster

The world's worst port explosion occurred during the First World War at Halifax, Nova Scotia, on 6 December 1917, when the French ship *Mont Blanc* loaded with 5000 tons of high explosive collided with the Norwegian *Imo* in the approaches to the port. The resulting explosion killed some 1500 people for certain, over half of them schoolchildren, and 8000 were injured. A further 2000 bodies were never found. The explosion which took place at Bombay on 14 April 1944 was almost as devastating, and like the Halifax one was not caused by direct enemy action. The ship at the centre of it all was the *Fort Stikine*.

Built at the Prince Rupert dockyard, British Columbia, and managed by Port Line Ltd, she was on her maiden voyage in early 1944. Her captain was forty-four year-old Alexander Naismith, whose first command it was. The ship arrived at Bombay from Karachi on 13 April 1944 and berthed alongside in Victoria Dock the following day. She had loaded a mixed cargo at Birkenhead two months earlier for ports in the Indian sub-continent, some of which had been discharged at Karachi where the vacated hold space had been filled with other cargo for Bombay. One of the British consignments not unloaded at Karachi, and which was stowed in a secure lock-up in No. 3 'tween deck, consisted of thirty-one crates of gold, each crate holding four 28lb bars. The gold consignment was worth in excess of £1,000,000 and was destined for Bombay, where it was to be sold to help pay for the Indian input into the British war effort. Another of the consignments from Britain still on board was 1395 tons of ammunition and explosives.

At Karachi the ship had loaded 3000 tons of Punjabi cotton, bags of dried fish, drums of lubricating oil, timber, and 900 tons of sulphur. It was reported that when Captain Naismith was informed of the nature of the cargo to be loaded there in addition to the ammunition already on board, he told his officers they would be transporting just about every commodity capable of burning or blowing up. The cargo plan for No. 2 hold, the largest of the five cargo-carrying compartments, provides a good example of a potentially lethal mix of commodities; most of the hold was filled with baled cotton which was overstowed with bags of dried fish, while the 'tween deck above contained cases of ammunition and 300 tons of TNT. On the face of it cotton might appear to be an innocuous cargo, but in fact it has an extremely bad reputation as a fire risk and insurers do not like it all. One spark or a carelessly-disposed-of cigarette butt can readily set it alight, and cotton fires are notoriously difficult to extinguish once they have taken hold. In happier times such a mix of cargo in one hold space would never have been permitted.

Article 24 of the British Merchant Shipping (Safety and Load Line Conventions) Act, 1932, which was still in force during the Second World War, prohibited the carriage of goods liable to endanger the safety of the ship unless 'for the public service of the State under conditions authorised by the Administration'. The definition of 'public service of the State' was stretched to the limit during the war, but perhaps never more so than in the case of the freighter *Fort Stikine*. Captain Naismith, being a prudent seaman, had put his foot down firmly when, in addition, he had been asked to load 750 drums of turpentine at Karachi. He may also have remonstrated over other consignments, but if so he was overruled, probably by the representative of the British Ministry of Shipping based in that port. On top of that, under normal circumstances the ship would never have been allowed to enter the Bombay port complex with ammunition and high explosives on board. They would have been discharged first into barges under controlled conditions at the Dangerous Goods Anchorage, which was situated well away from the port. But this was wartime and circumstances were far from normal.

Nevertheless, it must be said that had the Bombay port authorities deliberately set out to berth *Fort Stikine* in the most dangerous place should an accident occur, it is doubtful they could have chosen a more suitable one. The port complex consisted of two adjacent dock basins, one called Victoria and the other Princes, each having its own lock entrance from the sea, with a third lock connecting the two basins. *Fort Stikine* was berthed alongside the pier which separated the two docks, and astern of another British ship, *Jalapadma*. Another thirteen ships, including two moored to buoys in the middle of the dock, also lay in Victoria, whilst in Prince's there were a further ten vessels, including one in a dry-dock over in the far corner. Two more ships lay berthed alongside the outer walls of the dock basins, bringing to twenty-seven the number of ships in the close vicinity. On all sides except that facing the sea, the docks were surrounded by godowns, sheds crammed with cargoes many of which were highly combustible in their own right. Thus the stage was set for disaster.

Unloading of the ship commenced at 0800 hours on the 14th. The stevedores began on the dried fish in No.2 lower hold, leaving the dangerous goods in the 'tween deck until later. As a precaution, hoses from a hydrant ashore were led aboard and placed in handy positions, and the ship's own fire-fighting apparatus was put on stand-by. *Fort Stikine* did not display the customary red flag at the masthead which denotes 'I am loading or discharging explosives', probably because at the time in question she was not actually doing so. This point was made much of during the subsequent inquiry, although it is difficult to see in the light of events what *effective* precautionary actions other ships in the vicinity might have taken even had such a flag been displayed.

At 1330 hours a fire was discovered amongst the bales of cotton, which caused No. 2 hold to be evacuated by the stevedores in some haste. The crew began to tackle the fire with hoses from the ship's own mains, and only at 1410 hours was the Bombay Port Fire Service informed that a ship carrying explosives was on fire. The firemen arrived to find smoke pouring from the hold and got to work with the hoses connected to the shore. Fighting a cotton fire was not at all an unusual event for them; what made the *Fort Stikine* situation different was the type of cargo that lay immediately over the seat of the blaze. The Fire Brigade, led by Senior Fire Officer Raganath Singh, began the usual technique of flooding the hold with hundreds of tons of water in the hope that it would soak into the heart of the compressed bales and so dowse the fire. The General Manager of the Bombay Port Trust, Colonel J R Sadler, was very quickly on the scene. To advise him on matters concerning explosives and ammunition he had Captain Brindley Oberst of the British Army. Oberst, who knew a floating time bomb when he saw one, advised that the ship be immediately towed from the dock.

Colonel Sadler was faced with the awful dilemma that comes every time a ship catches fire in port. Should the ship be towed from the dock to some less dangerous position or should it be left alongside where the fire could be fought by professionals? If he made the former decision and *Fort Stikine* blew up during the lengthy process of getting her out through the lock he stood to be accused of taking her away from the hands of professional fire-fighters. In modern parlance, Sadler was in a no-win situation. He decided to leave her where she was. As it turned out, he was to be castigated later for leaving the ship *in* the hands of the professionals, though by that time he was not around to care.

Rather strangely, neither Sadler nor the other man in authority in the port, Harbourmaster Nicholson, saw fit to inform the Commodore, Royal Indian Navy, nor the Naval Officer-in-Charge in the area, about the fire. Under the Defence of India Rules then in force, both those officers had the authority to order a ship on fire in the docks to be moved, beached or scuttled where she lay. So, had Sadler seen fit to do so, he could have shared the decision-making responsibility with them. It seems that Captain Naismith may not have been particularly helpful in the decision-making process, possibly because this was his first command and he hoped it could be saved.

As the fire grew in intensity there was a debate over whether the ship should be scuttled, but that was effectively squashed when the Chief Engineer pointed out that the bilge pipes in the holds were fitted with non-return valves; they let water out, not in. The engine room and stokehold could both be flooded by opening sea-cocks, but that in itself would not be enough to sink the ship. Anyway, taking into considering the depth of water in the dock, it is unlikely that even had the ship settled bodily on the bottom the water level would have been sufficient to drown the fire. Someone put forward the idea that hawsers from the far end of the dock

should be used to haul the ship bodily on to its side, but that was considered impractical.

All the while the Fire Brigade was doing its best, but there was no sign
of the fire diminishing. So thick was the smoke it was becoming difficult
to see what was going on. At about 1500 hours a section of the hull plating
began to glow red-hot and the Fire Officer sent for the service's cutting
equipment in order to cut away the plating and so gain direct access to the
lower part of the hold from the shore. When it arrived the cutting equipment proved to be defective so the dockyard engineer sent for his, but by
the time that arrived the area of the hull was so hot that no one could get
within range of it with the cutting torch. At 1545 hours the smoke billow-
ing from the hold changed colour; now it was black, and Captain Oberst
announced that some of the explosives must have begun to smoulder. It
was obvious that the ship was doomed and might blow at any minute.
Nevertheless, the firemen stood to their task, now playing their hoses on
the cases of TNT in the 'tween deck in the hope of cooling them down. It
was a forlorn effort, for rising water in the hold was pushing burning
cotton bales up against the underside of that deck. When flames suddenly
shot in the air, Captain Naismith ordered his ship abandoned. Someone
ran along the quay to the nearby *Jalapadma*, where the captain did
likewise.

The evacuation of *Fort Stikine* took place rapidly and in some kind of
order. From the quay the firemen continued to play hoses on the ship as
Captain Naismith and Chief Officer W M Henderson made a final
round of the ship to make sure everyone was off. The pair had just
reached the quay when at 1607 hours the ship blew up in an explosion so
huge it cut her in two. A thousand miles away at Simla in the Himalayan
foothills the explosion registered on the seismograph there. The firemen
on the quay were killed outright and all that was ever found of those
brave men were their metal helmets. Harbour Master Nicholson and
Colonel Sadler were also killed. Captain Naismith, Chief Officer W D
Henderson, and a seaman called Jopp who had waited ashore for them
disappeared from the face of the earth. Metal and wood debris and
blazing cotton bales were flung high, to fall on and set fire to godowns,
dock offices and other ships in the port. So massive was the explosion
that *Fort Stikine*'s boiler, almost intact, was later found over half a mile
away in the city. The explosion generated a 60-foot tidal wave in Victoria Dock which tore every ship from its moorings before smashing
them back against the quays. Every ship that is, except two. One of
those, a large coaster, was actually swept out of the water to come to rest
atop the roof of a low building. The other was *Jalapadma*, which after
breaking adrift was unlucky enough to fetch up alongside what remained of *Fort Stikine*. Over the other side of the pier in Prince's Dock
the situation was almost as bad. There too, ships were torn from their
moorings and the heavens rained fire. The two ships moored on the
outer side of the dock basin wall were blown adrift.

Everywhere fire and chaos reigned, but the worst was yet to come. At 1633 hours a second enormous explosion came either from the remains of *Fort Stikine* or from *Jalapadma*, no-one ever knew for sure. Apart from pieces of debris there was now nothing left of *Fort Stikine*, and the mangled wreck of *Jalapadma* ended up on the quay, its master, Captain F T W Lewis, and the only other man left on board being killed in the process. Flames and black smoke shot almost 2000 feet into the air. Ten miles away in the hills behind Bombay eyewitnesses saw a huge mushroom cloud in the direction of the harbour. On Cumballa Hill, only four miles away, a horrified Mrs Jean Rasmussen began taking photographs of the terrible scene in the port below, photographs that were later used at the Official Inquiry.

That second explosion had finished the job. Once again, red-hot debris scattered everywhere. *Jalapadma*'s poop-deck, complete with a 12-pounder gun, was blown over a 40-foot high building to end up on the main road leading from the docks. In Frere Road, a quarter of a mile away, a man was sliced in half by a piece of flying metal. Every shed in the port was on fire and so dense and black was the smoke that to those unfortunate enough to be in the vicinity it seemed as if day had turned to night. Quayside cranes were lying every which way and others had been blown into the dock, Another batch of firemen engaged in fighting fires from the first explosion were either killed or injured by the second one, which meant that almost the entire force had been put out of action. Twenty-five ships were burning, some of them floating around the dock out of control.

Lloyd's Confidential Sheets for 17 April carried the following coldly factual report from the Lloyd's Surveyor in Bombay:

> A fire in cargo of cotton of British Steamer FORT STIKINE ignited explosives at 4p.m. on April 14th causing complete destruction of FORT STIKINE and setting on fire other vessels in Victoria Dock and Prince's Dock and extensive damage to dock installations, goods, and precincts.

Lloyd's Surveyors are never given to hyperbole, but that report seems to err somewhat in the other direction.

At the inquiry into the disaster it was assessed that 233 persons, including many merchant seamen, had been killed within the port area, and another 476 injured. Outside in the city the number of dead was estimated to be over 500 with 2408 injured. The exact death toll will never be known, for the streets around the dock area were virtually a shanty town, and no one had any idea of how many people lived there. One authority has given a final figure for deaths as around 1400. The tally of merchant-seaman deaths would have been far higher had not the two ships at the centre of the explosion, *Fort Stikine* and *Jalapadma*, been evacuated just in time. As it was, ships farthest from the centre of the explosion suffered more casualties; two Dutch ships, for example, losing twenty-two men between them.

The Allied cause had lost over 50,000 tons of shipping, to say nothing of the cargoes involved. *Fort Stikine* had completely disintegrated, and *Jalapadma* (Scindia Line) was also a total loss. A further eleven ships were write-offs; the *Kingyuan* (China Navigation Company), *Baroda Fort Crevier* and *El Hind*, all British, the Egyptian *Rod el Farag*, three Dutch vessels, *General Van Der Heijden, General van Sweitten* and *Tinombo* (all KPM Line), the Norwegian *Graciosa*, and two Panamanians, *Norse Trader* and *Iran*. Even that was not the end of the mayhem. The port's dredging vessel, *Spotbill*, was declared a total loss, and a further 50,000 tons of shipping were more or less severely damaged. Three ships of the Royal Indian Navy were either sunk or badly damaged, and some landing craft under construction in the port, which were to have been used by the British in the Burma campaign, were also lost.

Throughout the port, in which some 300 acres had been virtually flattened, people like Lieutenant Burke of the RINVR, who had been carrying out degaussing work on one of the vessels, disappeared never to be seen again The few warehouses which had somehow escaped being flattened were still burning four days afterwards, despite the best efforts of the Army, which was brought in to assist.

It was not only fire that rained down on Bombay that day. *Fort Stikine*'s strong-room had held 124 gold bars and several stories went around the city of those bars turning up in the most unexpected places. Most of the stories were probably apocryphal. However, some of the gold has not been recovered to this day. There is a possibility that some of it still lies in the silt at the bottom of Victoria Dock, where one bar is known to have been dredged in the late 1950s.

The gallantry of Senior Fire Officer Raganath Singh and his men has been properly commemorated. At Byculla Fire Station in Bombay there is a granite pillar to their honour, and another memorial to them is the preserved 1936 Leyland fire engine, the only survivor from those used during the disaster. Many other gallant deeds were done that day. Sub-Inspector William Greene of the Bombay Police and Captain John Dale, Royal Engineers, were both awarded George Medals for leading their men in battling against explosions and fires, and Sergeant Jones, Royal Indian Engineers, was awarded the BEM for bravery aboard one of the burning ships.

The report of the Commission of Inquiry into the disaster concluded that the most likely cause of the fire was the careless disposal of smoking material. Other factors that contributed to the scale of the catastrophe, the Commissioners held, were improper stowage, failure to appreciate from the start the seriousness of the situation, delay in summoning the fire brigade, and failure to cover the hatchways of other holds, which failure led to the fire spreading. The important observation was made that there was an absence of any centralised executive control in the port.

It took over six months, almost to the end of 1944 in fact, to get the important port of Bombay back into full operation. In the interim, many war cargoes had to be diverted to other ports. The indirect costs of the disaster probably exceeded the direct costs involved in the loss of ships and cargoes and the damage to the port structures. Persons who consider insurance companies to be greedy should note that although it would have been easy for Lloyd's and the other companies involved to plead that all losses suffered in the Bombay disaster should be the responsibility of the British Government, they did not do so. Instead they agreed to share the burden of compensation with the Government.

The final word on the *Fort Stikine* incident is left to the Supreme Allied Commander, South-East Asia, in whose command Bombay lay. In his diary entry for Friday 14 April 1944, the day of the explosion, Lord Mountbatten wrote that he heard the 'devastating news' that evening, adding, 'as if we hadn't enough troubles already without having a large part of the facilities of the only good port in India destroyed'. He went on to record what he called a 'curious side-light of this show'. His Chinese staff had been visiting the port when the explosion came, and the Chinese Naval Captain had been killed and the rest badly shaken up. Mountbatten commented that as the Chinese no longer had a navy of their own he could not understand why they had wanted to send him a Naval Officer 'and that his loss can hardly be said to be a disadvantage though he was a nice fellow . . .'.

Mountbatten visited the port himself on 4 October 1944. Although wrecked ships still lay all over the place, he noted that new dock walls were rising from the ruins of the old, and that reconstruction was now well under way. After recording that the reconstruction would bring about improvements to the port that must be seen to be believed, he commented that the old port had suffered from buildings and warehouses owned by vested interests and 'from which they could not be dislodged', and that the 'slum dwellings crowded round the docks' had also made any attempt at modernisation impossible. He wrote:

> Then, fortunately, an Indian coolie dropped a lighted cigarette on a bale of wool [sic], which caught fire, and in due course caused the ammunition in the ship to blow up, with these remarkably beneficial results. The fact that . . . lives were lost and that damage ran into millions of pounds sterling may well prove to have been a light price to pay for the vital modernisation at Bombay, as without this railway lines could not have been extended and the areas could not have been cleared for the vehicle . . . pools or for troop assembly points.

He went on:

> In fact, this explosion will immeasurably have improved Bombay as a military mounting port. No doubt the Chief Magistrate at Bombay had this in mind when last week, instead of giving five years hard labour to two coolies who were again caught smoking on board an ammunition ship, he gave them a five rupee fine . . .

About a year later, a disaster which might have developed into one of a similar scale was narrowly averted at Vancouver, British Columbia. On 6 March 1945 fire broke out aboard *Green Park Hill*, which was loading a cargo of timber and explosives alongside Pier B. An explosion in No. 3 hold was quickly followed by others, and soon the ship was a blazing inferno. Six stevedores and two of the crew died and others were injured, but only superficial damage was done to office and residential buildings in the area. As Vancouver's fireboat poured tons of water into her, the ship was towed away and beached in English Bay, where later she was declared a constructive total loss.

CHAPTER 25

'Sea-Pie'

'Sea-pie' is a sailor's dish of salt meat, vegetables and dumplings, and was also the name of a magazine dating from mid-Victorian times which dealt in nautical miscellanea.

We have already seen with the *Fort Stikine* incident at Bombay how some merchant ships were lost from indirect consequences of war rather than from enemy action. Another such incident, and one which took place much earlier, concerned the *Sirdhana*, a cargo liner belonging to the British India Steam Navigation Company. This ship sailed from Singapore's Keppel Harbour bound for Hong Kong on 13 November 1939, and was less than three miles offshore when she strayed off course and struck a mine in one of the British minefields protecting the port. The ship sank in under twenty minutes. She was carrying many passengers including, in a lock-up in the 'tween decks, 137 Chinese deportees from Malaya who were under the charge of an officer and two men of the Singapore Police. As the ship sank and at considerable risk to their own lives, Inspector Stanley Marsden, Detective Ng Kim Bok and Corporal Mustan Singh, made below and freed the penned-up men. Although twenty Asiatic deck passengers lost their lives, all of the deportees made it ashore. Marsden was awarded the King's Police Medal and his men received the Colonial Police Medal.

Deportations from Singapore and Malaya were a regular occurrence, those being deported being usually illegal immigrants, although Government officers in Malaya were also inclined to throw in any alleged Communists they came across. It is of interest to note that many of the illegals had originally landed from Chinese junks on the east coast of Malaya during the bad weather and poor visibility brought on by the north-east monsoon; those conditions making it easier for the junks to elude Customs and Police patrol launches. Yet, in the face of this knowledge, and in the face of reports from some of the more enlightened officers concerned, British military planners in Malaya held on to the belief that the Japanese would not be able to land troops on that coast during the same period of bad weather. The Japanese, of course, did exactly that.

One of the European passengers on board *Sirdhana* was Lieutenant-Colonel Billy Dawson. At the invitation of the ship's master, Captain Philip Fairbairn, Dawson was on the bridge at the time of the incident. He reported that there was a tremendous explosion after which he rushed to his cabin and managed to retrieve his cameras, a typewriter and some papers which he then passed down to one of the ship's boats which was in the process of being launched. He himself climbed down a ladder, but when half-way down had a Chinese child thrust at him. By that time the boat had pulled away from the ship's side, but Dawson managed to toss the child into the waiting arms of a sailor in it. Dawson had to leap into the water, but was safely picked up. The *Straits Times* reported that the rescue operation took place under the gaze of thousands of spectators on the water-front, brought there by the sound of the explosion.

At the Official Inquiry into the sinking held at Singapore, headed by a High Court Judge with three Master Mariners sitting as assessors, Captain Philip Fairbairn was held to be 'in wrongful default in not acquainting himself with the position of the minefield into which his vessel sailed'. The master's certificate, issued in 1925, of Captain Fairbairn, an experienced officer of forty-seven years of age, was suspended for one year, although it was recommended that he be allowed to act as mate during that period. (There is no indication in Lloyd's Captains Registers that Fairbairn sailed as master again, but those lists were discontinued in 1947.) One rather extraordinary fact which emerged at the Inquiry was that although Captain J W M Hipkin RA, the commander of one of the battery of guns which overlooked the harbour, saw the ship steaming into danger, he did not fire a warning shot. He said to have done so he would have needed to have obtained the permission from a senior officer at another post.

Ship losses from strandings and collision caused by the ordinary hazards of the sea did not diminish during the war. Indeed they were probably more frequent, for many coastal lights were either extinguished or were being run at reduced power, and buoys were removed from confined waters to prevent them being used as markers by the enemy. Out at sea, sailing in close convoy in bad weather, in fact in any weather, increased the chances of collision. These dangers are well illustrated by incidents that involved two ships of the Lamport & Holt Line.

Empire Ibex, once the American freighter *Edgefield* and since being renamed placed under the management of Lamport's, was homeward bound in mid-1943 with a cargo of grain, tanks, guns and cased aircraft which had been loaded at Portland, Maine. She was under the command of Captain Sweeney. At Halifax, Nova Scotia, she became part of a convoy of twenty-four merchantships. One of the escort vessels was the MAC ship (Merchant Aircraft Carrier) *Empire MacAlpine*. On 1 July the ships were sailing in six columns of four vessels, *Empire Ibex* being the rearmost ship in the starboard line. The weather was fine and the visibility excellent when, at about six in the evening, *Empire MacAlpine* decided to proceed through the convoy from starboard to port, her apparent intent being to pass ahead of *Empire Ibex*. As the *MacAlpine* drew closer it became obvious to Chief Officer Ansdell on the bridge of *Ibex* that the two ships were on a collision course. He blew a single blast on the ship's whistle and ordered the helm hard-a-starboard. *MacAlpine* made no signal but altered course to port, causing her to strike *Ibex* a glancing blow on the port side. Although the blow was not heavy, *MacAlpine*'s paravane apparatus (a paravane is a fish-shaped device towed from the bow to deflect mines and sever their moorings) cut a 90-foot gash in *Ibex's* hull, which sank the following day, her crew being rescued by the Convoy Rescue Ship *Perth*. At a later Inquiry *Empire MacAlpine* was held to be at fault for not following the Rules of the Road, an error that had led to the loss of a ship and a vital cargo.

Lamport & Holt's *Browning* under the command of Captain Thomas Major sailed from Liverpool for Buenos Aires on 20 January 1942. She was carrying a general cargo in the holds and, in stalls erected on the after well deck, a number of thoroughbred polo ponies together with some prize bulls being exported to Argentina for breeding purposes. She joined up with a convoy, and at about 0230 hours on the following morning, in pitch darkness and foul weather, she and five other ships piled up on the unlit shores of County Down, Northern Ireland. Captain Major ordered 'snowflake' rockets to be fired. These were parachute rocket flares of high intensity and designed to show up lurking submarines. On this occasion they had a dual effect, the intended one of lighting up the beach, and the unintended one of calling the local populace to arms. In next to no time, citizens began arriving on the beach armed to the teeth with shotguns and pitchforks. It was not long, however, before they realised they were dealing with stranded British ships and not a German invasion fleet. The rockets, the noise of the surf, and the general hullabaloo had shattered the nerves of the highly-strung polo ponies, and Captain Major had no recourse but to have them shot by his DEMS gunners. The bulls were quieter, and this comparative docility saved their lives.

Aboard *Browning*, Third Officer Ken Maguire was ordered to get the cadets and other young members of the crew ashore by breeches-buoy, and very soon the gear had been rigged across the very rough stretch of intervening water with the help of the by now friendly natives. Ken says: 'The first cadet got into the breeches-buoy and was pulled towards the shore but due to the large belly in the rope he disappeared beneath the waves and was eventually dragged ashore like a drowned rat. The others, seeing this, refused to abandon ship in this manner.'

At daybreak the local lifeboat came alongside and took off most of the crew. The bulls were eventually landed too and, it is reported, were used to good effect by the local farmers, one assumes after the animals had an appropriate period of rest and rehabilitation. *Browning* was salvaged and repaired in time to take part in the invasion of North Africa. However, on 12 November 1942 she blew up after being struck by a torpedo off Oran. The master of the ship at the time was Captain Sweeney, who had earlier in the year been in command of the *Empire Ibex*.

Among the worst war casualties not due to enemy action was the loss of the tramp steamer *Ashbury* (Alexander Shipping Company). At the end of 1944 she was badly in need of repairs, and so left the port of Workington for the shipyards on Tyneside, sailing via the Pentland Firth. She joined a convoy at Loch Ewe which sailed on 6 January 1945. By the following day the weather had become as atrocious as it only can in that strait between Scotland and the Orkney islands, with a high steep sea whipped up by a Force 9 northerly, which had brought with it snow showers and bad visibility. Very soon *Ashbury* and another ship, the Norwegian *Bestik*, had lost touch with the convoy. Both ships fought against wind and weather which was forcing them close to the shore off the entrance to the Kyle of Tongue. Both ships had their anchors down, but whilst the engines of *Bestik* were in good enough shape to allow her to steam full ahead to ease the strain on its anchor cables, *Ashbury*'s were not. With his ship out of control and drifting ever closer to the shore, Captain David Morris radioed for urgent assistance. The call was answered by the Canadian frigate *Ste Therese* which made several attempts to pass a line in the early hours of the 8th despite being in danger of being herself driven ashore. It was all to no avail, and by 0400 hours the frigate had lost contact with *Ashbury*, which struck Black Rocks at the entrance to the Kyle of Tongue, and foundered. There were no survivors from the crew of forty-two, although over the following days, twenty-six bodies were washed ashore. The graves of some of those can be seen in the cemetery at Thurso. The names of the men never found appear on the memorial at Tower Hill, London.

Several examples have been given in this book of the lengths to which some shipmasters would go to save men from another ship, especially when the victim was from the same shipping line. Another example involved two Elder Dempster ships, and it is worthy of note not only because of the heroism displayed, but also for the brilliant seamanship involved. The incident took place on 15 November 1940 about 200 miles west of the Irish coast. Two Elder Dempster ships, the *Apapa* and *Mary Kingsley*, were in a convoy making for Liverpool when the former was attacked by a lone German aircraft. One of the two bombs dropped penetrated *Apapa*'s No. 3 hatch, blasting a great hole in the hull and causing the palm kernel cargo in that hold to catch fire. The ship was soon afire from stem to stern, but that did not stop the master of *Mary Kingsley* from bringing his ship stern on to *Apapa* and skilfully holding her there. So close were the ships, that many of *Apapa*'s crew and passengers were able to leap on to the after deck of the rescue ship. Twenty-three passengers and crew were lost, but the toll would certainly have been much higher but for the action of the *Mary Kingsley*. *Apapa* eventually broke in two before sinking.

The stories of several very young heroes of the war at sea have already been related in this book, but there is one more which must be told. On 14 May 1941 the freighter *Dalesman* (T & J Harrison, Liverpool) was attacked by German aircraft and sunk at Suda Bay on the north coast of Crete. There were some fatalities amongst the crew but fifty-six survivors got ashore. The army on Crete made use of the men by forming them into anti-paratroop patrol groups, although they were not armed in accordance with the international conventions on the use of civilians in war. Amongst the survivors was seventeen year-old Cadet J H Dobson.

Towards the end of the month the commander of the British forces on the island, General Bernard Freyberg, began to withdraw his army, but many men did not get off in the main evacuations which ended on 1 June, and they fell into German hands. Dobson and the other men from *Dalesman* were amongst them. The Germans herded their prisoners together and began to march them to a prison camp. Cadet Dobson was having none of this and grabbed a machine gun and turned it on his captors before making off into the hills with some of his shipmates. Somewhere in the interior of the island they fell in with men from a New Zealand artillery battery, and eventually they all reached the south coast of the island. They found an abandoned LCT (Landing Craft Tank) on the beach and managed to get its engine working. As the nearest thing they had to a navigator, Dobson was elected to take charge of the navigation. He managed to get the craft to Egypt and was awarded a well-deserved BEM for his efforts. Throughout the entire saga, young Dobson was suffering from a rumbling appendix. Not only that; it was his first trip to sea.

The bravery shown by women at sea, crew and passengers alike, has been touched upon. One special lady must be mentioned here, special for several reasons including the fact that she was the only British sea-going women engineer of the times. Her name was Victoria Drummond, and she was a god-child of Queen Victoria. Between the wars she had served with Blue Funnel Line and had gained her Second Engineer's Certificate. During the war she saw service in an unarmed neutral ship. Such ships were not at all immune to attack by German U-boats and aircraft even when sailing well-lit at night and with their national flag emblazoned on each side of the hull. More than a few were sunk, some disappearing without trace. In consequence, many neutral ships sailed part of the voyage in convoy with Allied ships. Victoria's ship, the *Bonita*, had detached from such a convoy and was making for its destination when it came under attack by a German bomber. As the ship's captain skilfully evaded the bombs by frequent changes of course, Victoria stayed glued to the controls in the engine-room, milking the last ounce of horsepower from the engines to such good effect that the eighteen year-old ship's usual speed, described as a 'miserable' 9 knots, rose to 12.5 knots for the first time in her life.

The ship had several close shaves, one bomb dropping so close it shook the ship so violently that Victoria was flung against the control levers as scalding steam hissed out of a fractured pipe directly over her head. She stayed at her post throughout, not leaving it until the plane flew off. It was reported that the speed was still going up when Victoria eased down the engines on receiving the 'all clear'. For her bravery Miss Drummond was awarded Lloyd's War Medal for Bravery at Sea as well as the MBE. The citation read, 'Her devotion to duty saved the ship from more serious

damage, and her disregard of danger inspired all on board.' When asked
by a brother officer how she got the extra speed out of the engines, the
lady replied: 'Oh! I just talk nicely to them. You can coax or lead engines
to do what you want; you must never drive them.'

Service on tankers was possibly the most hazardous part of the job of
merchant seamen during the war, yet many men served throughout only
on that type of ship. Early in 1941 the crew of the *Chesapeake*, one of four
loaded tankers being escorted by an armed trawler between Belfast and
Avonmouth, watched in horror as the Eagle Oil Company's vessel *San
Conrado* disappeared in a blazing inferno during an attack by Heinkel
bombers. They were only too well aware that their own ship was carrying
a similar cargo of petrol. The bombers then concentrated on the Norwegian *Kaia Knudsen* which caught fire but did not blow up because she
was carrying a heavy grade of fuel oil. Then it was *Chesapeake*'s turn, but
she was extraordinarily lucky. Although struck by armour-piercing cannon fire and ending up with a large hole in her starboard side from some
sort of missile, the ship did not catch fire, although for the remainder of
the voyage she was leaving behind a wake of petrol and the air around was
full of fumes. After discharge at an oil installation off the port of Avonmouth, an unexploded 300lb bomb was discovered lying in one of the
tanks. Experts concluded that the bomb had hit the sea and ricocheted
into the ship's side, passing through three internal bulkheads before
coming to rest. Even as the *Chesapeake* was discharging, Avonmouth was
subjected to several air attacks and some incendiaries landed on her deck,
but still the ship refused to catch fire.

Because they blew up so easily, tankers were the especial prey of enemy
U-boats and aircraft. British Petroleum lost a total of thirty ships during
the war, most of them to U-boats but some to mines and aircraft, and two
to Armed Merchant Raiders. Eagle Oil Company, the line which owned
the *San Demetrio* which managed to reach England after being damaged
in the famous *Jervis Bay* convoy, lost nine tankers which took to the
bottom with them some 300 men. Tankers became even more attractive
targets when fitted with an extra top deck constructed from timber on to
which were loaded planes, landing craft, tanks, and even depth charges –
the latter with their detonators removed. (Such cargo-carrying innovations on specialised ships which carried no cargo-handling gear of their
own, posed problems at the unloading end of the voyage, of course, and
barges fitted with heavy-lift cranes and manned by merchant seamen and
dockers were regularly moved from port to port to help them.)

It is fitting to end this 'sea-pie' chapter with the story of the last British
ship to be sunk in the war by enemy action. It is also fitting that the little
Seamen's Mission at Methil on the Firth of Forth features in it. On 7 May
1945, the day before VE-Day, a general cease-fire had been ordered by the
Allies after the German leadership had agreed to unconditional surrender. One German submarine commander decided to ignore the cease-
fire, and at 2300 hours that night, off the Isle of May which lies in the

entrance to the Firth of Forth, it torpedoed and sank the British *Avondale Park* and the Norwegian *Sneland I*. Lay Reader Stanley Price of the Methil Mission was in nearby Leven at the time and looking out over Largo Bay at the many ships anchored there which were celebrating the end of the war by letting off flares and rockets. He heard the two heavy explosions from seaward as the torpedoes struck home. He did not then know the cause, but intuition told him he was needed and he hurried back to Methil. Sure enough, the police were waiting for him with the news that fifty-four survivors from the two ships were being brought in. Stanley Price wrote of that night:

> We got a band of ladies together to prepare meals and hot drinks. I was on the pier just after midnight to receive the men, and about 2 a.m. a very pathetic stream of seamen poured into the building, wet, half-dressed, covered in oil and filth from the explosions. In the British ship two men had been killed, nine were lost in the Norwegian; three were badly injured, one of them dying from shock as he lay on board the drifter which was bringing them into port.

As the lady helpers gave first-aid to the injured, a local tailor and a grocer opened their shops and gave all the help they could with clothes and provisions. The Lay Reader continued:

> Coming out of the docks at 10 o'clock in the morning – it was now VE-Day – we saw the townspeople getting out their flags and a band was playing victory music, all unconscious of the drama that had been enacted right under their windows as they slept. War had gone out, as it had come in six long years before by the sinking of a merchantman far out on the Atlantic trade routes, by a last vicious attack on merchant shipping, a heavy blow beneath the belt when the gloves were off.

But the final part of the drama had yet to be played. Late in the afternoon of VE-Day, after Churchill's victory message had been broadcast and as, despite the bitter cold, people carried on dancing, singing and cheering in the streets, the bodies of two merchant seamen were washed ashore. They beached on a lonely stretch of sand near St Monance some eight miles from where the last two Allied merchant ships to be sunk by a German submarine went down. 'The sea,' wrote Lay Reader Stanley Price, 'had given them back – was it as a reminder of the sacrifice of their thirty thousand mates who had made the same trip?'

CHAPTER 26

Epilogue

May 1945 had brought the end of the war with Germany, but that still left the matter of dealing with the Japanese on the other side of the world. The Pacific was still largely an American theatre of war as it had been from the start of hostilities there, although the Southeast Asia area had been left as a mainly British affair. British merchant ships were included in Admiral Mountbatten's invasion fleet formed in August 1945 to retake Malaya in what was known as Operation 'Zipper'. As it turned out, the landings on Morib beach on the west coast of Malaya were unopposed, for by the time the fleet arrived off that beach, the Americans had dropped the atom bombs on Japan and the war in the East was over. (It is perhaps as well those landings were unopposed, as Mountbatten's planners had not done some of their homework properly. To the casual eye Morib beach looks like a long stretch of firm, golden sands. However, that appearance is deceptive, for although the infantry landed in good order, the heavy equipment did not, much of it, including tanks, sinking through the thin layer of sand into the quagmire beneath.)

Despite the cessation of hostilities there was still much work in Eastern waters for British merchant ships, not least in helping to re-establish British control of Hong Kong. Warships on duty with the British Pacific Fleet, which had been working very much as a junior partner alongside the American Pacific Fleet, had been detached to race for Hong Kong when it became known that the Americans had secretly negotiated a deal with Generalissimo Chiang Kai Shek that the colony be handed over to the Chinese and not back to the British. (One historian has remarked of the wartime relationship between Britain and America that the pair 'were Allies of a kind'; blame for the lack of trust which sometimes plagued the relationship between the two nations can be attributed to both sides.) In addition to the warships, British merchant ships were also hastily diverted to the colony with the ostensible purposes of carrying food and supplies to the hungry populace and to help fetch away the many Allied prisoners of war and internees there, who were in a most wretched condition. Another immediate purpose however, was to serve notice on the world, and to the United States and China in particular, that trade and commerce in, and the governance of, the Crown Colony were back as they were before the war began.

All over the world the Merchant Navy was engaged in the homeward movement of troops and former prisoners of war, and in carrying much-needed food and supplies to many countries. Very often the ships engaged in these operations were in danger of running into uncharted minefields or, almost as bad, into rogue mines that had broken from their moorings. In fact, mines were to remain a hazard to shipping for many years to come, and the British Admiralty was still issuing mine warnings in the shape of so-called 'Nemredi' reports, until at least as late as the 1960s. (Second World War minefields exist to this day in some of the more remote parts of the world. Mines laid by the Japanese in the strait that leads to the Indonesian port of Surabaya were left in situ after the war, probably because they were considered too dangerous to move. Those mines are probably harmless by now, but even so, when it was decided to re-lay a telegraph cable in that strait recently, naval experts from Britain were flown out to pass judgement on any residual risk.) One indication of the dangers at sea which still abounded after the war was that the monthly War Risk Money paid to merchant seaman was still paid and still called that for several years after the war ended, though eventually the payment was incorporated into the standard wage.

There were other hazardous war legacies in the seas, legacies potentially as dangerous as those mines in Indonesian waters. Some exist to this day. Perhaps the best known of those in the West is the hulk of the American Liberty ship *Richard Montgomery*, which lies off the Isle of Sheppey in the Thames Estuary. That ship crossed the Atlantic in Convoy HX301 and arrived off Southend in August 1944. Loaded with a cargo of 6862 tons of high explosive bombs, bursters and fuses, she was ordered to anchor off the northern edge of Sheerness Middle Sands, there to await a convoy for the Normandy beachhead. The water off Middle Sands is shallow, and at a low tide on 5 September the ship took the bottom, hogged, and broke her back, the crew promptly abandoning ship. Admiralty salvage teams managed to remove about half of the cargo, but over 3000 tons of it is still there. The ship is listed, with good reason, as a Protected Wreck and is well marked by buoys and is regularly inspected.

The seas of the world are littered with ships sunk in the war and with the bodies of men who went down with them. Many of the ships disappeared without trace, some no doubt lost to the elements but most of them victims of enemy action. The naval records of the Axis partners were scrutinised after the war and, in consequence, the fate of many of the missing ships was discovered. However, the words 'lost without trace' still appear in the official list of ship losses against the names of a substantial number of them.

We have seen in the case of the *Empress of Asia* that some of that ship's crew downed tools and mutinied as the ship approached the doomed fortress of Singapore in February 1942. At various times during the war there were other similar incidents, and it has been said that strikes and desertions, particularly amongst Asian seamen who made up a substantial proportion of merchant navy crews during the war, were on an unprecedented scale. These incidents and the general morale of merchant ship crews were a cause of much concern in Whitehall and to top officials elsewhere. We have noted one particular instance of official concern that stemmed from the pen of Admiral Sir James Somerville in mid-1944, in which he aired his anxiety that when news of Japanese atrocities against the crews of Allied ships in the Indian Ocean leaked out, there might be a reluctance to sail in unescorted ships. He was right, for a certain reluctance did manifest itself amongst the crews of some ships.

However, all that must be put in perspective. Desertions and/or mutinies also occurred during the war in the armed services, not only of Britain, but other Allied countries as well, so it is scarcely surprising that such incidents also sometimes arose in the Merchant Navy. The great losses in ships and men were at some periods and in certain waters alarmingly high; alarming not only to those in Whitehall engaged in conducting the grand strategy of the war, but more pertinently, to the men manning the ships. What is more, a goodly number of those recruited to make good the losses in personnel were 'hostilities only' men with little of the tradition of sea service running in their veins. (Many such men quickly learnt those traditions and to this day are rightly proud of the four or five years they spent at sea.) The desertions, mutinies and strikes which did take place, together with an occasional reluctance to sail in some waters, do not detract much from the overall conclusion that the great majority of British merchant seamen in the war carried out their duties in a way consistent with both the age-old traditions of the sea and with the proud traditions of the service in which they worked and, moreover, did so in the face of the most appalling dangers. Who can doubt the courage of men aboard those ships which were either too fast, or, much worse, too slow, to voyage in escorted convoys? From the numbers of those independently routed vessels came no less than 60 per cent of all ships sunk by U-boats. And what of the men who sailed the coastal waters of Britain during the winter months of 1939, when from lack of expertise and sweeping ability the magnetic mine took such a toll? A similar situation arose during the following winter when the Germans first introduced the acoustic mine, but still merchant seamen put to sea.

Time and time again during the war, merchant sailors, sometimes against standing orders, risked their lives to save men from other ships. There were many instances, a few of which have been mentioned in this book, when men of this non-belligerent service took on a more aggressive role, and took it on most successfully. Who can doubt the courage of the men who ran the blockade to Sweden? And those who sailed to take aid to Malta, even though sometimes their efforts came to naught, like those of the gallant crew of the tiny, rust-covered *Parracombe*?

In general the men of Britain's Merchant Navy served their country and the Allied cause splendidly during the Second World War. For a few years after it, up until about the mid-1950s, they were rewarded by high employment as nations everywhere went about recovering from the ravages of war. After that period which has been termed the 'halcyon years' by several shipping historians, the British Merchant Navy went into a decline from which it has never recovered. There were many reasons for this. They included the rise of nationalism in the Third World; the expansion of the use of so-called flags of convenience; the rules some countries promulgated regarding the carriage of their own produce; containerisation, which so dramatically reduced the world's overall requirement for ships; the failure of British shipowners, compared with those of some other nations, to recognise changing trading conditions in good time; and the failure of British governments of whatever political persuasion to give much in the way of aid to the industry.

Britain had entered the war in 1939 as the world's premier maritime country with about 50 per cent of the world's shipping tonnage under her flag. By the time the Falkland Islands conflict came along in 1982, Britain had to charter in foreign ships as its Merchant Navy could not supply all the vessels needed. The spirits of the seamen who died during the Second World War must, wherever they lay, have stirred in concerned wonderment in the knowledge that the service they had so proudly served had by then been reduced to a position well down the world's maritime league table.

Bibliography

Primary Unpublished Sources

Public Record Office
ADM199/526, 1009, 1011, 1025, 1032, 2147
MT9/3679
PREM3/88-3
WO193/712

Imperial War Museum
Mrs M Baker 88/42/1
Captain M J Curtis 87/25/1
Lieutenant-Colonel W C P Dawson P440
Captain S F Nicolson 98/1/1
Owen Rutter 85/10/2
J F Sweeney 85/18
Peter Wood 94/43/1

Private Collections
Captain R W Armstrong
Sam Harper
Ken Maguire
Dr Doreen Rippon
William Mutimer

Books
Anon, *Britain's Conquest of the Mediterranean, Key to Hitler's Defeat* (London c1945)
—, *Merchantmen at War, the Official Story of the MN 1939-1944* (HMSO, London 1944)
—, *Merchant Shipping (Losses) 1914-1918* (HMSO, London 1919)
—, *British Merchant Vessels Lost or Damaged During the Second World War* (HMSO, London 1947)
Atherton, Louise, *SOE Operations in Scandinavia – Guide to records in the PRO* (London 1994)
Atkinson, Tony, and O'Donoghue, Kevin, *Blue Star* (Kendal 1985)
Barker, Ralph, *The Blockade Runners* (London 1976)
—, *Goodnight, Sorry for Sinking You* (London 1984)
Cowden, James, and Duffy, John, *Elder Dempster Fleet History* (Norwich 1986)
Credland, Arthur G, and Thompson, Michael, *The Wilson Line of Hull 1831-1981* (Beverley 1994)
Dear, Ian, *The Ropner Story* (London 1986)
Dobbie, Sybil, *Grace Under Malta* (London 1943)
Elliott, Peter, *The Cross & The Ensign* (London 1982)
Elphick, Peter, *Singapore, The Pregnable Fortress* (London 1995)
—, *Far Eastern File* (London 1997)

Ennis, John, *Bombay Explosion* (London 1959)
Fisher, Admiral of the Fleet Lord, *Memoirs* (London 1919)
Fredh, Terje, *Kullagertrafiken (The Blockade Runners)* (Lysekil, Sweden 1975)
Grove, Eric J (ed), *The Defeat of the Enemy Attack on Shipping 1939-1945* (Aldershot 1997)
Havilland, Charlotte (ed), *The China Navigation Company Limited* (London 1992)
Heaton, P M, *Reardon Smith Line* (Pontypool 1984)
Hocking, Charles, *Dictionary of Disasters at Sea*, 2 vols (London 1969)
Hope, Ronald, *The Merchant Navy* (London 1980)
Hoyt, Edwin P, *Death of the U-boats* (New York 1988)
Infield, Glenn B, *Disaster at Bari* (London 1971)
Kennedy, Joseph, *British Civilians and the Japanese War in Malaya and Singapore* (London 1987)
Kerr, J Lennox (ed), *Touching the Adventures* (London 1963)
Kohler, Lawrie, *A Life At Sea* (Hull 1983)
Middlemiss, Norman L, *Travels of the Tramps*, 2 vols (Newcastle-upon-Tyne 1989-1991)
Mohr, Ulrich, and Sellwood A V, *Atlantis – The Story of a German Surface Raider* (London 1955)
Mountbatten, Lord Louis (ed Philip Ziegler), *Personal Diary* (London 1988)
Nilsson, Lars-Axel, and Sandberg, Leif A, *Blockade Runners* (Orebro, Sweden 1994)
Rogers, H C B, *Troopships and their History* (London 1963)
Rohwer, J, and Hummelchen, G, *Chronology of the War at Sea*, 2 vols (London 1972)
Rutter, Owen, *Red Ensign – A History of the Convoy* (London 1943)
Sawyer, L A, and Mitchell, W H, *The Liberty Ships* (Newton Abbot 1970)
Simpson, Michael (ed), *The Somerville Papers* (Navy Records Society 1995)
Strong, L A G, *Flying Angel* (London 1956)
Syrett, David (ed), *The Battle of the Atlantic & Signals Intelligence* (Aldershot 1998)
'Taffrail' (Capt. Taprell Dorning), *Blue Star Line at War 1939-1945* (London 1973)
Taylor, James, *Ellermans – A Wealth of Shipping* (London 1976)
Thomas, Gabe, *Milag: Captives of the Kreigsmarine* (Milag POW Association 1995)
Tomlinson, H M, *Malay Waters* (London 1950)
Tracy, Nicholas (ed), *The Collective Naval Defence of the Empire* (Aldershot 1997)
West, Frank, *Lifeboat Number Seven* (London 1960)
Woodman, Richard, *Arctic Convoys 1941-1945* (London 1994)

Articles
Sainsbury, J D, 'For Gallantry & Initiative in Hazardous Circumstances', *Journal of the Orders & Medals Research Society* (Winter 1982)
Uhl, Robert, 'They got it all, and they ain't *too* holy', *Seaport Magazine* (South Street Seaport Museum, New York, Fall 1984)

Index